TRIPWIRE

TRIPWIRE

Korea and U.S. Foreign Policy
in a Changed World

Doug Bandow

CATO
INSTITUTE
Washington, D.C.

Library of Congress Cataloging-in-Publication Data

Bandow, Doug.
  Tripwire : Korea and U.S. foreign policy in a changed world / Doug
Bandow.
    p.   cm.
  Includes bibliographical references and index.
  ISBN 1-882577-29-9. — ISBN 1-882577-30-2
    1. United States—Foreign relations—Korea (South).   2. Korea
(South)—Foreign relations—United States.   I. Title
E183.8.K6B36   1996
327.7305195—dc20   96-7916
                                                                 CIP

Cover Design by Mark Fondersmith.

Printed in the United States of America.

CATO INSTITUTE
1000 Massachusetts Ave., N.W.
Washington, D.C. 20001

To Shelly and Birkley Wical
who are serving God, loving their family,
and defending their country

Contents

Preface

I began political life as a fairly typical conservative, committed simultaneously to limited government and a big military. But I soon developed gnawing doubts: If government in general didn't work well, why did I believe that the Department of Defense worked better? If bureaucrats manipulated domestic programs, why couldn't they do the same with overseas initiatives? If social spending wasted valuable resources, why were military outlays any different?

Of course, the existence of the Soviet Union required maintenance of a sizable military, despite the costs. However, it became increasingly obvious over the years that America was spending as much money to defend its allies as itself and that doing so discouraged them from doing more for themselves. That phenomenon was evident in Europe, where the West European countries had a much larger gross domestic product than the Soviet bloc and were capable of far greater military exertions. It was also obvious on the Korean peninsula.

When I wrote my first article on the Koreas in 1983, the Republic of Korea (South Korea) enjoyed a gross domestic product estimated at five times that of the Democratic People's Republic of Korea (North Korea). In 1987, when I did my first Cato Institute study on the subject, the disparity had grown to nearly seven to one. Now it is 18 to 1, or thereabouts.[1] Over the same period the South, with twice the North's population, began to pull away on virtually every other measure—international support, technological advance, democratic development. In short, the ROK seemed to be handily winning the contest between the two countries.

Yet the gap in military capabilities between North and South never seemed to close. And Pyongyang's edge was ritualistically trotted out as justification for America's military commitment, embodied in the Mutual Defense Treaty, and troop deployment, with U.S. soldiers constituting a literal tripwire between the Demilitarized Zone and Seoul, thereby ensuring American involvement in any war. Indeed, the very unanimity of specialists in the field was suspect.[2] The idea of disengagement had not so much been debated and discarded as simply assumed away. It was as if security analysts and especially government officials believed that the ROK's military inferiority was an immutable principle of geography, that the nation to the south had to have fewer tanks than the one to the north. Thus, America had to stay.

An even more curious evolution has been taking place during the 1990s, particularly within South Korea. So dramatic is the South's growing advantage that it is hard for anyone, no matter how committed to the status quo, to argue that Seoul is helpless in the face of an impoverished, faltering DPRK. So officials in the South have gone off in search of new enemies from whom to be protected by America. Perhaps not surprisingly, Japan tops the list, but China and general instability run close behind. In short, argues the ROK today, even if the North Korean regime disappears and the peninsula is reunited, the U.S. defense guarantee and troops will still be needed. And officials in Washington are only too happy to agree. If universal peace ever descended upon the globe, defenders of the status quo would undoubtedly find new reasons to keep America's military presence unchanged.

Obviously, Korea is not the only or even the most important outdated U.S. military commitment. But it has received less attention than America's relationships with Europe and Japan.[3] It is also a simpler case, a good starting point for reconsidering overall U.S. foreign policy. After all, if disengagement makes sense in the ROK, then why not in Japan? Why not in Europe? Even if the answer is that those cases are different, and I don't believe that they are, the questions should still be asked. So I'm asking.

Acknowledgments

Many people have contributed, both directly and indirectly, to this volume. Most obviously deserving credit (or blame in the view of those who don't like my thesis) is the staff of the Cato Institute. Its president, Edward H. Crane, and executive vice president, David Boaz, have generously supported my research and writing. The Institute has published several of my studies and underwritten visits to both North and South Korea. I've had help from Gregory F. Taylor, director of information services, and a host of interns, most recently Aaron Lukas, who located much of the necessary information; my editor, Elizabeth W. Kaplan, who corrected my grammar and clarified my prose; Mark Fondersmith, design director, who designed the cover of this book; and David Lampo, publications director, who handled production and promotion.

Special thanks go to Ted Galen Carpenter, Cato's vice president for defense and foreign policy studies. He has long been an inspiration, developing and articulating a new foreign policy that defends U.S. interests and promotes international cooperation without attempting to police a de facto global empire. He has helped find the third way between traditional isolationism, which fears everything foreign, and Wilsonian internationalism, which idealizes humanitarian militarism. Carpenter encouraged me to write this book; offered advice and helpful editorial suggestions; and, most important, somehow convinced me to agree to a deadline so I had no choice but to complete this long-delayed project. Not only is he a valued colleague; he and his family are also valued friends.

I appreciate, too, the help of colleagues who have offered advice and criticism and forced me to sharpen my arguments. Selig Harrison and Ed Olsen commented on a draft of the manuscript; Gari Ledyard, Chae-Jin Lee, Patrick Morgan, Burton Yale Pines, Steve Rollins, Christopher Sigur, Steven Sudderth, and Dae-Sook Suh have provided me with forums in which to discuss these ideas. Kim Changsu and Park Hong-Kyoo helped me learn about their country even as they criticized my proposals. Many others have engaged in intellectual combat at conferences and through publications, forcing me to hone my analysis. But in the end, of course, only I bear responsibility for my views and any mistakes in this volume.

Finally, I want to thank my parents, Don and Donna Bandow, and my sister and brother-in-law, Shelly and Birkley Wical, for their continuing love and support. My father took time to review the manuscript for sloppy grammar and reasoning. More important is the fact that they all helped to remind me about the most important things in life.

1. Korea and America's International Role

On June 25, 1950, U.S. foreign policy changed almost as dramatically as it had on December 7, 1941. Whereas the Japanese attack on Pearl Harbor had brought the United States into the second great global conflict of this century, June 25, 1950, ensured that Washington would adopt a garrison-state policy even during peacetime. More than any other development, the events of June 25, 1950, inaugurated the Cold War. On that day North Korea's Kim Il Sung launched a full-scale invasion of South Korea, and one of America's client states was at war.[1]

Washington's intervention was not foreordained. The Korean peninsula had no intrinsic value to American security—it was, after all, several thousand miles away from U.S. territory and had long been the focal point of struggles among three important Asian powers, China, Japan, and the Soviet Union. That point was acknowledged by Gen. Douglas MacArthur and the Joint Chiefs of Staff, as well as implicitly by Secretary of State Dean Acheson in his famous defense perimeter speech. Nevertheless, President Harry S. Truman viewed the attack as part of a larger, more serious Soviet global threat and quickly made Seoul's cause the United States' and the United Nations' own by dispatching forces to assist South Korea.

U.S. entry into the war blunted the North Korean drive and then routed Pyongyang's forces; by late September, Kim Il Sung's army was broken and streaming northward. General MacArthur, the overall UN commander, seized what appeared to be an easy opportunity to reunify the peninsula under South Korea's anti-communist president Syngman Rhee.[2] That attempt backfired, however, leading to Chinese intervention, a near disaster for the allies, and what MacArthur would soon call "an entirely new war."[3] By mid-1951 the lines stabilized roughly where the war had begun, but two years of bloody trench warfare followed. An armistice was finally reached, but with the collapse of negotiations on a peace treaty, the Korean peninsula

1

lapsed into a cold war as frigid as that between the two Germanys. Washington then extended a security guarantee to the ROK (a "mutual" defense treaty in name only, since the obligations were entirely one-sided).

New Global Responsibilities

The Korean War was much more than the simple defense of one small nation far from America's shores. Between 1950 and 1953 America essentially adopted as its responsibility the defense of the entire globe—at least that portion not already under communist domination. And that role would not be seriously challenged for four decades, until the collapse of the Soviet Union and international communism in the early 1990s.

The United States emerged from World War II as the leader of the "free world" and the only power strong enough to contain a seemingly aggressive and threatening Soviet Union. America began to implement its policy of containment through a global network of alliances, bases, and forward deployments, literally ringing the USSR and its new ally, China. The Rio Pact was established with 22 Latin American states in 1947; two years later came the North Atlantic Treaty Organization (NATO), to protect Western Europe. Mutual defense treaties were negotiated with Japan and the Philippines in 1951, along with the Australia–New Zealand–U.S. pact.

Yet the original goals of the Truman administration seem, in retrospect, rather modest—to maintain a "defensive perimeter," as Acheson called it, even while shrinking the military and resisting Pentagon pleas for larger budgets. The problem was simple: a system of worldwide commitments does not come cheap. In the 1930s Washington spent an average of $740 million (8.65 billion 1996 dollars) annually on defense and fielded an armed force numbering about 250,000 active-duty personnel. America's participation in World War II led to a 12.8-million-man military (supported by another 1.9 million civilians), and in 1945 defense expenditures reached $83 billion (988.4 billion 1996 dollars).

Although Washington rapidly cut force levels after the war, they remained high by historical standards: the military averaged 1.64 million personnel, and the budget was $13.7 billion in 1950 (114 billion 1996 dollars). After initiating a substantial build-up from 1948 to 1949 (following the spending trough in 1947), President Truman sharply slowed the growth of defense spending. At the time, reports an official Pentagon history, "his commitment to fiscal restraint remained strong and unyielding."[4] That commitment was one reason for the decision to withdraw America's 45,000 soldiers from South Korea in 1949.[5] Truman's hope, of course, was to spend just enough to deter the Soviets, thus both avoiding renewed war and minimizing America's economic burden.

NSC Memorandum 68

However, administration advocates of a major military build-up remained active. In early 1950 the president approved a joint State-Defense Department working group "to undertake a reexamination of our objectives in peace and war and of the effect of these objectives on our strategic plans, in light of the probable fission bomb capability and possible thermonuclear bomb capability of the Soviet Union."[6] Chosen to head the review was Paul Nitze, director of the State Department's Policy Planning Staff. The result was National Security Council Memorandum 68. Shrill even by Cold War standards, the document spoke in cataclysmic terms and proposed a massive conventional military build-up, which would cost as much as $50 billion, according to the study team. However, the authors left specific budget figures out of the report since their inclusion "might have jeopardized the study's acceptance," according to historian Steven Rearden.[7] Secretary of Defense Louis Johnson, who had warned the services to hew to a $13 billion budget ceiling, was hostile; officials such as State Department counselor George Kennan and Ambassador Charles Bohlen were also critical. Although President Truman seemed sympathetic to at least some of the recommendations, he deferred and ordered further study of the issue.

What Truman—and Congress—would ultimately have decided to do will never be known, though historians consider anything more than a modest build-up to have been unlikely.[8] In the words of historian William Stueck, the North's invasion of June 25, 1950, provided "the spark necessary" to turn NSC 68 into Washington's de facto blueprint for foreign and military policy for decades to come.[9] On July 19 President Truman called for an emergency supplemental appropriation of $10 billion; by 1953 military spending had escalated fourfold. Truman also proposed doubling the armed forces to 3 million.

Thereafter commenced a global military build-up. Observes Stueck, "Not only did the United States intervene in Korea, it stepped up aid to anti-Communist forces in Indochina and to the beleaguered government of Elpidio Quirino in the Philippines. It also announced that it would defend Taiwan."[10] Even as it poured ground forces into Korea, the Truman administration decided to send several divisions to Europe.[11] And after the war in Korea came more alliances and commitments, including the Southeast Asia Treaty Organization, an amalgam of Asian, South-Pacific, and Western states, including the United States; and the Central Treaty Organization, consisting of several Middle Eastern states and Great Britain, that Washington supported. Those organizations, which were, in effect, multilateral facades for U.S. defense guarantees, were dissolved in 1977 and 1979, respectively.

Hostile Peace

Although America continued to acquire new client states—Iran and Vietnam, to name two—it never seemed to drop any. Instead, Washington's defense guarantees became permanent. Indeed, the hostile peace of 1953 on the Korean peninsula persists today. Along the so-called Demilitarized Zone are lined up more troops with more armaments than were formerly between the two Germanys and almost as many as there once were along the entire Soviet-Chinese border. China withdrew her forces from the North in 1958, but America has left her soldiers in place. Without them, the Republic of Korea—for years underdeveloped, with a repressive and unpopular government—would have been vulnerable to another invasion.

But in the 1960s the balance of economic power began to shift, and with it the political and military dynamic. The ROK gained an ever-growing economic edge over its northern neighbor; Seoul also moved toward a stable democracy and international respectability, while the DPRK's rigid totalitarianism earned increasing scorn even in the Third World. By the 1980s the U.S.-Korean Mutual Defense Treaty was making ever less sense. Seoul outstripped the DPRK financially, technologically, and diplomatically. The South also had a bigger population, greater access to foreign markets, and the ability to outspend Pyongyang on defense. By the end of the decade even the North's allies were changing sides, as both the Soviet Union and China recognized the ROK.

As If Nothing's Changed

Officials in Washington act as if they are unaware that much of anything has changed since 1953. President Reagan's defense secretary, Caspar Weinberger, once assured the ROK government that U.S. forces would remain as long as Seoul wished. Similar pledges were made by Presidents George Bush and Bill Clinton. When the latter visited the South in 1993, he told the Korean National Assembly that "the Korean Peninsula remains a vital U.S. interest."[12] And when South Korean president Kim Young Sam journeyed to Washington in 1995 to celebrate the dedication of the Korean War Memorial, Clinton promised not to leave the ROK undefended.

In fact, many analysts in both countries hope to retain U.S. forces on the Korean peninsula even if the two Koreas reunify. In the view of some Americans, such an advanced posting gives Washington a base from which to project power in the region.[13] That seems to be the view of the Clinton administration, which in early 1995 proclaimed, "Even after the North Korean threat passes, the United States intends to maintain its strong defense alliance with the Republic of Korea, in the interest of regional security."[14] A number of Koreans, too, want Washington to stay, particularly as long-term insurance against any future Japanese aggression.[15]

However, the collapse of the USSR and end of the Cold War provide America with a unique opportunity to reassess its role in the world. For nearly five decades the United States acted more like an empire than a republic, creating a global network of client states, establishing hundreds of military installations around the world, conscripting young men to staff those advanced outposts and fight in distant wars, and spending hundreds of billions of dollars annually on the military. Indeed, that globalist foreign policy badly distorted the domestic political system, encouraging the growth of a large, expensive, repressive, secretive, and often uncontrolled state.

The justification for the interventionist military strategy, so alien to the original American design, was the threat of totalitarian communism. With that threat gone, the United States should return to its roots, rather than look for another convenient enemy. It should become, in the words of former U.S. ambassador to the United Nations Jeane Kirkpatrick, "a normal country in a normal time."[16]

And that requires a foreign policy with much more limited ends. The ability to project power in Northeast Asia may have been important when the United States feared that a North Korean attack would be merely the opening salvo of a general communist offensive in the region. An American tripwire in the ROK served a purpose when Washington feared Soviet- and Chinese-backed aggression against Seoul; placing troops in Japan was a logical response to the need to protect a nation disarmed at the end of World War II; and bases in the Philippines had value in supporting American naval operations to contest control of the Indian and Pacific Oceans. But the demise of the USSR has turned all of those old Pacific war scenarios into little more than lurid and paranoid nightmares.

Fiscal Black Holes

All of America's one-time security assets around the globe are now fiscal black holes, commitments of little value that cost the United States billions annually. The Pentagon's hypothetical threats—including a Russian attack on Lithuania and a coup d'état in the Philippines, advanced to justify a large budget—are embarrassingly strained.[17] Even if an authoritarian regime eventually gains control in Moscow, it will not be able to replicate the threats posed by a unified USSR acting in the name of an expansionist, terrorist ideology.

Not surprisingly, then, the threat of a major war in the Pacific seems smaller than it has in five decades. Russia's attention is focused on the Soviet Union's one-time constituent parts, particularly in Europe and the Transcaucasus; much of the Red Navy is rusting in port. The leaders of a faction-ridden and still relatively poor China are squabbling over economic reform and face an uncertain future in the ongoing leadership struggle. Japan has achieved, peacefully, all of the plausible goals it sought in the 1930s when it forcibly established the Greater East Asia Co-Prosperity Sphere. Australia and New Zealand enjoy splendid isolation; the Philippines faces only internal enemies; and continuing instability in Burma and Cambodia, while tragic, threatens no one outside those countries. Only in Korea does a significant armed conflict seem even remotely possible. But while a North Korean attack on the ROK remains plausible, it has become both increasingly improbable and increasingly unlikely to be successful.[18]

That is reason enough to end American defense subsidies. Although "Dear Leader" Kim Jong Il retains the capability to at least try to reunify the peninsula by force, the DPRK's quantitative military advantages are counterbalanced by the South's qualitative superiority and far greater economic strength. Moreover, the North seems to lack the will to gamble everything on an invasion. And that's not surprising: the odds of succeeding long ago shifted against Pyongyang. To roll the die of war today would be astronomically risky, given the DPRK's virtually bankrupt economy, hungry population, and lack of outside support.

ROK Advantages

Most important, focusing on the threat side of the equation misses the change in the overall balance of power. With a gross domestic product estimated at about 18 times that of North Korea, the ROK looms over the DPRK rather like the United States overshadows Mexico. Seoul has outspent the North on defense since the mid-1970s and could now devote the equivalent of the entire DPRK economy to the military by roughly doubling its defense outlays. Why, then, should the United States maintain forces for use in Korea when the South is capable of raising an overwhelming military on its own?

It is true, of course, that Pyongyang retains a quantitative advantage in manpower and materiel: 1.128 million men and 3,940 tanks versus 633,000 men and 2,050 tanks, for instance.[19] But such numbers alone, while not meaningless, are not dispositive. Observed analyst Stephen Goose, a host of "nonquantifiable factors," including "quality of weapons and personnel, degree of readiness and sustainability, number and readiness of reserve troops, nature and quality of command, control, and intelligence, reliability of allies, and degree of economic and industrial power," all favor Seoul.[20]

Moreover, the quantitative imbalance is not inevitable, not an immutable aspect of the political geography of the Korean peninsula. Rather, the South possesses a smaller military because it has chosen to do so. And it has been able to adopt that risky policy because the U.S. tripwire acts as a supplemental deterrent to North Korean aggression. That the relationship is beneficial to the ROK is obvious. That it is in America's interest is not.

After all, providing defense guarantees—and maintaining the forces necessary to back them up—is not cheap. The most obvious expense is financial: it costs upwards of $15 billion annually to maintain the units based in Korea, as well as those destined to intervene in the event of war. The issue is not merely the expense of basing the units overseas, since the ROK and Japan, in particular, provide significant "host-nation" support. Rather, the real issue is the cost of the units themselves, which exist only to back up the security commitment embodied in the defense treaty. In short, military spending is the price of America's foreign policy.

Billions in defense subsidies to allied nations (South Korea is merely one beneficiary) have a dual impact. One is on domestic economic policy, since such outlays further inflate government borrowing, diverting credit from more productive private investment today and requiring higher exactions on taxpayers tomorrow. Perhaps even more serious is the international impact. American defense subsidies not only impoverish U.S. taxpayers; they simultaneously enrich foreign nations that are major trade competitors. Allowing South Korea (as well as Japan and a host of European nations) to concentrate domestic resources on economic pursuits rather than military spending has put American enterprises at a disadvantage. That cost was modest and probably worth enduring during the early days of the Cold War, given the magnitude of the Soviet threat and the economic weakness of U.S. allies. But there is no longer any reason to indirectly underwrite large Korean, Japanese, and European businesses as they compete with U.S. firms.

Also significant are several more intangible costs. Happily, the ROK's move to democracy has largely eliminated the identification of Washington with military dictators, once a serious problem. For instance, a number of Koreans long blamed America for complicity in the 1980 massacre in the city of Kwangju by South Korean government troops.[21] Many pro-democracy demonstrators in 1987 believed that the United States could dictate policy to President Chun Doo Hwan and criticized Washington for not forcing the Chun regime to accept free elections.[22] They overestimated Washington's influence, of course, but their belief, though erroneous, that the United States was responsible for domestic repression harmed America's reputation.

Military Dangers

More important is the military risk of U.S. security ties. Although the American commitment probably helps deter North Korean aggression, it ensures that the United States will be involved if hostilities should recur. Indeed, the 37,000 U.S. soldiers are a tripwire that makes intervention automatic. Although the risk of war seems slight at the moment—in late 1995 famine in the North and political scandal in the South did raise tensions—the consequences would be horrific. And the possible acquisition by North Korea of atomic weapons increases the potential costs exponentially. If a conflict erupted, perhaps over the nuclear issue should the current agreement with Pyongyang break down, the American troops would become nuclear hostages.

There are obviously times when the nation must risk war. But this is not one. There are no vital American interests at stake that warrant such a risk. The mere fact that the United States fought in Korea nearly 50 years ago does not mean it should prepare to do so again; the best way of honoring the sacrifice of so many soldiers in that war is to ensure that no Americans will be forced to fight and die in a similar future conflict. That is not to say that Washington has no interests at stake on the peninsula—the U.S.–South Korean cultural and economic ties are real, though modest—but they do not warrant a security guarantee and troop presence. In any case, America no longer needs to provide a military commitment to secure its interests. South Korea is now fully capable of defending itself.

So, why is Washington risking the lives of U.S. soldiers in Korea? Put bluntly, would it dramatically affect American interests if war broke out on the peninsula and produced the worst-case scenario— a North Korean conquest of the ROK? Since the Korean War killed an estimated 1 million Koreans and Kim Jong Il's regime is the last best replica of Stalinist totalitarianism, such a conflict and outcome would obviously be tragic.[23] But tragedy alone is not sufficient to warrant U.S. intervention, otherwise America would have invaded the USSR and, later, China to stop mass murder greater than that which occurred in Nazi Germany. America would also have occupied Angola, Bosnia, Burundi, Liberia, Sudan, and a host of other smaller hellholes around the globe. While moral concerns tug at our hearts, they are not enough to warrant committing 260 million Americans to war, risking unknown amounts of treasure and numbers of lives. In the case of Korea, we should ask, would U.S. security be seriously affected by a war (assuming no American tripwire was present to automatically trigger U.S. involvement)?

No Threat to America

The answer is no. Kim Jong Il's forces would pose no credible military threat to the United States. And, unlike the situation in 1950, a successful North Korean attack, highly unlikely given the South's capabilities, would be unconnected to a larger, hegemonic international threat to America. A united communist Korea would lack the wherewithal even to threaten its closest neighbors, China and Russia. Given the low quality of the North's military, and Pyongyang's economic travails, as well as the intensified international isolation that would greet the DPRK as a result of renewed aggression, even the unlikely worst-case scenario would be a tragedy confined to the Korean peninsula. A victorious North Korea would face insurmountable difficulty developing the military capability to intervene overseas, against, say, Japan. Pyongyang's possible possession of nuclear weapons would rightly frighten Tokyo, but the latter's development of a countervailing weapon, while unsettling to its neighbors, would deter any adventurism.

South Korea is a major trading partner of the United States; combined trade in 1995 ran $42 billion. Yet that is only 3 percent of all American trade and little more than one-half a percent of America's GDP. Thus, the economic impact on the United States would be minor. The loss of access to Hyundai automobiles, for instance, would be irritating, not catastrophic, given the many alternatives available. Millions of Americans with relatives in and ties to the South would be understandably grieved, but that hardly warrants treating the ROK as a vital U.S. interest. For that reason, Ted Galen Carpenter of the Cato Institute calls Korea a "peripheral interest," one that "does not warrant either the expense or the risk that the U.S. military commitment entails."[24]

Indeed, were it not for the existence of the Soviet Union in 1950, policymakers then would probably have written off the Korean conflict. In September 1947, for instance, the Joint Chiefs of Staff declared the Korean peninsula strategically unimportant. In the view of the Joint Chiefs, U.S. airpower based in Japan would be sufficient to neutralize the impact of a communist takeover of the peninsula.[25] And while Secretary Acheson's speech treating South Korea as outside the U.S. defense perimeter is quite famous, less well known is the fact that before the war General MacArthur also didn't believe that the ROK warranted defense by the United States.[26] Indeed, the

Pentagon supported the withdrawal of U.S. forces from South Korea in 1949 because it considered the country of "little strategic interest," even though it recognized that Soviet domination of the ROK thereafter would "have to be accepted as a probability."[27] Similarly, Washington later refused to carry the war into China and accepted a negotiated settlement, both pragmatic decisions that suggested that policymakers understood that the conflict affected no vital U.S. interests.

International Symbolism

What motivated U.S. military intervention in what was essentially another people's civil war was the belief that enormous symbolic and psychological damage would be done to the policy of containment if the United States allowed a Soviet proxy to swallow an American client state. In his memoirs, for instance, President Truman discusses, without disagreeing with, the Pentagon's conclusion that the peninsula was of little military value.[28] However, when the attack occurred, Truman assumed—erroneously, it turns out—that the invasion was Soviet inspired (as opposed to approved), "a repetition on a larger scale of what had happened in Berlin. The Reds were probing for weaknesses in our armor."[29] In short, he sought to send an international signal via intervention in Korea.

> Our allies and friends abroad were informed through our diplomatic representatives that it was our feeling that it was essential to the maintenance of peace that this armed aggression against a free nation be met firmly. We let it be known that we considered the Korean situation vital as a symbol of the strength and determination of the West. Firmness now would be the only way to deter new actions in other portions of the world. Not only in Asia but in Europe, the Middle East, and elsewhere the confidence of peoples in countries adjacent to the Soviet Union would be very adversely affected, in our judgment, if we failed to take action to protect a country established under our auspices and confirmed in its freedom by action of the United Nations. If, however, the threat to South Korea was met firmly and successfully, it would add to our successes in Iran, Berlin, and Greece a fourth success in opposition to the aggressive moves of the Communists. And each success, we suggested to our allies, was likely to add to the caution of the Soviets in undertaking new efforts of this kind. Thus the safety and prospects for peace of the free world would be increased.[30]

11

In retrospect, those sentiments seem questionable, since it appears that while Joseph Stalin did nothing to discourage the proposed attack, he neither planned the invasion nor intended it as a first stage in a program of global conquest, and he consequently distanced himself from it. Further, the Soviets were apparently surprised by the invasion's timing, since the USSR's ambassador was boycotting the UN Security Council (because of failure to seat the representative of the People's Republic of China). Moscow also later made it clear to the United States that it did not intend to enter the war (except, perhaps, in response to the defeat of China and a second advance to the Yalu).[31] Finally, Stalin, for all of his brutality, had no known plan for further direct or indirect aggression against any other allied state.

No International Puppeteer

But the argument had superficial appeal at the time, especially given the postwar advance of communism into Eastern Europe and China. Today, however, the world looks very different. Without the existence of a central puppeteer orchestrating probes for weaknesses, as Truman called them, around the world, all aggression now is local, dictated by the specific circumstances and histories of particular rivalries. Thus, in the absence of backing from an analog of the Soviet Union, an attack by Pyongyang on South Korea would be just that—an attack by Pyongyang on South Korea.

While the lack of larger consequences would make the event no less horrifying, it means that no vital U.S. interests would be at stake. That in turn indicates the absence of any justification for sacrificing U.S. lives and wealth and taking the other risks—terrorism and the proliferation of weapons of mass destruction—that could arise from intervening in what would otherwise be a sub-regional conflict. Of course, the collapse of communism has led to a frantic search for new justifications for old commitments—regional stability, containment of China or Japan, and even promotion of political and economic liberty, to name a few.[32] None of those proposed justifications offers a serious replacement for the Soviet menace, however. Containment was neither cheap nor risk free, but for 40 years there was a global threat to be contained. Today there is no commensurate need for the United States to subsidize nations that could defend themselves were they required to do so. Having sacrificed some 113,000 lives, spent some $13 trillion (in 1996 dollars), and accepted creation of the authoritarian and bloated national security state in order to win the Cold War, the American people deserve to reap the fruits of their victory.

A Changed World

Such a harvest requires Washington to adapt its foreign policy to a changing world. A good place to begin that shift would be Korea. The prospect of a major-power confrontation in the region has virtually disappeared; the bilateral balance has shifted irrevocably toward America's ally; and a successful disengagement would provide a model for eliminating other, similarly outmoded, commitments in the region. Such a policy shift should hold particular attraction for conservatives, who most loudly proclaim their commitment to smaller government, fiscal responsibility, and individual liberty.

It should also appeal to South Koreans. Although entrepreneurial, resilient, prosperous, and rightly proud, they will continue to be treated as children by Washington so long as they rely on their American "big brother" for protection. As the Ministry of National Defense of the ROK has rightly observed, "A sovereign state should be able to defend itself independently, without relying on foreign assistance."[33] That is especially true when a significant number of Koreans doubt the foreign nation's willingness to fulfill its commitments.[34] The key to South Koreans' military security and international growth will ultimately be Seoul, not Washington.

Today there is no Soviet Union to contain, and regional quarrels are no longer of vital concern because they are part of the overall Cold War. Moreover, those who were once possible victims of aggression—not only underdeveloped Korea but also defeated Germany and Japan and war-torn Britain and France—are all now stronger than their potential foes. The United States needs to develop a new military strategy of strategic independence, or benign detachment.

2. The U.S.-ROK Relationship

The Korean peninsula has long been a pawn in a larger regional game of power politics. Surrounded by China, Japan, and Russia, for centuries Koreans have found themselves dominated by one imperial power or another. The United States, in contrast, was a latecomer to the contest for influence over the peninsula. Although America's seizure of the Philippines as part of its war against Spain and its assertive Open Door policy on China in the late 1800s brought Washington a measure of influence in the Pacific, the United States lacked the proximity, ability, and commitment to impose its will in East Asia.[1]

America's first contacts with Korea were innocent enough: a ship that docked in what is now Pusan in 1853 was visited by local officials, and four deserters from the whaling ship *Two Brothers* swam ashore in 1855, only to be sent back to America via China. In 1866 came tragedy, however, when the schooner *General Sherman* sailed up the Taedong River near Pyongyang carrying cotton products, glass, and tin plate. Apparently the captain's actual intention did not match the ship's official commercial purpose. According to Richard O'Connor, "What the owner and crew of the *General Sherman* actually planned was to loot the tombs of Korean royalty and hold their contents for ransom."[2] The plan failed when the ship ran aground; natives burned the ship and killed the crew. Secretary of State William Seward proposed a joint punitive expedition to the French (who had their eyes on the Korean peninsula as well as Indochina). The French refused, and a year later Seward proposed sending a naval task force to blast open the markets of the so-called Hermit Kingdom. That effort, too, was stillborn, given the perceived strength of Korea's defenses. In 1870 an expedition finally did set sail, modeled after Com. Matthew Perry's famous "black ships" that had ended Japan's international isolation 16 years before. All too typical of the times, the American forces got into a scrap and launched a retaliatory expedition that captured a fort and killed 350 Korean defenders. Instead of capitulating, however, the Korean government simply ignored the U.S. forces, dismissing their demand for a commercial treaty. Too weak to conquer the peninsula, the Americans finally sailed away. The xenophobic regent for King Kojong branded the Americans "pirates" and "sea-wolf brigands" and put up tablets to warn "our descendants for ten thousand years to come" of the need to resist any further invasions.[3]

That was hardly a promising beginning for a friendly relationship. However, King Kojong, who soon supplanted his regent, proved more open to foreign influences. Moreover, China saw the possibility of using Washington as a counter to ever more aggressive Japan. After Tokyo concluded the oppressive 1876 Kanghwa Treaty, which opened Korean ports to Japan, the United States used Chinese intermediaries to initiate relations with Korea, despite the strong opposition of many Korean traditionalists, including Confucian scholars. Negotiated in China (America had to steadfastly resist that nation's pressure to include a clause recognizing Korea's dependence on Beijing), the Treaty of Peace, Amity, Commerce, and Navigation was signed by the United States and Korea on May 22, 1882. In an accord modeled after a similar U.S.-Chinese agreement, Korea granted the United States commercial privileges and extraterritorial status (protection from arrest and regulation); the United States offered its "good offices" to help Korea resist foreign oppression.

Regional Counterweight

Korea hoped that the United States would become a useful regional counterweight; indeed, reports former Korean ambassador to the United States Pyong-choon Hahm, "The Korean leaders read into the Korean-American treaty of 1882 something that was not there: a strategic commitment on the part of the United States to intervene to preserve the sovereignty and political independence of the Kingdom of Korea."[4] Over time, Korea's pathetic pleas for assistance grew ever more insistent.[5] However, America's interests were too slight to warrant serious engagement in a potentially violent struggle with China, Japan, and Russia. When U.S. envoy Horace Allen attempted to assist Korea, observes Dae-Sook Suh of the University of Hawaii, "he was reminded that intervention in Korean political affairs was not one of his assigned duties."[6] First Russia and then Japan exercised dominant influence. In 1905 Washington agreed to Japanese predominance in Korea in exchange for Tokyo's promise not to dispute American control of the Philippines. Despite the appeal of the Korean emperor, the United States terminated the U.S.-Korean treaty and closed its Korean legation in November 1905. That action still rankles some Koreans. Writes historian James Matray, "Today, most Koreans no longer blame the United States for *acquiescing* in Japanese annexation. Instead, they believe that Roosevelt *authorized* Japan's conquest of Korea."[7] Five years later, Japan formally swallowed the peninsula as a colony.[8]

For the next 35 years Korea essentially disappeared as an issue for Washington, except for a private campaign, waged by émigrés and American supporters, on behalf of Korean independence. Immigration to Hawaii for plantation work began in 1903; other Koreans, such as Syngman Rhee, traveled to America for schooling and stayed to organize politically. Missionaries to Korea proved to be particularly influential. As Suh relates, "It was said that politically Korea was nil, but in missionary circles Korea was a first-rate power."[9] Nevertheless, Washington remained aloof from such efforts. Even Woodrow Wilson refused to extend his promise of "self-determination" under the 14 Points to nonwhites, especially those under the rule of a nominal U.S. ally.

Then came World War II. Exiles like Rhee clamored for U.S. support for Korean liberation, but initially they received little attention.[10] As the collapse of Japan became imminent, policymakers in Washington finally became concerned about the disposition of Korea—though, according to one famous story, Secretary of State Edward Stettinius Jr. had to request a map to locate the nation. At Yalta in February 1945, Washington and Moscow agreed to a four-power trusteeship for the peninsula but left the details to a committee; Harry Truman, who became president in April, was skeptical of the proposal, which was subordinated to plans for the final defeat of Japan.

British opposition to the trusteeship, combined with the evident lack of American planning for a military occupation of Korea at the 1945 Potsdam conference, alerted Moscow that it might be able to play a significant role on the entire peninsula, then ruled by Japan, a nation with which the Soviet Union was not yet at war.[11] The United States was not prepared for Stalin's declaration of war against Japan, and, with Soviet troops racing for the peninsula, U.S. officials requested that Moscow halt at the 38th parallel, for what was to be a temporary division of the peninsula. Washington chose that line because it was as far north as policymakers thought the USSR would accept (in fact, there was some surprise when Stalin acceded to the U.S. proposal); the suggested boundary made no other sense.[12] The two occupiers agreed to establish a provisional government under a five-year trusteeship (reflecting Washington's view that the Koreans were not ready for full freedom), with independence to follow. For the Koreans it was a good news, bad news situation: "Korea was liberated but not independent."[13]

Yalta Breakdown

The U.S.-Soviet partnership quickly broke down in Korea as well as in Europe. Plans for peninsula-wide administration and elections went unfulfilled as both superpowers proceeded to create client states in their own images.[14] The USSR promoted communist and anti-Japanese guerrilla Kim Il Sung, while the United States relied on conservative nationalists, like Rhee (though he was not initially America's preferred candidate, given his irascibility, rigidity, and unpredictability), to the exclusion of local leftist leaders.

South Koreans praised the United States for liberating them from Japan, but numerous conflicts arose from the significant cultural differences—after all, most of Koreans' prior contacts with Americans had been with diplomats and missionaries, not war-hardened soldiers. Washington's military rule and decided preference for Rhee, a brutal right-wing nationalist, created additional problems.[15] Observes Edward Olsen of the Naval Postgraduate School, "American haste to wash its hands of Korea induced a willingness to accept 'stability' at the cost of political pluralism."[16] Indeed, the average South Korean could be forgiven for believing that the United States liked democracy only as long as it produced a compliant regime.[17] Moreover, the division of the peninsula, though not intended by the United States to be permanent, stung. Observes Olsen, "While many South Koreans are grateful for all that the U.S has done to keep their country alive and well, they also know that few of those dilemmas would have occurred had the U.S. not contributed to Korea's division."[18] At the time, many Koreans mouthed a popular slogan: "Don't rely on the United States, don't be deceived by the Soviets; Japan will rise again."[19]

Still, Seoul had little practical choice but to rely on America. The North refused to participate in UN-supervised elections, thus solidifying the peninsula's partition. The Republic of Korea, with Rhee as president, was created in August 1948; the Democratic People's Republic of Korea, led by the even more vicious Kim, emerged in December.[20] Both regimes claimed to represent the entire peninsula. "The ultimate result of great power rivalry, therefore, was to institutionalize the civil war in two contending states, both committed to the cause of unification," observes Callum MacDonald, a lecturer at England's University of Warwick.[21]

With no Demilitarized Zone to divide the country, the peninsula witnessed a southward population migration. The two countries settled into a rather hot cold war, with frequent cross-border raids and more serious military clashes. Moscow withdrew its troops from the North in late 1948; America's last forces left the South in July 1949.[22] Although Pentagon defense planners recognized that there was a risk that the North might invade the South, they did not intend to unilaterally commit U.S. troops in the event of war. Given America's expanding military commitments and declining force levels, the U.S. reaction was to be an appeal to the United Nations.[23]

Defense Perimeter

In his famous speech to the National Press Club on January 12, 1950, Secretary of State Dean Acheson excluded the ROK, along with the rest of the Asian mainland, from America's strategic "defense perimeter" and said that those nations should look to the United Nations for help in deterring communist aggression. Although Acheson was only reiterating the stance of the Pentagon and even Gen. Douglas MacArthur, he was widely blamed for having given the DPRK the go-ahead for war. The actual impact of his speech is difficult to gauge; Truman appeared to veer away from its noninterventionist line shortly thereafter, and Acheson later denied that he had meant that Korea would not be defended, though Senate Foreign Relations Committee chairman Tom Connally had publicly taken much the same position.[24]

In any case, despite the frequent border clashes and North Korea's military build-up, the Pentagon resisted proposals to increase military assistance to Rhee. The thuggishness of Rhee's administration was one problem; moreover, Washington overestimated the ROK's military readiness.[25] Perhaps most important was Rhee's repeated threat to retake the "lost territories" of the North. As historian James Matray puts it, "Once Rhee had sufficient military power, there could be little doubt that he would attempt forcible reunification."[26] For that reason, Washington refused to equip the ROK's military with aircraft (either bombers or fighters), tanks, and other heavy equipment and decided to limit ammunition stocks. By the summer of 1950 the North possessed a decided military edge. Writes historian William Stueck,

> Supplied generously by the Soviet Union, North Korea had 150 medium-sized tanks and a small tactical air force; South Korea had no tanks and virtually no military aircraft. North Korea had a three-to-one numerical advantage in divisional artillery, and its best guns far outranged those of South Korea. Although both sides had a relatively equal number of contestants, tens of thousands of Koreans, hardened by combat in the Chinese civil war, filled North Korea's lead divisions. The war began with Koreans fighting Koreans, but the inequality of the contest had much to do with the relative support given the two sides from beyond Korea's boundaries.[27]

The Coming of War

On June 25, 1950, the North Korean People's Army crossed the 38th parallel.[28] The Truman administration responded almost immediately. Although Washington's judgment that the ROK itself was not strategically significant had not changed, officials feared the impact on Japan, then seeking greater autonomy from U.S. occupation authority; the implication for the global struggle between Washington and Moscow; and the possibility of a similar attack by East Germany on its western counterpart. As historian Glenn Paige puts it, "The President and his advisers had no doubt whatever that the North Korean invasion had been inspired and controlled by the Soviet Union."[29] As a result, the example of appeasement of Nazi Germany—and the threat of sharp criticism from conservative Republicans—apparently weighed heavily on Truman. In fact, however, the invasion was not a Soviet project. The attack was Kim Il Sung's idea and he initiated the war, though he acted with the acquiescence if not the active support of China and the USSR. (While Joseph Stalin certainly would not discourage the "liberation" of an American client state, he was always a cautious predator wary of confrontation with the United States.[30] In contrast, in 1953 he impeded armistice negotiations because he believed the continuation of the conflict tied down U.S. forces and precluded any rapprochement between the United States and China.)[31]

President Truman attempted to contain the invasion first by supplying equipment to the ROK and then by launching naval and air strikes. But the South Korean army was overwhelmed by both surprise and tanks; it yielded Seoul in only three days. So Truman sent in American troops in what he termed a "police action." U.S. forces began arriving in July and were soon joined by 15 small foreign contingents under the aegis of the United Nations. (At the time, the Soviets were boycotting the Security Council over the failure to seat Beijing's ambassador in place of Chiang Kai-shek's representative and therefore were unable to veto the enabling resolution.) Nevertheless, by September most of the ROK was in North Korean hands; only a small beachhead around the southeastern port of Pusan was under allied control. However, with the dramatic landing at Inchon, near Seoul behind North Korean lines, Gen. Douglas MacArthur reversed the tide of battle; within a month the UN troops had crossed into the DPRK.[32]

Rolling North

Although the UN resolution merely called for restoration of the ROK, Washington—or rather, General MacArthur—was effectively running the war. Observes historian Clay Blair, "As it happened, the invasion of North Korea actually began without regard to these elaborate directives and the diplomatic nuances. It was led by the ROK 3d Division, which was speeding up the east coast highway against slight to no opposition. . . . This remarkable feat rendered academic all debate about crossing the parallel. Nonetheless, Washington and Tokyo proceeded with the diplomatic formalities. At the UN the British delegate introduced the vaguely worded resolution which, in effect, authorized crossing the parallel."[33]

China provided a number of signs—some intentional, some not—that it would not countenance American forces on its border. For instance, Premier Chou En-lai summoned Indian ambassador Kavalam Panikkar (Washington and Beijing had no means of direct contact) to a midnight interview to issue an explicit warning to the United States. The Chinese also launched a series of limited attacks on allied forces in October, before fading away, which indicated their presence and Beijing's irritation at the allied advance.[34] U.S. leaders ignored those signs of trouble—with disastrous results. As the allied forces, split between Gen. Walton (Johnnie) Walker's Eighth Army and Gen. Ned Almond's X Corps, neared the Yalu River, which marks the Korean-Chinese border, in November, about 300,000 Chinese "people's volunteers" struck the unprepared allied forces.[35] In the ensuing retreat, which at times verged on a rout, Seoul fell a second time, only to be recaptured by UN forces, which retook and then lost Pyongyang, the North's capital, a second time. By mid-1951 the front had stabilized near the original dividing line at the 38th parallel and Truman had fired MacArthur for insubordination.[36]

Painful Negotiations

Two years of negotiations that were both tortuous and torturous followed; particularly difficult was the issue of forced repatriation of prisoners. An armistice was finally signed on July 27, 1953. Rhee, who had never been an easy wartime partner, resisted. Writes Clay Blair, "He never relented in his efforts to sabotage the armistice. Throughout the talks he had demanded that no concessions whatsoever be granted the Communists, that the [Chinese forces] be expelled from North Korea, that the NKPA be disarmed, and that all Korea be united under the ROK government. [When] the armistice appeared to be impervious to sabotage, Rhee declared that South Korea would not honor its terms and that he might detach the ROK Army from the UN command and continue the war alone."[37] In the end, Rhee did not, though along the way he freed North Korean prisoners of war and otherwise attempted to undermine the armistice negotiations.[38] Promises of a U.S. defense guarantee and financial aid mixed with threats to let the ROK face the North and China alone (buttressed by covert planning for an American-backed coup) ended Rhee's resistance. Still desiring to liberate the entire peninsula, however, he refused to sign the accord.

At 10:00 p.m. on July 27 the guns fell silent. The war had cost America some 54,246 lives (including nonbattle deaths), 103,284 nonfatal casualties, and $75 billion—a significant 5.6 percent of the aggregate U.S. gross national product between 1950 and 1953.[39] Total UN force casualties (killed, wounded, and missing) ran nearly

1 million; the toll for China and North Korea was an estimated 1.4 million. The highest cost was borne by Koreans of South and North alike: 3 million dead, wounded, and missing; 10 million families broken up; 5 million refugees; and as much as one-fourth of the total population unable to support itself.

Discussions on the terms of a permanent peace treaty, including troop withdrawals and the reunification of the peninsula, began in October 1953 but quickly proved fruitless. A formal conference was also held in Geneva between April 26 and June 15, 1954, without result.[40] Left in place was the Armistice Agreement, along with the Military Armistice Commission and the Neutral Nations Supervisory Commission, tasked with enforcement of the accord.[41] Despite numerous violations over the years, that temporary peace regime has survived. In 1995, however, it came under renewed pressure as the North pushed to replace the armistice with a formal peace treaty with the United States.

As a cold peace descended on the peninsula, Washington negotiated a defense treaty with South Korea, or, as Youngnok Koo of the University of Michigan puts it, Rhee "extracted" the agreement, which the United States used to mollify his dissatisfaction with the war's indecisive outcome.[42] The Mutual Defense Treaty, ratified in January 1954, does not explicitly guarantee U.S. military assistance to the ROK; rather, it states that each party "would act to meet the common danger in accordance with its constitutional processes," which later caused Seoul to request a strengthening of the clause.[43] However, the continued presence of U.S. soldiers in the ROK has acted as a tripwire that would make American participation in combat automatic.

International Bonding

What had once been an indifferent relationship thus became an exceedingly close one. As Suh puts it, "Unlike the political impartiality and indifference that marked its policy at the time of the demise of the Korean kingdom, the reaction of the United States in 1950 was decisive. . . . The bond between the peoples of Korea and the United States was renewed and strengthened."[44] Washington's modest commitment of only four years before had become essentially unlimited. Although it took 70 years, Korea achieved its original objective of gaining the United States as its protector.

After the war America continued to support the ROK despite Rhee's despotic and erratic rule. In 1954 Rhee visited Washington and pleaded for financial help. Congress responded with a billion-dollar, multiyear development program (unfortunately, it did little to lift the ROK economy). And though the United States drew down its troop levels, which had peaked at 360,000 during the war, it left two divisions (about 60,000 troops) after 1957.

With little regret in Washington, Rhee and the so-called First Republic ended on April 19, 1960, in the wake of student demonstrations that the military refused to curb.[45] Civilian Chang Myon (educated in the United States, as reflected by his American name of John), a leading opposition figure, eventually took power but was ousted in a coup d'état by Maj. Gen. Park Chung Hee the following year. Although initially displeased with the coup, the Kennedy administration soon supported Park, who visited Washington shortly after taking power and was narrowly elected president in 1963 in elections that appeared to be relatively free and honest.[46]

U.S. financial aid and military support continued without question throughout the Park era, because the peninsula was regarded as an integral part of the Cold War struggle. Explained John Spanier of the University of Florida, "The Asian balance depended upon the United States until the non-Communist states of the area became economically developed and possessed sufficient capabilities of their own. Commitments . . . were interdependent. The United States could not choose to defend West Berlin and Quemoy but not Matsu and South Korea."[47]

In 1963 Pentagon planners considered reducing U.S. forces in South Korea but held off after Seoul dispatched some soldiers to Vietnam (in part to forestall any American drawdown). Park and President Lyndon Johnson exchanged visits in 1965 and 1966. U.S.-ROK ties were further reinforced by North Korean terrorism and adventurism—an assassination attempt against Park, the seizure of the USS *Pueblo*, and the shooting down of an American EC-121 reconnaissance aircraft, for instance. The United States continued to fund the bulk of South Korea's defense effort; in fact, it was 1969 before U.S. military aid accounted for less than 50 percent of the ROK's defense expenditures.[48]

The Nixon Doctrine

In early 1970 President Richard M. Nixon decided that additional troop reductions in Asia were desirable; he withdrew the Seventh

Army Division the following year, leaving about 40,000 personnel stationed in Korea. That decision caused consternation in the ROK, which had grown accustomed to American protection. The prime minister went so far as to threaten to resign over the issue, stating that "if GIs go, I go."[49] The Park government not only cited the North's military superiority but also claimed that only an American presence could deter Chinese and Soviet support for a DPRK invasion.[50] However, Nixon helped purchase Korea's acquiescence, if not assent, to the pullout by authorizing a $1.5 billion, five-year military modernization program for the ROK forces. (Additional U.S. force withdrawals were to begin in 1973 but were never carried out as the Watergate scandal consumed the Nixon presidency and North Vietnam conquered the Republic of Vietnam.) Nixon also studiously avoided raising human rights issues despite the Park regime's egregious conduct.[51]

President Gerald Ford followed his predecessors in visiting South Korea but abandoned any further force cuts. Although the Ford administration admitted that Chinese intervention in any conflict was increasingly improbable (in light of the growing rapprochement between Washington and Beijing), it contended that the U.S. commitment to the ROK remained necessary "to serve as a symbol of America's continued interest in the overall stability of that part of the world during a period of some tension."[52] Most of those tensions, of course, were linked to the Soviet Union.

The U.S.-ROK relationship faced a serious test in the late 1970s. Much of the problem was Park, who made no pretense of being a democrat. In late 1972 he declared a state of emergency and suspended most political freedoms. In 1973 the Korean Central Intelligence Agency kidnapped Kim Dae Jung, who had nearly defeated Park in the presidential election two years before, from Japan and placed him under house arrest in Seoul. Moreover, President Park

> instituted a powerful domestic surveillance organization to suppress popular dissent. Contrary to his original pledge and in contravention of constitutional limitations as well, President Park amended the constitution to prolong his tenure in office. He declared martial law to enable him to institute the so-called October Revitalization Reform of 1972 that virtually assured him the presidency for life. The powerful government intelligence agency made frequent arrests of dissidents, suppressed newspapers, jailed students and writers, and allegedly kidnapped political opponents.[53]

25

Congressional Alienation

Although Park's ugly record did little to disturb the support of GOP administrations, it did alienate Congress, which cut back administration aid requests and held hearings on human rights abuses. Then came the Korean influence-peddling scandal involving lobbyist Tongsun Park (which ran from 1976 to 1978) and, even more important, President Jimmy Carter's campaign pledge to sharply downsize the U.S. military commitment to the South, discussed in more detail in chapter 5. In 1978 President Carter pulled 3,600 soldiers out of South Korea, the first step of his plan to remove all ground forces (leaving 14,000 U.S. Air Force personnel and logistics specialists) by 1982. He, too, attempted to buy Korea's sufferance of a troop reduction, through a $2.2 billion, five-year program of credit and weapons transfers. However, opposition to the president's plan emerged in the military, Congress, and his own administration. Again, Korea was linked to the hegemonic threat to America in the larger Cold War. Sens. John Glenn (D-Ohio) and Hubert Humphrey (D-Minn.) argued that the Soviet Union and China might still back the North in a war. Retired Gen. Richard Stilwell, who had commanded U.S. forces in Korea during the 1970s, pointed out that "North Korea is linked by land to her Communist allies, whereas several thousand miles of water separate South Korea from the California coast."[54] Under congressional pressure Carter put his plan "in abeyance."

Throughout most of that period there was virtually no U.S.-DPRK contact outside the armistice commission. Such incidents as the 1968 *Pueblo* seizure and the 1976 ax murder of two servicemen who were trimming a tree in the DMZ firmly established the image of the DPRK as an outlaw nation. Yet for a long time the United States proposed cross-recognition—that China and Russia recognize South Korea and that Japan and the United States recognize North Korea. In 1975 Secretary of State Henry Kissinger proposed a four-power conference of the armistice powers in an attempt to move beyond the armistice accord. The Carter administration shifted policy slightly: it lifted the ban on private visits to the DPRK, allowed Pyongyang's foreign minister, Ho Dam, to visit New York for a meeting of the nonaligned nations, and sent a team to the 1979 World Table Tennis Tournament. The administration did not, however, initiate direct talks; moreover, Carter's postponement of his withdrawal plan cooled Northern ardor for better relations.

Tempestuous Relationship

For a time in the 1980s it looked like U.S.-ROK relations might become even more tempestuous. The assassination of President Park by his trusted head of the KCIA, Kim Jae Kyu (who favored more liberal political policies), in October 1979 led to brief civilian rule. Kim Dae Jung, former presidential candidate and kidnap victim; leading opposition legislator Kim Young Sam; and Kim Jong Pil, who had helped orchestrate Park's 1961 coup, all maneuvered for power. But the electoral process, which the military had vowed to respect, turned chaotic, with violent demonstrations and even more brutal repression. Gen. Chun Doo Hwan ended up arresting all three Kims and seizing power, with the assistance of military academy classmate Roh Tae Woo; along the way Chun used military special forces to suppress an uprising in Kwangju, in Cholla province, a political stronghold for Kim Dae Jung. Estimates of the number of deaths, officially set at about 200, range up to 2,000. Many Koreans blame the United States for the incident, because at that time an American general headed the Combined Forces Command— though, in fact, he had no operational control over the units sent to Kwangju. Unfortunately, explains Edward Olsen, "despite widespread, and vigorous, U.S. denials, the circumstances surrounding the Kwangju incident have haunted U.S.-R.O.K. relations and provided invaluable leverage for North Korean propagandists."[55] The Chun regime sentenced Kim Dae Jung to death for opposition activities but later commuted his sentence and allowed him to go into exile in America. As a signal of disapproval, President Carter halted bilateral economic talks and pushed the Asian Development Bank to halt new loans in an attempt to pressure Seoul to end martial law and institute other reforms.

But in 1981 President Carter was gone, the victim of an electorate angered by economic stagflation and the humiliating taking of hostages in Iran. President Ronald Reagan, who considered the ROK a frontline state in the struggle against global communism, immediately moved to improve relations with Seoul, reaffirming America's commitment to the ROK's defense and inviting South Korean president Chun to be the first foreign head of state to visit during his administration. In so doing, writes one observer, Reagan "in effect gave his seal of approval to the military regime."[56] Disputes over trade grew somewhat rancorous, but Reagan visited the ROK in

27

1983, and in 1986 Secretary of Defense Caspar Weinberger pledged that American troops would remain there "as long as the people of Korea want and need that presence."[57] At the same time—little more than a decade ago—conservative analysts were saying that the alliance was as important as ever and warning that China and the USSR were still likely to back a Northern attack, which could lead to both conquest of the ROK and "Finlandization" of Japan.[58] As for the DPRK, the Reagan administration maintained support for the traditional formula of cross-recognition but indicated its willingness to talk with North Korea only in the presence of the ROK. Left unhindered, however, were private contacts, begun during the Carter years.

Still, some tensions began to surface in the U.S.-ROK relationship. Between 1985 and 1988 a number of radical student organizations targeted American citizens and institutions for protests, taking over the offices of the Chamber of Commerce and U.S. Information Agency, for instance.[59] As street demonstrations escalated during the summer of 1987, many protestors blamed America not only for the political intransigence of the Chun government but for its very existence. At the same time, the Reagan administration became more interested in human rights and pressed the regime to forge a peaceful, democratic solution.[60] Then the 1988 Olympics showcased obnoxious behavior by some U.S. athletes—two swimmers stealing a hotel statue, for instance—which generated public disapproval. And acrimonious trade disputes over automobiles, food, and other products have continued to elicit public censure. After the fall of the Berlin Wall, polls found that many younger Koreans blamed the United States for impeding reunification of the peninsula.

Military Disputes

Strains in the U.S.–South Korean relationship also became evident in a series of government-government disputes over Washington's military presence. The ROK army resented the fact that the Combined Forces Command, with nominal authority over most South Korean forces, was still headed by an American (a Korean has since taken over). Many conservative businessmen as well as radical students were irritated by the presence of a U.S. base near the center of Seoul (South Korea later agreed to pay to move the facility). And many Koreans were angered by the special treatment accorded

American soldiers accused of crimes. (That issue has not been resolved: a 1992 case involving a serviceman who murdered a prostitute led to huge anti-American demonstrations. Even relatively minor conflicts—a subway brawl in the summer of 1995, for instance—have raised popular discontent with the dominant U.S. presence in Korea.)[61]

However, troublesome human rights issues at least have now largely passed from the scene. Roh Tae Woo, elected president in 1987, provided the needed transition from military to civilian rule; five years later his successor, Kim Young Sam, became the first genuine civilian president in three decades. Kim began purging the military and defanged the ruling party, having joined it, along with Kim Jong Pil (who later split off), in 1990. True, government officials still act in a high-handed and arbitrary fashion; for instance, Samsung Corporation learned the limits of free speech after Chairman Lee Kun Hee criticized the Kim administration.[62] Nicholas Eberstadt of the American Enterprise Institute writes of the difference between democracy, which the ROK has achieved, and a rule of law, which the South is still seeking.[63] Nevertheless, the possibility of a return to military rule seemed slight after Roh's presidency, and the United States, with more than its share of imperious government officials, had little about which to complain. (The prosecution of former presidents Chun and Roh vividly demonstrated how far the South had come in a decade.)

Moreover, despite disputes over command structure and base location, the two nations' security ties have remained largely inviolate. Shortly after taking office, President George Bush promised to maintain America's troop presence "as long as they are needed and as long as we believe it is in the interest of peace to keep them there."[64] President Bill Clinton has maintained a similar policy: preserving existing military deployments and promising to do so as long as the ROK desires. When the administration's bilateral discussions with North Korea over Pyongyang's nuclear program and decision to move toward diplomatic relations caused disquiet in the South, Clinton went out of his way to reaffirm his commitment to Seoul. Indeed, his administration actually halted the Pentagon's planned troop drawdown to 30,000 and beefed up the U.S. forces in response to North Korea's intransigence on the nuclear issue. Explained the Defense Department in early 1995,

Our security relationship with the Republic of Korea continues to be central to the stability of the Korean Peninsula
and Northeast Asia, as it has been for over forty years. The
Republic of Korea–United States combined defense structure
rests on three strong pillars: the 1953 Mutual Defense Treaty,
Combined Forces, and the annual Security Consultative
process. . . .

The relationship between the United States and the Republic of Korea is more than a treaty commitment, it is a vital
component in our national objective of supporting and promoting democracy. Even after the North Korean threat passes, the United States intends to maintain its strong defense
alliance with the Republic of Korea, in the interest of
regional security.[65]

Private Ties

Complementing the ties between the two governments are extensive private cultural and economic relationships among individuals,
businesses, universities, and other institutions. Indeed, the human
ties between the two nations are quite strong. No longer is the
primary connection a few American missionaries. More than 1 million U.S. citizens have served in the military in Korea, for instance,
and American businessmen are regular visitors to the South.

Flowing the other way across the Pacific have been hundreds of
thousands of Koreans, many to settle here permanently. As of 1990
some 800,000 Americans of Korean extraction lived in the United
States, more than double the number 10 years earlier, which itself
was a quintupling of the 69,130 counted in 1970. Indeed, reports
one expert, "The Korean population in the United States has become
one of the fastest-growing ethnic minorities. Over 80 percent of the
current Korean population in the United States is composed of these
post-1965 immigrants."[66]

Moreover, like Syngman Rhee, many Koreans—over 30,000 since
1960 alone—have been educated in the United States and returned
to the ROK. Equally significant are the thousands of Korean students'
children born in America and therefore eligible for U.S. citizenship.
That educational link has been expanding for a century and has
helped to fill influential positions in academia, business, and government in South Korea with Americophiles.[67]

Further, the ROK is one of America's largest trading partners,
generally ranked seventh in both exports and imports. Total U.S.

trade with South Korea in 1993 was almost $32 billion. As the ROK continues to grow wealthier, it is likely to become an even more important market for American goods and producer of quality products for U.S. consumers.

Where Next?

American-Korean relations were born in violence and disappointment, but a bloody war forged a relationship that remains close today. What, however, of the future in a post–Cold War world that is so very different from the environment in which the U.S.-ROK alliance was formed? Unfortunately, security ties remain dominant, as a result of the threat of renewed aggression from the North. Yet those links are growing increasingly fragile, since the raison d'être for Washington's security guarantee and domineering role has disappeared. Although officials on neither side of the Pacific are ready to concede the obsolescence of the security structure that they have so laboriously constructed, it is bound to collapse. A 1995 poll found that only South Koreans 40 years old and older supported a continuing U.S. troop presence. By increasing margins, people in their 30s and 20s opposed it.[68] Either the two governments will agree to an amicable separation, or, as the ROK grows richer, the DPRK reforms (or dies), America tires of underwriting a defense treaty that is mutual in name only, and South Korea no longer wishes to be treated as a protectorate, the divorce will be nasty.

A planned and positive transition from a relationship of parent and child to one of equal partners would be to both nations' benefit. First, it would be more likely to preserve a friendly working relationship between the two governments on political and security issues. Second, such a denouement would strengthen the increasingly important private, nonmilitary ties between Americans and South Koreans. It would help emphasize the links—cultural, economic, and personal—that are most relevant and bound to grow only stronger in the future.

3. The Costs of Commitment

If the promiscuous manner in which Washington hands out security guarantees is any indication, American policymakers appear to believe them costless. And if they were, there would be little reason not to hand them out indiscriminately. After all, a promise by America to defend another nation, be it South Korea, Germany, or Saudi Arabia, reduces the likelihood of attack on that nation. That is why other countries desire U.S. protection.

But security commitments are not costless—for America, at least. To the contrary, such promises not only entail financial expenditures and military risks; they often create economic and political problems as well. In the post–Cold War world, Washington needs to reweigh the costs and benefits of its security commitments. In the case of Korea, the United States should preserve its troop presence and underlying treaty guarantee, not "as long as the Korean people want them," as sundry U.S. officials have said, but only as long as doing so serves the interests of the American people.

"Vital" Alliance?

Of course, official Washington claims that the Korean commitment does serve U.S. interests. According to the Department of Defense, the alliance "is a vital component in our national objective of supporting and promoting democracy."[1] Yet that argument—which, notably, does not claim that Korea's protection is vital to the *security* of America—appears to be little more than an afterthought. The continuing U.S. commitment seems to largely reflect the power of inertia. In early 1995 the Department of Defense declared, "Our security relationship with the Republic of Korea continues to be central to the stability of the Korean Peninsula and Northeast Asia, as it has been for over 40 years."[2] While America's presence probably was central to the maintenance of peace 40 years ago, it is not obviously so today.

Indeed, the burden of proof surely lies with those who would retain the existing arrangement. In 1953, after the South had been devastated by war and Chinese forces remained in North Korea, there was a strong argument for America's defense guarantee. But that was more than four decades ago. The ensuing years have rendered obsolete every assumption underlying the Mutual Defense Treaty. First, there is no more Cold War, during which Washington assumed that any regional conflict had global implications. A North Korean invasion—unlikely, given the shifting balance of power on the peninsula—would no longer be tied to an expansive, hegemonic threat to the United States.

Second, Pyongyang can no longer expect support from China and Russia, which armed and supported the DPRK during the Korean War. In fact, South Korea has been forging close relations, including some military ties, with those two giant neighbors. Third, the ROK is no longer backward economically or politically. It vastly outstrips its northern antagonist and could easily achieve an overwhelming military advantage if it so desired. Fourth, East Asia is no longer filled with weak neighbors, such as Japan and the Philippines, vulnerable to communist aggression. Finally, the war in which tens of thousands of young Americans perished to preserve the South's independence, and which created a strong emotional barrier to any change in the two nations' relationship, is now more than 40 years rather than a few months or years old.

In short, *none* of the original arguments for America's security commitment, backed not only by the 37,000 soldiers on the peninsula but also by the full military faith and credit of the United States, now applies. If there is a case for continuing the ROK's security dependence on America, it must be made anew. And it must take into account the substantial costs of retaining Seoul as a de facto protectorate.

The Existing Commitment

The U.S. commitment to South Korea reflects both an implied promise to go to war—the Mutual Defense Treaty—and the means to do so—military forces on the ground in Korea and throughout the Pacific and the United States to act as reinforcements. The treaty says,

> Article 2. The Parties will consult together whenever, in the opinion of either of them, the political independence or

security of either of the Parties is threatened by external armed attack. Separately and jointly, by self-help and mutual aid, the Parties will maintain and develop appropriate means to deter armed attack and will take suitable measures in consultation and agreement to implement this Treaty to further its purpose.

Article 3. Each party recognizes that an armed attack in the Pacific area on either of the Parties in territories now under their respective administrative control, or hereafter recognized by one of the Parties as lawfully brought under the administrative control of the other, would be dangerous to its own peace and safety and declares that it would act to meet the common danger in accordance with its constitutional processes.[3]

Soldiers and arms are, of course, necessary to back up America's implicit promise to intervene. That is why military spending is the price of a nation's foreign policy. Washington's direct military commitment to South Korea is not large: one infantry division, two air wings, and sundry smaller detachments, for a total of about 37,000 personnel.[4] Most of the soldiers are members of the Second Infantry Division, which is part of the Eighth U.S. Army. (Germany is the only other foreign nation in which Washington stations at least a full division.) The air units come under the U.S. Seventh Air Force and are headquartered at Osan. All told, American forces occupy some 40 military installations. Until 1991 Washington also stored an estimated 150 tactical nuclear warheads (aircraft bombs, artillery shells, and land mines) in the South.

If war were to come, however, thousands more troops would follow. The two air wings and one Marine Expeditionary Force (20,000 Marines) stationed in Japan, for instance, are intended more to reinforce America's position in the ROK than to defend Japan, which today faces no serious threats. Additional forces in the United States are also implicitly intended for the defense of Korea. Although divining the purpose of any particular unit is difficult, especially since troops may have multiple roles, Georgetown University professor Earl Ravenal calculates that the East Asia obligations account for about three divisions.[5]

The treaty does not formally require American intervention, let alone use of combat forces, in a war, but the commitment is structured to make involvement automatic. Indeed, that is the purpose of stationing U.S. troops in Korea. One infantry division, all the American ground forces likely to be present in the event of a surprise North Korean attack, adds little to the ability of the ROK's 520,000-man army to stop an invasion. Observed Gen. John Bahnsen, the chief of staff of the ROK/U.S. Combined Field Army during the early 1980s, "The wisdom of maintaining any U.S. infantry in a country so rich in manpower is purely political."[6] What those 26,500 soldiers, still centered around Seoul and the Demilitarized Zone, do is guarantee immediate American casualties, making it unlikely that any administration would fail to order full-scale participation and any Congress would challenge such a decision. Thus, while the treaty gives a perfunctory nod to the operation of America's constitutional processes, particularly the requirement that Congress declare war and fund military operations, the practical implementation of the treaty would effectively short-circuit those requirements.

The Costs of Commitment

America's apparently small and simple security umbilical cord to South Korea is actually quite expensive to maintain. The consequences of America's promise to go to war on the ROK's behalf could be expensive financially and catastrophic in human terms, given the potential casualties of any war. The annual budgetary impact, even in the absence of war, is serious. Moreover, Washington bears a political cost for its defense ties, though that price has fallen as the South has moved from dictatorship to democracy. Should the ROK's form of government ever change, however, America would undoubtedly bear, fairly or not, a large share of the popular blame.

The Korean commitment also contributes to the overall expense of maintaining an oversized military more appropriate for an imperial than a republican foreign policy. That is, the Mutual Defense Treaty is one of Washington's many unnecessary military guarantees that collectively have deformed the nation's constitutional system by promoting the growth of state power at the expense of civil and economic liberty. Even more serious is the economic price paid by the United States for subsidizing the ROK, along with other increasingly productive trade competitors. All told, Washington's promises to Seoul are far more expensive than even most policymakers, let alone U.S. citizens, realize.

Military Risks

The cost of the Korean War was horrific for the United States: 138,000 American casualties and more than $360 billion (1996 dollars) in both direct and indirect expenses.[7] The risk of involvement in another conflict is the most important cost of the present commitment. True, the presence of U.S. troops in the ROK reduces somewhat the likelihood of a North Korean invasion. However, the placement of American soldiers between the two potential combatants also ensures that the United States would be deeply involved in a war between the two Koreas.

Any such conflict would be extremely bloody. The concentration of military power in Korea is unparalleled elsewhere in the world; roughly 1.5 million troops face each other across a 155-mile border, in contrast to only 2 million soldiers along the entire 4,600-mile Sino-Soviet border when those two nations were involved in serious border skirmishes. In fact, the two Koreas are technically still at war because Seoul never signed the 1953 armistice; since 1953 more than 1,000 South Koreans and 90 Americans have died in incidents along the Demilitarized Zone. As late as 1984 a firefight erupted when a Soviet student defected. A decade later the DPRK shot down a U.S. helicopter that strayed over the border. There is no more sensitive flash point for U.S. troops.

Presumably the toll would not match that of the first Korean War, in which America's technological lead was not so great, the South was far less prepared to defend itself, and China intervened on the DPRK's side. Indeed, the general consensus is that the allies would prevail quickly, perhaps within three months instead of three years, though there are some dissenting voices.[8] The North's qualitative inferiority, lack of combined forces exercises, inadequate training, and centralized command structure would all hinder any attack. And for Pyongyang, speed would be of the essence. South Korea alone vastly outstrips the North in virtually every measure of national strength; the longer a conflict continued, the more those advantages could be brought to bear.

Nevertheless, if Kim Jong Il unleashed his million-man army (roughly 10 times the size of the DPRK's first invasion force), 4,000 tanks, 7,500 artillery pieces, and assorted other weapons, the United States would be involved in a serious war over rough terrain where its air advantage would count for less than it did in the Iraqi desert.

Casualties would probably be far higher than those suffered in the Persian Gulf War. The military risks would be greatly exacerbated if Pyongyang developed even a small nuclear arsenal, since U.S. forces would provide a tempting target. Indeed, nowhere else on earth are so many Americans so conveniently clustered as a target for a power that might feel it had nothing to lose.

There is another military cost of Washington's security guarantee—the consequences of discouraging the development of the ROK military. If America were truly concerned about the fate of allied nations, it would encourage them to become strong enough to deter and contain regional threats. Yet the U.S. tripwire not only allows, but positively encourages, the ROK to spend less on the military than it otherwise would.

Intangible factors may also play a role. Melvyn Krauss of the Hoover Institution argues that because of Washington's dominant role, the South Koreans suffer "from a psychological inferiority complex and inadequate political will because they are constantly reminded of their extraordinary dependence on a foreign power for their survival by the presence of American ground forces in their country."[9] Any such feelings are obviously hard to measure and probably have lessened as the ROK has achieved so much economically and diplomatically, and particularly since it has created a functioning democracy so quickly.

Necessity

More significant is the simple question of need. So long as Seoul can rely on the United States, it has little incentive to devote more resources to defense. ROK officials would be foolish to spend the full amount needed for national security when Uncle Sam is willing to pick up much of the check. As long-time Korea watcher Selig Harrison put it in 1980, "The combined economic subsidy represented by U.S. forces, U.S. bases, U.S. military aid, and such ancillary economic aid as Food for Peace has enabled the South to have a maximum of security with a minimum of sacrifice."[10] ROK officials now naturally balk at increasing that level of sacrifice. At a conference hosted by the U.S.-Korean Security Council in late 1989, one member of the South's ruling party rejected a suggestion that his nation spend more on military research and development (R&D), explaining that "we have needs in health and education that must be met."[11] (At that time, one estimate—different sources vary—was that Seoul was devoting about 4 percent of its gross national product to the military, compared to nearly 6 percent spent by the United States and as much as 20 percent by North Korea.)

Obviously, the ROK cannot do nothing—America would not long maintain the Mutual Defense Treaty in the face of such blatant free riding, and few Korean citizens would tolerate being so helplessly dependent on a foreign power, whose policy could change overnight.[12] Nevertheless, South Korea spends significantly less—3.5 percent of GNP in 1994—than one would otherwise expect of a nation facing such a critical threat to its security, probably the most serious threat anywhere in the world. Israel, for instance, has consistently spent more than 10 percent of GNP, and often far more than that, on defense. Moreover, Seoul's military suffers from specific deficiencies, such as air-to-ground support, as a result of overreliance on America. Observes Henry Rowen, a former president of the Rand Corporation who also served in the Defense Department and the Bureau of the Budget, "Seoul's present military deficiencies exist because of earlier decisions that South Korea would rely on the United States in those areas. So long as a decision has been made to develop R.O.K. capabilities in these areas, it should not be difficult to overcome these weaknesses."[13]

The practical test of the South's willingness and ability to strengthen its military is provided by its response to previous U.S. troop drawdowns. As discussed in more detail in chapter 5, every force reduction or proposed reduction has resulted in increased South Korean defense efforts. For instance, President Richard M. Nixon's withdrawal of an Army division helped to trigger a nearly 10-fold increase in ROK military spending over 15 years.[14] President Jimmy Carter's proposal to pull out all Army personnel, though limited and ultimately abandoned, also helped to spur ROK military outlays.[15]

Although dependence on America may have been at least in the ROK's short-term interest, especially in the republic's early days of poverty, the long-term impact is likely to be less positive. It is, after all, hard to be simultaneously a fully independent participant in the world system and a de facto protectorate. More important, creating an international security dole on which allied nations wish to stay is surely not in Washington's interest, either short or long term. It is bad enough to risk being drawn into war. It is ridiculous to simultaneously risk being drawn into war and discourage the nation being defended from protecting itself.

Budgetary Consequences

The direct marginal cost of stationing 37,000 troops in Korea is small by Washington standards—about $3 billion.[16] In fact, U.S. officials have claimed that "the relative cost to the United States of our military presence in Korea is among the lowest of all foreign countries where we have stationed troops."[17] One reason for that is that the ROK theoretically offsets roughly half of America's cost. The cash offset was only about $300 million in 1995, but it is to gradually rise to $399 million by 1998. For the rest, reports the Department of Defense, Seoul "provides rent-free bases and facilities and forgoes taxes and customs on American troops."[18] However, while some of those expenses represent genuine opportunity costs for Korea (the land could be put to commercial use, for instance), they do not help the United States cover its expenditures. Moreover, not charging another nation for the privilege of offering military protection is hardly an act of charity, especially when the presence of that other country's soldiers generates over $1 billion annually in economic benefits.[19]

In any case, the most important expense is not deploying troops but raising and equipping them. A typical division costs from $5.7 billion to $6.8 billion annually to maintain; an air wing, of which there are two in the ROK, runs between $2.4 billion and $3.0 billion.[20] Thus, creating and sustaining the relevant units cost substantially more than the specific costs associated with stationing them in Korea—probably at least $10.5 billion to $12.7 billion more.

Moreover, as Ravenal observes, "The continued commitment of one ground division is just the tip of the iceberg."[21] The expense of all the military units—Army, Navy, Marine Corps, and Air Force—that are earmarked for a Korean conflict must also be included. In 1990 Ted Galen Carpenter of the Cato Institute estimated that cost at about $16 billion (in 1996 dollars). Adding in a proportionate share of the Pentagon's overhead, though no easy task, boosts the figure. In 1991 Ravenal figured the total cost of defending East Asia at about $39 billion (46.1 billion 1996 dollars).[22] Korea's defense accounted for about half of that outlay.[23] Thus, while the exact cost of America's Korean guarantee depends heavily on the parameters of one's analysis, it is clearly well above the oft-cited $3 billion. And the Clinton administration is committed to maintaining the status quo not just in Korea but throughout East Asia.

It is America's defense promise to, not its military presence in, the ROK that creates most of the expense. Merely withdrawing U.S. troops from the South without demobilizing them would save little money; in fact, redeploying them elsewhere might actually increase the cost, since there would no longer be any Korean and Japanese basing support. (Tokyo pays a substantially larger portion than does Seoul of the direct cost of stationing U.S. forces on its soil.) But Washington cannot disband the forces so long as it maintains its military guarantee. Only by terminating the security commitment can any significant savings be achieved. Failure to address that point was the most important flaw in the Carter withdrawal proposal.

Political Damage

The U.S. political record in Korea is not particularly honorable. After occupying the southern half of the peninsula at the conclusion of World War II, Washington ended up backing Syngman Rhee because, according to historian Callum MacDonald, it considered his regime "an instrument of containment" and "the only reliable barrier against communism."[24] Unfortunately, Rhee at times appeared to be trying to emulate the North's Kim Il Sung. Rhee's regime slaughtered an estimated 50,000 political prisoners before Seoul fell, for example, and mistreated DPRK civilians when the war moved to the North.[25]

Nevertheless, the Korean War helped America's reputation, because Washington had saved the South from Kim's brutal, totalitarian "paradise." The good feeling has been fading, however, since more than two-thirds of South Koreans were born after 1953. Their memories of America's role are rather different. "It's not that we don't like Americans," explained one demonstrator in July 1987, "but for 37 years you've been supporting the wrong guy here."[26]

The record extends well past Rhee. Barely a year after his fall in 1960, the military seized power from the civilian leadership. The United States accepted Park Chung Hee with few public qualms until the Carter administration. Although the assassination of Park in 1979 eliminated that blight on America's record, another soon followed: President Chun Doo Hwan.

Blind Support

Many Koreans suspect America of having been involved in Chun's 1980 coup. Although Gen. John Wickham, then U.S. commander in the ROK, said that he had no opportunity to block the move, and it is doubtful that Korean field officers would have refused to obey orders from their own commanders, he fanned suspicions by saying that Koreans were "lemming-like" and needed "a strong leader," among many other things.[27] Perhaps an even worse blow to America's reputation was inflicted later the same year by the Chun regime's brutal suppression of the student demonstrations in Kwangju. Many residents blamed Washington. Linda Lewis, an American anthropologist in Kwangju at the time, writes of "the oft-repeated expectation that the American government would (and should) actively intervene."[28]

It was almost certainly unfair for Koreans to accuse the United States of complicity in the Kwangju massacre. Wickham did not have operational control of the special forces that crushed the demonstrations, and, again, it is unlikely that U.S. disapproval would have stopped Chun from using the Korean military to bolster his control. But the fact that Wickham raised no objection to Chun's use of the troops and later publicly stated that the Koreans were not ready for democracy made it appear that Washington would blindly support any pro-American government regardless of its cruelty.[29]

The Reagan administration was even friendlier to Chun's regime, though amid rising civil disorder Washington ultimately encouraged Chun to implement democratic reforms.[30] Koreans may be forgiven their irritation at America's ambivalence. After all, observes Edward Olsen of the Naval Postgraduate School, "South Korea is joining the ranks of democratic nations," but more despite than because of the United States.[31]

Since the ascension of Kim Young Sam to the Korean presidency, fears of American interference in the ROK's internal political affairs have diminished. Yet even today, notes historian James Matray, "burning the American flag, carrying banners denouncing the United States, and chanting anti-American slogans have become standard features at student demonstrations regardless of the issue."[32] Moreover, while South Korea's future looks bright, there are no guarantees. Should the unlikely happen—a renewed military bid for influence or some bitter electoral infighting in a system that

42

continues to revolve around several polarizing political figures—Washington would once again risk being drawn into the vortex. So long as it is viewed as providing a bulwark for the ROK, the United States will not be able to escape perceived responsibility for domestic political events.

Moreover, democracy has magnified another problem inherent in America's military role: cultural conflicts. To place some 37,000 soldiers—largely young, single, and male—in a foreign nation guarantees social friction. In particular, issues of crime and punishment, easily handled by a military dictatorship, have become explosive for a democratic government facing elections. For instance, in the summer of 1995 a subway melee gave rise to bitter controversy. South Koreans protested the Status of Forces Agreement (SOFA), which outlines special treatment for U.S. soldiers by the Korean judicial system.[33] Washington blamed the ROK media for sensationalizing the incident and pointed to the fact that four Americans but no Koreans were indicted for the subway brawl as evidence that some protection of U.S. personnel is required, though Secretary of Defense William Perry later promised to consider changes in the SOFA.[34]

Whatever the merits of that particular case, it created serious discontent. Explained a student leader at Yonsei University, "The problem is not in the crime itself, but in the criminal process. This process reflects the imperialist characteristics of the U.S. government."[35] His opinion may be extreme, but he is not alone in his unhappiness about the present U.S.-ROK relationship. One activist collected 40,000 signatures demanding revision of the SOFA. Moreover, with the local media citing a supposed wave of 800 crimes in the past year (most were traffic violations), public opinion polls showed a 20-point plunge in public support for maintenance of the American forces.[36] Even U.S. ambassador James Laney acknowledged that "the Korean public is led to believe that these things are getting out of hand, and it's affecting our welcome here. It's cause for great concern."[37]

In short, Washington's security guarantee with its troop backstop creates significant social costs. Although the end of military rule has eliminated the most serious sources of tension, anger persists over U.S. support for past military regimes.[38] Moreover, the ROK's very success makes its dependence more insufferable. Opines Manwoo

Lee, "Anti-Americanism in Korea symbolizes a renaissance of Korean nationalism."[39] His argument appears to be supported by poll data. The United States long ranked at or near the top of the list of nations admired by Koreans. However, during the 1980s America slipped dramatically, falling to number nine in 1988, rebounding a little, and then sliding to number eight in 1992.[40] Ominously, America is rated lowest by urban dwellers, professionals, and the young. Thus, although the Northern threat forced South Koreans to accept an unnatural relationship of dependence, an older, independent heritage is reasserting itself. That only means more trouble in the future.

Domestic Costs

The direct costs are not the only price that Washington pays for defending the ROK. America's Korean security guarantee is also the keystone of a more expansive foreign policy that is expensive in other, more general ways. In those cases the Mutual Defense Treaty is a contributing rather than the sole cause.

Constitutional Distortions. Our domestic freedoms inevitably suffer as a result of America's many military commitments. World Wars I and II resulted in direct and massive assaults on civil liberties, including the suppression of dissent and free speech, and culminated in the incarceration of more than 100,000 Japanese-Americans. Much more modest, but still unsettling, was the anti-Arab sentiment unleashed during the short war against Iraq.[41] Moreover, the panoply of security restrictions that grew out of the Cold War continues to limit our freedom.[42]

The two World Wars also vastly expanded the government's economic powers. Federal spending in 1916 was just $713 million; it shot to $18.5 billion in 1919 and eventually settled back to the $3 billion level, more than quadruple its prewar level, throughout the 1920s. Similarly, federal outlays in 1940 were $9.5 billion. Spending increased nearly 10-fold, to $92.7 billion in 1945; fell to $29.8 billion, triple prewar levels, in 1948; and then began its inexorable growth upward. Observes Burton Yale Pines, formerly at the conservative Heritage Foundation, "Today's mammoth federal government is the product not so much of the New Deal but of the massive power assembled in Washington to wage World War II and the Cold War."[43] Some of the government's wartime regulations were never reversed.

New York City, for instance, still suffers from the destructive effects of rent control, a supposedly temporary wartime measure. Former Federal Reserve chairman Arthur Burns warned of the impact of military spending on the independence of businesses and educational institutions, pork-barrel abuses, and violations of privacy and liberty.[44]

All told, writes historian Robert Higgs, after World War II,

> a host of legacies remained: all the government-financed plants and equipment and the military-industrial complex to continue operating them; important postwar legislation inspired by wartime practices, including the Employment Act, the Taft-Hartley Act, and the Selective Service Act of 1948; the GI Bill and the new middle class it fostered; a voracious and effective federal income-tax system; a massive foreign aid program. More importantly the war left the constitutional structure of the country deeply altered in the direction of judicial abdication and excessive autonomy; the nation no longer possessed a "peacetime Constitution" to which it could return. Most significantly the war moved the prevailing ideology markedly toward acceptance of an enlarged governmental presence in the economy. At last even the majority of businessmen had come to accept, and often to demand, Big Government.[45]

Similarly, America's interventionist foreign policy has upset the constitutional balance within government. We have seen both the centralization of power in the federal government and the aggrandizement of the presidency. How far we have come is reflected in the fact that serious thinkers who purport to believe in jurisprudential interpretation based on the original intent of the Framers backed President Bush's contention that he could move more than 500,000 soldiers across the globe and launch a war against another sovereign state without congressional approval.[46] After the White House changed hands in 1993, both parties shamelessly flip-flopped when it came to the need for congressional authorization for involvement in Bosnia, Haiti, and Somalia.[47] And although U.S. participation in formal United Nations' peacekeeping operations is rather limited, it represents an even greater abrogation of Congress's authority, since interventionists claim that America's UN membership supersedes the need for a declaration of war to deploy U.S. troops.

In the case of Korea, the Clinton administration considered launching military strikes, without legislative assent, in response to the North's refusal to allow international inspection of its nuclear facilities. The administration was also prepared to seek UN sanctions against the DPRK, which might have triggered military action by Pyongyang—a development that would have automatically resulted in American casualties and thus full-scale military involvement, all without Congress's assent.

Obviously, America's security guarantee to Korea did not alone create—and today does not alone preserve—an expansionist, expensive, repressive, and secretive state apparatus. But it is an important part of the problem, since the principles behind the Mutual Defense Treaty are the same ones that underlie commitments elsewhere around the globe. Thus, so long as Washington follows a larger interventionist strategy, the American people will continue to suffer under an outsized government. One current example is the Clinton administration's attempt to control sales of encryption technology abroad and require private entrepreneurs to turn over to the government the "keys" to such technologies used domestically, despite the end of the Cold War.[48] So much for the end of the national security state.

Financial Costs. America's extensive military commitments to the ROK and other nations also impose a significant burden on the U.S. economy. Such costs are impossible to apportion to specific treaty partners, like Seoul, but the Korean security guarantee is emblematic of the larger problem faced by the United States.

Some defense spending is necessary, of course. How much is necessary should be determined by the global threat environment. Yet today, despite the end of hegemonic communism, a substantial share of U.S. military outlays is devoted to defending other nations, such as South Korea, rather than America. Observed Gen. Wallace Nutting, former commander in chief of the U.S. Readiness Command, "We today do not have a single soldier, airman, or sailor solely dedicated to the security mission within the United States."[49] House Speaker Newt Gingrich has conceded much the same point: "You do not need today's defense budget to defend the United States. You need today's defense budget to lead the world. If you are prepared to give up leading the world, we can have a much smaller defense system."[50]

By one measure, about 46 percent of America's 1995 military budget was primarily for the benefit of other nations. Put another way, America is spending roughly 85 percent more on the military than is necessary to defend this nation—roughly $260 billion compared to the $140 billion that would be necessary to maintain a 850,000-man military, 6 carrier groups, and 15 air wings.[51] Such an expenditure would still put the United States far ahead of Russia and equal to Britain, France, Germany, and Japan collectively.

There are some advocates of *increased* military spending who point to the Department of Defense's "Bottom-Up Review."[52] However, there are a number of serious flaws in such analyses. The most important is that they measure the current budget against the status quo policy that presumes military intervention in a host of potential conflicts irrelevant to U.S. national security.[53] In East Asia alone those responsibilities, which grew out of the Cold War, are immense. As historian Paul Kennedy noted, "Even a mere listing of those obligations cannot fail to suggest the extraordinarily wide-ranging nature of American interests in this region. A few years ago, the U.S. Defense Department attempted a brief summary of American interests in East Asia, but its very succinctness pointed, paradoxically, to the almost limitless extent of those strategical commitments."[54] That is, a commitment to, for instance, defend "stability" in East Asia implies a willingness to intervene in a score of local conflicts revolving around border disputes, ethnic divisions, and other parochial squabbles.

Imperial Overreach When There Is No Threat

Why are such commitments necessary in the absence of a hegemonic threat? Even military men recognize that the world has changed a bit over the last decade. As Gen. Colin Powell observed in 1991, "I'm running out of demons. I'm running out of villains. I'm down to Castro and Kim Il Sung."[55] Instead of assuming that present foreign policy is sacrosanct and must be fully funded, policymakers should reconsider their assumptions, including the assumption that the United States must defend South Korea.

Their refusal to do so will continue to be costly. After all, America's policy of promiscuous intervention, by bloating the military budget by more than $100 billion, accounts for the lion's share of the federal deficit (about $160 billion in 1996). In effect, the United States is borrowing from allies for the privilege of defending them and racking up interest charges in the process. In some years Japan, the biggest buyer of U.S. government bonds, has financed a third of Uncle Sam's red ink; up to 80 percent of individual debt issues have been purchased by Japanese investors. All told, the opportunity cost of those expenditures, along with the interest that will eventually come due—the real financial burden borne by America—is huge.

The result will not necessarily be as dramatic as the deleterious impact of "imperial overstretch" on dilapidated empires such as the Hapsburg, which Kennedy described in great detail in *The Rise and Fall of the Great Powers*. But it is still significant. The harm caused by the national security state, created to defend South Korea and a host of other nations around the world, to the American economy has been pervasive. As Higgs puts it, fighting the Cold War "brought about massive changes in the allocation of resources, with effects on many dimensions of the nation's economic performance."[56] The problem is not so much the dollar amount—generally a few percent of GDP (though during the early years of the Cold War and the height of the Vietnam War it hovered around 10 percent). Rather, explains economist Lloyd Jeffry Dumas, it is government's manipulative role that is decisive: federal spending "may be small relative to the total economy, while at the same time diverting substantial amounts of critical economic resources."[57] Conscription, large-scale civilian hiring, massive military procurement, creation of entire security-related industries, and sustained higher rates of taxation to pay for the Cold War military all worked to reduce U.S. economic growth rates. The impact has been particularly dramatic in some areas of the economy. For instance, during the Cold War Washington "assumed major responsibilities for decision making, for finance, and even for the use of the 'output' of scientific research," report economists David Mowery and Nathan Rosenberg.[58]

Illusions of Prosperity

Military spending does sometimes create the illusion of prosperity.[59] For instance, it is widely believed that World War II brought America out of the Great Depression. But the economy was already recovering in 1940, and real personal consumption and private investment actually fell during the war.[60] A similar misperception of the beneficial effects of military spending occurred during the

Cold War. The Cold War creation of what President Dwight D. Eisenhower called the "military-industrial complex" generated a lot of highly visible jobs in security-related industries, such as aerospace. Unfortunately, the price of creating those jobs was even greater job losses elsewhere, as money was withdrawn from other sectors of the economy.

There is little doubt that in the short term the transition to a less militarized economy would be painful. One estimate is that up to $60 billion in plant and equipment may have been rendered obsolete by the end of the Cold War.[61] Examples of serious human dislocations are evident in southern California and elsewhere.[62] In the longer term, however, most citizens will benefit as the economy grows faster, especially as that growth effectively compounds (like interest). Numerous analyses have predicted that cutting military spending further would increase employment, almost irrespective of how the money was used.[63] As the Congressional Budget Office reported in 1992, then-planned budget cuts "would increase national savings and investment and would therefore benefit the economy. By the next decade the dividend realized . . . could result in a permanent increase in GNP of around $50 billion a year (in 1992 dollars)."[64]

The financial problem of subsidizing the defense of allies is twofold. First, as has long been said, there ain't no such thing as a free lunch. Unless the funds to pay for the military units stationed in Korea, Japan, and Europe are being provided by a grateful emir, emperor, king, president, prime minister, sultan, or other party, they are being extracted from the American economy. Both taxing and borrowing generate economic costs that are greater than the more visible benefits of military outlays. Explains economist William A. Niskanen, "Additional defense expenditures are not a good investment in terms of the marketed output of the business sector."[65] Depending on other economic policies, higher military spending can also contribute to inflationary pressures and other economic problems.[66]

Opportunity Costs

Spending on the military generally carries a high opportunity cost, that is, the uses to which the funds could have been devoted— private investment, R&D, and the like—are more valuable than the use to which the money is actually put. As one analysis of America's entry into World War II explained, "The immediate practical task of war financing consists largely in reducing civilian use of resources needed for the military program."[67] Unfortunately, the substitution of military for civilian uses is quite costly.

For one thing, military spending tends to create fewer jobs per dollar than does normal private economic activity.[68] Even more important, defense outlays are what Dumas calls an "economic parasite."[69] For example, building tanks and paying soldiers to patrol Korea's Demilitarized Zone, whether or not necessary for America's defense, have never added anything to the nation's wealth, as would have, say, manufacturing washing machines and paying construction workers to build houses. Such forgone goods and services are the real price of Washington's expansive defense guarantees.

The cost in consumption is high. Political scientist Bruce Russett has figured that every additional dollar in military outlays cuts civilian consumption by 42 cents. But America's defense subsidies do more. They diminish investment in the future—in R&D, business plant and equipment, education, training, and the like. Indeed, in the mid-1980s the book value of the military's physical capital was almost half that of all U.S. manufacturing establishments, an incredible diversion of otherwise productive resources.[70] Russett estimates that an extra dollar for the military reduces private capital investment by about 30 cents. Since total investment is lower than consumption, defense spending has a disproportionately negative impact on the former. Assuming marginal productivity of capital is between 20 and 25 percent, every $1 billion in additional military spending permanently lowers economic output by roughly $65 million annually.[71] (Civilian government programs have proved to be far more resilient than have private expenditures in the face of increased military outlays.) Other studies, too, note the significantly negative impact of military spending on private investment.[72]

High-Tech Drain

Of particular concern, given the growing economic importance of high technology, is the drain on R&D caused by military expenditures to defend other nations, such as the ROK. Although America's outlays for R&D have long been higher than those of Japan and Western Europe, a much larger share of the U.S. effort is devoted to defense; military R&D by South Korea and Japan, in particular, is minimal. Thus, for years America's most important industrial competitors, Germany and Japan, have actually been devoting a larger share of their GNPs to civilian R&D spending than has the United States.[73]

Unfortunately, despite some specific and occasionally dramatic civilian applications derived from security research, studies have found little overall economic benefit from military R&D for the United States or other nations.[74] To the contrary, America lost much of its competitive and technological edge during the 1970s despite continued high expenditures on defense-related R&D.[75] Moreover, research on cutting-edge technology has increasingly shifted from the Department of Defense to private firms. As a result, the Pentagon "has become a net user of civilian research," says former Council of Economic Advisers chairman Murray Weidenbaum. He reports that Secretary Perry, before taking office, cited

> the example of semiconductors, where the differences between defense and commercial technologies are not very great. Extremely detailed military specifications have isolated defense production, dividing the U.S. industrial base between defense and commercial uses. Perry believes that, due to the rigidity of military specifications and requirements, chips made for the Defense Department are ten times more expensive and nearly two generations behind their commercial counterparts.[76]

Yet military R&D spending competes directly with civilian projects. The ratio of defense to civilian R&D expenditures went from 1.2 to 2.6 between just 1980 and 1984.[77] Although Department of Defense retrenchments have since reversed that trend (the ratio was back to a still high 1.2 in 1995), growing pressure to balance the budget after the 1994 election caused science advocates to complain about reductions in civilian R&D. For example, in 1995 the GOP majority in Congress proposed cutting federal R&D outlays from $32 billion annually to about $25 billion a year by 2000. The American Association for the Advancement of Science warned of "the most significant across-the-board funding cuts to the R&D enterprise in the post–World War II era."[78] (In fact, there is no reason to assume that reductions in government expenditures are bad, since taxpayer-funded research is afflicted by the perverse incentives that bedevil all public institutions, as detailed by public-choice economists.

51

Observes economist Paul Romer of the University of California, Berkeley, "We've been saying 'More bucks now!' for 40 years. Now is an opportune time to fine-tune these institutions.)[79]

Even worse, unnecessary military spending, most obviously to sustain outmoded commitments such as that to Korea, drains resources from private research outlays as well. The problem is not just inadequate funds; the defense sector has also proved to be a tough competitor for a relatively limited pool of skilled labor. Early in the Cold War, and later during the Reagan administration's military build-up, two-thirds of R&D scientists were working for security-related enterprises.[80] As Arthur Burns explained, "Many civilian-oriented laboratories of business firms have found it difficult to match the salaries or the equipment that subsidized defense firms offer to scientists and engineers."[81] That has been a recurrent problem; during the Reagan build-up in the early 1980s, firms were using headhunters to acquire, not just senior management, but machinists and computer technicians.

American subsidies for the defense of other nations, including some of its most aggressive trading partners, such as South Korea and Japan, have another pernicious effect. Not only do they divert U.S. resources from other pursuits, but they free foreign funds for other nations to use in competition with America. Every dollar that the South Koreans and the Japanese, for instance, do not spend on the military can be spent to advance economic, social, and other goals. Over the years America's defense guarantees have given other industrialized nations a huge advantage over the United States. As economist Otto Eckstein, president of DRI, warned in 1980, "If we're going to have an age of defense step-up, we'll lose competitive edge, vis-à-vis Japan and Germany, if we allow them to maintain their 1 to 4 percent [military spending] share of GNP."[82] Cross-national comparisons make the same point: in general, countries with higher military expenditures invest less, which lowers productivity and slows economic growth.[83]

U.S. Subsidies for Seoul—And Others

Consider the ROK. Although Seoul spends considerably more of its GNP on defense than do Japan and most NATO countries, it trails the United States, 3.6 percent to 4.7 percent by one measure and 4.2 percent to 4.6 percent by another, even though it confronts a far greater direct military threat.[84] In fact, measured as a percentage of GNP, the South's effort has been *falling* for more than a decade, dropping from a high of 6.1 percent in 1981.[85] Decreasing effort may make sense for America and Western Europe, where serious security threats have essentially vanished in the aftermath of the collapse of the USSR. But that is not the case for Seoul, since the DPRK, though not likely to invade, retains a potent and aggressively positioned military.

The financial disadvantage suffered by America as a result of its Korean protectorate is dramatic. In 1981 the United States spent about $799 per capita on defense, compared to $113 spent by South Korea. In 1994 America's per capita military outlay ran $1,079, compared to $311 in the ROK. Obviously, the South's lower expenditures in part reflect its lower per capita GDP, though in the same years per capita defense spending by the much poorer North Korea was a good deal higher—$175 in 1981 and a comparable $229 in 1994. More important, the gap between Seoul and America *actually widened* over a decade when the South was enjoying much faster economic growth. It was one thing for America to accept that sort of economic disadvantage in the 1950s and 1960s to encourage economic growth in what was a desperately poor nation. Such a policy today, when profitable Korean manufacturers successfully compete in most major American markets, is frankly inane.

And America's protection has been critical to the ROK's competitive success. Without U.S. defense subsidies, the South could not have promoted industrialization with as much fervor as it did during the 1970s, nor would it have been likely to create entrepreneurial incentives, such as tax breaks.[86] Equally important, Seoul probably could not have begun in the early 1990s what one reporter calls "a spending binge" on R&D "to become more self-reliant."[87]

South Korea is merely one part of a global problem for the United States. The South has been moving in the same direction as Japan, with even higher annual economic growth rates. Indeed, one analyst argues that Korea's goal is to "do what the Japanese have done, but do it cheaper and faster."[88] Ernest Oppenheimer, a former investment banker, observes of Japan,

> From 1981 through 1994, the U.S. spent $3.5 trillion on defense, or $14,000 per capita. In the same interval, Japan devoted about $2,500 to this task. The $11,500 per capita

difference constituted a $1.4 trillion financial advantage to 120 million Japanese. These funds represented a form of free financing, which was channeled into the creation of superior products and state-of-the-art manufacturing facilities that gave Japan a competitive advantage in the global marketplace.[89]

Tokyo's dramatic economic success over the last two decades is all too obvious. One recent review documented "Japan's advantage with the subcontracting system and in factory efficiency in the large-scale assembly type industry and . . . the drag of elderly capital vintages in the United States."[90] One reason American industry took longer than it should have to accumulate the capital necessary to upgrade its physical plant is the higher taxes used to finance the defense of allied nations. Another problem has been the role of the Department of Defense as direct purchaser in reducing the price sensitivity of U.S. industry.[91] Although the pressure of international competition has ultimately forced domestic firms to become more competitive, the process has been slowed by Washington's placing a relatively higher defense burden on the U.S. economy and reducing the burden on allied nations.

Washington's European allies have benefited nearly as much as their East Asian counterparts. Daniel Burstein writes that Germany "is much like Japan in the sense that it has welded productivity, technological excellence, a high savings rate, and a strong currency into a tower of economic strength."[92] Equally important has been America's defense guarantee, which enabled German military spending to fall to an anemic $32 billion in 1996. The benefits go not just to such economic powerhouses as Germany and Japan; Britain, France, and others have enjoyed a financial windfall because of Washington's military generosity. In the end, Americans have paid twice: first as taxpayers and again as producers in an increasingly competitive world.

None of that is to suggest that South Korea or Japan is set to become a colossus likely to turn America into an economic colony— or even to go to war against the United States—as is suggested by some alarmists.[93] Indeed, it wasn't that many years ago that Europeans feared America's economic strength.[94] Japan has suffered, and is still suffering, its share of economic difficulties this decade, just as America has.[95] As the ROK matures economically, it is also certain to see its growth rate slow. Nevertheless, the underlying point is valid: America has imposed artificial burdens on its economy and conferred equally artificial advantages on the economies of allies by subsidizing their defense.

The response of some members of Congress has been to wish America's allies ill. For instance, Rep. Patricia Schroeder (D-Colo.) once proposed imposing a defense fee based on each defense dependent's trade deficit and military expenditures. That was never a real solution—in fact, trade deficits are little more than statistical artifacts, and charging other countries for America's protection would be essentially "hiring out" U.S. soldiers as quasi-mercenaries. But such initiatives reflected Congress's frustration with other nations' taking advantage of America's unfair military burden. A better response would be to stop subsidizing foreign manufacturers to the detriment of American producers. Ending the U.S. security commitment to South Korea, thereby permitting Washington to reduce military outlays and forcing the ROK—as well as Japan and other allied nations—to increase defense expenditures, would make the U.S. economy more competitive internationally.[96]

Contrary to the routine assertions of successive administrations and assorted policymakers, Washington's promise to defend South Korea is not cheap. It creates significant military risks, generates excessive budget expenditures, and engenders corrosive political tensions. Moreover, the Korean commitment is merely one of a number of outmoded security guarantees that collectively deform America's constitutional system and burden America's economy. All told, the costs of the Mutual Defense Treaty are actually quite high.

That a military guarantee is expensive does not necessarily mean that it is not worth sustaining, of course. But a serious weighing of the costs against the purported benefits is in order. The military balance 40-odd years ago, when America initiated its alliance with the ROK, no longer matters, since the existing situation is vastly different. If the advantages don't add up and the tally today turns out to be decidedly negative, as I contend in the following chapter, it is time to reconsider, not just troop deployments on the peninsula, but also the security treaty itself.

4. Reappraising the Security Relationship

The costs of America's security guarantee to the ROK are painfully obvious—increased military risks, perpetually higher taxes, and messy political entanglements, as well as lost economic productivity and domestic freedoms. It is time to ask two questions: what is the United States receiving in return? and is it enough to compensate for the costs of commitment?

The Myth of Leverage

Although economic ties are among the strongest aspects of the existing relationship between America and the ROK, Washington's security promise provides the United States with no tangible economic advantages. After all, U.S.–South Korean trade is valuable but not critical, accounting for about 3 percent of America's total trade and only a bit more than one-half a percent of its gross domestic product. Bilateral trade would be affected by the removal of U.S. troops only if the ROK was overrun, an exceedingly unlikely prospect for a nation so much more advanced than its adversary.

The mere presence of 37,000 U.S. soldiers in the South does not materially strengthen Washington's hand in any trade dispute. To the contrary, Seoul has long resisted trade liberalization by claiming that any step that hurt its economy would undercut American security goals. Some ROK officials argue that South Koreans prefer U.S. goods to competing products out of gratitude for American military support, though such an impact, impossible to measure if present, is modest at best. The ROK does not import a disproportionate number of American products, ran a string of trade surpluses in the 1980s, and continues to impose numerous barriers against U.S. imports.[1] Short of marching on the Blue House, home of the South's president, American soldiers can do little to enhance access for, say, U.S. cigarette exporters. The knowledge that American taxpayers are paying to protect a nation that closes parts of its market to the

United States causes U.S. negotiators to be more petulant, not more persuasive.

In fact, after more than four decades of protecting South Korea, Washington continues to fight South Korean barriers to such American products as automobiles. Complains Paul Pheby, a managing director of Peregrine Investment Holdings Ltd., "These days, it's not so easy to tell which of the two Koreas is open and which is more closed."[2] Washington might exercise greater influence if it seriously threatened to bring home its troops, but it would have to be prepared to follow through, which, of course, would give the lie to the argument that the security commitment serves important American interests. For that reason, William Taylor of the Center for Strategic and International Studies has warned that "a linkage between trade and troop deployment will seriously undermine U.S. interests in the region."[3]

And the United States could ill afford to promiscuously issue that most serious of threats; to do so would quickly complicate relations with Seoul, perhaps even causing South Korea to respond to the attempted blackmail by demanding the troops' withdrawal. Even the sort of run-of-the-mill pressure presently exerted by Washington to encourage agricultural liberalization, for instance, has caused significant popular indignation. Sung-Hoon Kim, dean of the Graduate School of Social Development at Chung-Ang University, warns that "quite a few people . . . resent U.S. pressure." Indeed, he adds, "In recent years the traditionally conservative farmers (23 percent of the total population) have rushed to join the radical anti-US group."[4] In September 1995 radical students rallied in the city of Kwangju against America's perceived role in the 1980 military crackdown on advocates of democracy, a traditional cause, and U.S. demands that the ROK open its auto market. To play politics with what Koreans view as their security lifeline would greatly exacerbate that sort of resentment.

Conversely, a withdrawal not linked to economic disputes would offer clear economic advantages for America. The result would be either détente on the peninsula or a substantial South Korean military build-up. The first course would open new markets for America in the North.[5] The second would eliminate Seoul's artificial economic advantage, due to Washington's defense subsidy, in international markets and probably lead to additional weapons purchases from U.S. manufacturers.

It has been argued, of course, that the trade, not just of Korea, but of all of Asia depends on the stability ensured by American forces. That the U.S. presence is comforting to other nations is obvious, but, as discussed in chapter 7, a general East Asian war is not threatening to break out, and regional institutions, too, could be used to promote stability. Although a wild daisy chain can be constructed to "demonstrate" that an American withdrawal from Korea might lead to, say, a war between China and Japan, it is no more persuasive than were claims that the fall of Vietnam would result in the neutralization of Japan or more recent claims that the Serb-Muslim conflict in Bosnia was likely to lead to World War III.

Regional Political Frictions

Regional political frictions might increase, but a modest military build-up by Japan, probably inevitable anyway, would act as a healthy constraint on China, potentially the more disruptive power. In any case, the end result, again, would be economically beneficial to this country. America's lower military spending would reduce the burden on U.S. exporters while our international competitors would have to bear the full burden of their nations' defense costs. Allied nations would also be likely to recycle some of their foreign exchange earnings to American firms as part of any defense build-ups.[6]

Another contention of defenders of the status quo is that increased military spending by America's allies would hurt their economies and thus, presumably, eventually harm that of the United States. The South Korean government explains that one reason it does not possess a "completely independent military capability" is because it has "considered the burden of [its] defense budget to [the ROK] economy."[7] Indeed, Koreans seem to regularly poormouth their nation's economic prowess. Although the ROK had enjoyed decades of record growth, one South Korean analyst complained in 1990 that his nation was "facing one of its worst situations in 10 years" with "a worrisome plunge in economic growth."[8] The following year the South's economy grew 9.1 percent.

Some Americans, too, have advanced that argument. For instance, in its fiscal year 1987 defense budget proposal, the U.S. Department of Defense argued, "If the ROK spent much more on defense than it does now (about 6 percent of gross national product) it could damage its economy."[9] That curious contention was later repeated by William Taylor and Michael Mazarr of the Center for Strategic and International Studies; they warned that sharp increases in defense spending "would deeply wound the ROK economy."[10] Notably, those arguments were being voiced while the South was enjoying double-digit economic growth rates, from 1986 to 1988. In 1989 Seoul suffered a dip to a mere 6.5 percent increase before rebounding to 9.6 percent 1990.[11] The ROK's economy grew more than 7 percent in 1995.

The spectacle of American administrations and defense analysts being more concerned about the state of their allies' economies than about that of their own nation's was odd enough. The claim that the South was incapable of spending more on defense was even stranger. Certainly, increased military spending would have put a burden on the South Korean economy, but even a decade ago the ROK had a GDP six to seven times the size of that of the North and was in the middle of an extraordinary boom. Had the ROK's growth rate fallen from 12 percent to, say, 10 percent, that would have been a modest price to pay for that nation's covering more of its defense costs. And today, with the ROK's GDP approaching $400 billion, the potential economic burden of greater defense outlays is not a serious concern.

Political Penance

The alliance brings some benefits. The absence of an American security guarantee would obviously reduce Washington's ability to influence the ROK. But that presumed clout was difficult enough to exercise even during the Korean War, when the Rhee regime depended on Washington for its survival. Indeed, Washington could barely restrain Rhee from upsetting the entire armistice. On matters important to Seoul—such as preservation of military rule by the Park and Chun dictatorships—Washington's influence has long been minimal. Even personal pressure from President Gerald Ford achieved no practical results, despite his belief that Park "would modify some of his more repressive policies."[12] Secretary of State George Shultz later complained that "you can't snap your fingers and make people do what you think."[13] And America's ability to influence events has diminished still further in today's Korean democracy.

Moreover, as argued earlier, any attempt to use clout derived from the security commitment not only requires a willingness to walk away from the peninsula but is bound to anger Koreans in and out of government. Nationalism is hardly a new phenomenon in Korea. Interestingly, during the massive 1987 protests against the Chun regime, resentment against America abounded on both sides. One government official complained, "We're tired of being treated as a colony of the United States."[14] His opinion differed little in substance from that of the student who told U.S. reporters, "We are trying to free the Korean peninsula from American imperialist influence."[15]

Those sentiments are surely understandable in the context of a relationship in which the United States has long loomed disproportionately large. Consider columnist Joseph Harsch's defense of American meddling in Korea's political affairs: "The U.S. has the right of any imperial power to intervene in the internal domestic affairs of one of its proteges and clients."[16] In practice, the U.S. government's attitude was little different. Indicative of the official attitude was the Combined Forces Command, long headed by an American and called "the most remarkable concession of sovereignty in the entire world" by one U.S. commander.[17] Although the command is now headed by a Korean, other vestiges of U.S. domination—a separate, English-language television channel operated by the U.S. Armed Forces, for instance—remain.

Making and exercising threats to end security subsidies unless ROK concessions were forthcoming would also prove to be self-defeating. The ultimate sanction would be to withdraw U.S. forces, but what administration would be willing to do so? "Short of pulling out troops," stated one U.S. diplomat after Chun Doo Hwan consolidated his dictatorial power in 1980, "which is out of the question, there is blessed little we can do about it."[18] And even if a president were willing to follow through, his threat to withdraw alone would diminish the value of Washington's commitment and therefore encourage the South to build up its own forces and act more independently. At the same time, the ROK would grow ever more resentful and recalcitrant. The United States could end up paying a far higher political price than any benefits it arguably receives from its defense commitment.

Washington's security guarantee has one, and only one, significant benefit: it reduces the likelihood of a North Korean attack on the

South. But that benefit accrues primarily to the ROK, not to America. Moreover, the American commitment is not necessary for Seoul's defense, since South Korea is eminently capable of creating an adequate deterrent on its own. As a result, the military gains to the United States are largely illusory.

Does Korea Matter?

A willingness to go to war for another nation represents a momentous commitment. During one of the periodic cycles of crisis during the North Korean nuclear controversy, President Clinton wrote to ROK president Kim Young Sam, stating that Washington would treat any attack on the South as an attack on America.[19] That was not the first time that a U.S. official had made a promise that bordered on the bizarre. Before the war Gen. Douglas MacArthur told Syngman Rhee, "If Korea should ever be attacked by the Communists, I will defend it as I would California."[20] But policymakers from the president on down need to remember that while its security is vital to the ROK, it is far less important to America. More realistic was the Joint Strategic Survey Committee that in 1947 ranked Korea 15th of 16 on a list of nations relevant to U.S. security.[21] Even the very unlikely worst case of a North Korean takeover of South Korea would be a human tragedy to, not a military disaster for, America.

Indeed, Washington's tendency to intervene everywhere suggests a failure to rank interests by importance—that is, to establish strategic priorities. The United States does have vital security concerns, but they are few in number, given America's relative geographic isolation and dominant economy. The only current threat to the nation's survival, independence, or constitutional system—the appropriate test of whether or not a vital interest is endangered—is a nuclear attack. Other unlikely possibilities include a hegemonic power's gaining control of the Eurasian land mass and an enemy state's overrunning Canada or Mexico, or both, thereby exposing the United States to conventional assault. An attack on South Korea is not in the same league.

In fact, the ROK doesn't even come up to the standard of an important interest—one that would materially affect America but not threaten its survival as an independent republic. Examples of that sort of interest include the maintenance of open sea lanes and

Western Europe's independence, for instance. In contrast, the preservation of a midsized trading partner surrounded by competing great powers in a distant region is not strategically important.[22] (Obviously, for the South Koreans their survival is not only important but vital; the fact that it is vital to them does not automatically make it vital or even important to us, however.) Rather, the ROK is what Cato's Ted Galen Carpenter calls a peripheral interest, one of many "assets that marginally enhance America's security but whose loss would constitute more of an annoyance than a serious setback."[23]

U.S. officials obviously reject such an assessment; they often portray South Korea as an advanced base for America, allowing the projection of U.S. power into East Asia. But traditional arguments about how deployments in Korea constrained the Soviet Union obviously no longer apply.[24] Creative policymakers have had to look elsewhere for justification; for example, Assistant Secretary of State Richard Holbrooke went so far as to contend that the loss of Korea "would be the end of our position in the entire Pacific."[25] William Gleysteen, former U.S. ambassador to the ROK, said the alliance contributes "importantly to the regional balance of power."[26] Similarly, Heritage Foundation president Edwin Feulner once called the Mutual Defense Treaty "a linchpin for stability in the entire Northeast Asian region."[27] In 1990 Secretary of Defense Richard Cheney warned that a U.S. withdrawal would be followed by a power vacuum. As a result, "there almost surely would be a series of destabilizing regional arms races, an increase in regional tensions, and possibly conflict."[28] In early 1995 the U.S. Department of Defense made much the same pitch, promising to maintain the alliance "even after the North Korean threat passes . . . in the interest of regional security."[29]

None of those arguments suggests that any vital American interests are at stake. Thus, the most obvious reason to threaten to go to war does not apply to Korea. Rather, America's second most important and costly commitment (after Europe) is rooted in the more nebulous concept of regional "stability." But the "stability" argument fails to distinguish between U.S. influence in East Asia and a defense commitment to the ROK. The latter is not necessary for the former.

First, the Mutual Defense Treaty yields America little benefit. As noted earlier, while a commitment to defend Seoul from North Korea helps stabilize the peninsula, the benefits of doing so accrue mostly to the ROK and to a lesser degree to neighboring nations. The advantages to America, based on proximity, if nothing else, are much more modest. Second, a militarily stronger South Korea, the probable consequence of a U.S. withdrawal, would promote regional stability almost as much as could the U.S. presence, by deterring aggression by not only Pyongyang but also by China, Japan, or Russia. (Those nations will always be able to outdo even a united Korea militarily, but the latter could make the prospect of war too expensive for any of them to seriously contemplate.) At the same time, it is hard to imagine even a more powerful Korea being in a position to threaten any of its major neighbors.

Useless Troop Presence

The U.S. troop presence in the ROK offers America little advantage. One infantry division in Korea would play no useful role in any conflict with, say, China. Nevertheless, Joseph Nye, assistant secretary of defense for international security, argues that pre-positioning equipment "is a terrific force multiplier" allowing one to "add tremendous additional capability in a very short time."[30] U.S. access to South Korean bases—which actually would not require a permanent troop presence—might be useful in a full-scale war in the region, but it is hard to imagine what interests would warrant U.S. participation in such a conflict. An attack on Manchuria in retaliation for China's sinking of a Filipino warship off the Spratly Islands? An expedition to help Japan forcibly wrest the Kuril Islands from Russia?

Further, that kind of U.S.-ROK cooperation would depend, not on past American support, but on shared interests at the time the conflict erupted. Seoul might be reluctant to join in a military crusade against a neighboring power or powers, however much it currently enjoys being defended by Washington. After all, South Korea has to live with China, Japan, and Russia while Washington can leave whenever it chooses. Moreover, it would be hard to preserve an isolated forward outpost like the ROK in any serious conflict; in 1950 Pentagon planners worried that the United States could maintain military superiority on the peninsula only by using atomic weapons on Siberia if the USSR entered the Korean War.[31] In short, using Korea as an advance military outpost could prove to be more costly and less beneficial than currently assumed.

Moreover, neither an infantry division nor bases in the ROK are likely to do much to suppress nationalistic sentiments and conflicts throughout the region. If Vietnam, the Philippines, and China slide toward war over the Spratly Islands, only an American threat to intervene, not the mere U.S. presence in Korea, is likely to deter them. Yet there is precious little evidence either that America is better able to solve regional problems than are the parties involved or that the United States has sufficient interests to warrant military action in response to the few problems that might spin out of control. The United States might have been the key to regional stability 40, 30, and even 20 years ago. That it was even 10 years ago is doubtful, and that it is today is very unlikely indeed.

Regional Cooperation

Withdrawing troops from the ROK would not preclude U.S. involvement in regional organizations, promotion of reconciliation and cooperation between tense neighbors, preservation of access to bases in an emergency, and naval visits to show the American flag. U.S. economic, cultural, and political ties would remain strong. Washington, with a strong mid-Pacific presence, would retain the option of becoming reinvolved in East Asia if it desired. As Carpenter puts it,

> Only if it could be established that the fall of South Korea would lead inexorably to the neutralization or subjugation of Japan and America's other trading partners in the Far East would the ROK itself be more than a minor stake. Taken *collectively*, the nations of the Pacific Rim constitute (as do the nations of Western Europe) a limited rather than merely a peripheral U.S. security interest—primarily because of economic considerations. But the notion that a North Korean conquest of the South would lead to the collapse of capitalist East Asia is little more than an updated version of the simplistic and discredited domino theory.[32]

The only plausible argument that Korea's fall could trigger such a disaster—that phasing out an antiquated defense guarantee to a small nation across the Pacific Ocean would unhinge the entire region's stability—requires the existence of the sort of aggressive, hegemonic threat once posed by communism. But the Soviet Union is gone and the People's Republic of China is a poor substitute. As discussed in greater detail in chapter 7, while Beijing's military is growing, its capabilities remain modest; moreover, so far the PRC's ambitions appear limited, though Beijing is more assertive than in the past. Even if the ROK, by virtue of its highly symbolic role in the Cold War struggle with Moscow and China, was important in 1950, it is not today.

In fact, the Truman administration originally didn't believe that South Korea's survival was vitally important even then. In September 1947, as the Cold War was deepening, the Joint Chiefs of Staff declared that the Korean peninsula was strategically unimportant. Before the invasion, General MacArthur maintained that the United States needn't defend the ROK.[33] Dean Acheson excluded the South from America's so-called defense perimeter, as did Senate Foreign Relations Committee chairman Tom Connally.[34] Republican members of Congress were no more enthused about acquiring another expensive client state.[35] The Pentagon actually acknowledged that an American military withdrawal, which it nevertheless advocated, meant that Soviet domination of the South would "have to be accepted as a probability."[36]

Soviet Inspiration?

Although the Truman administration shifted course after Pyongyang's invasion of the South, it did so because of the erroneous belief that the invasion was Soviet inspired. (Moreover, as Carpenter observes, Washington limited its prosecution of the war, which suggests that it implicitly recognized that the stakes in Korea itself were modest.) President Truman believed that the conflict was important for America's position in the Pacific and especially in Europe. The argument that the geopolitical stakes were that high was dubious in 1950. They certainly are not today. A decidedly unlikely North Korean victory over the ROK would be a triumph for an isolated and impoverished Stalinist state, not international communism or any other hegemonic threat.

Ironically, a united, communist Korea would probably follow the ROK in seeking a positive relationship with America in order to put distance between it and its neighbors. The DPRK seemed interested in maintaining such a balance even during the Cold War. Observed one South Korean scholar in 1984, "North Korean officials have reportedly told American visitors that North Korea does not want to be under pressure 'solely from the north,' implying that meaningful relations with the United States and Japan could be used to counter-balance relations with the Soviet Union or China."[37]

Of course, America has interests other than security in Korea. The U.S. Department of Defense has spoken of the role of the U.S.-Korean alliance in "supporting and promoting democracy."[38] What that means isn't clear, since Seoul has already moved to democracy and has done so in spite of American support for a succession of authoritarian rulers. The continuing presence of U.S. forces on the peninsula seems unlikely to speed the arrival of political liberty in China, North Korea, Singapore, or anywhere else. In any case, that goal, along with humanitarian concerns about a nation with which we have important cultural ties, does not warrant today's military commitment and threat to go to war. If it did, Washington would have to garrison half of the globe for the same reasons.

Can't South Korea Defend Itself?

The assumption that an independent Korea is important to America today does not end the analysis. The question is, why must the United States provide a treaty and troops to ensure South Korean independence? Why can't the ROK defend itself?

Oddly, American policymakers apparently never ask that question. Rather, they appear to accept Southern military inferiority as a given, like a feature of geography. Or perhaps as a necessity of history—the ROK was beaten by Pyongyang in 1950 and therefore would be defeated again. Yet as South Korea's Ministry of National Defense has admitted, "The current picture of North and South Korea's relative military strength is not a mere accident but the inevitable results of different national strategies and the systems of the two sides."[39] In assessing Seoul's alleged need for American support, it is time to review both sides of the equation—the threat and the resources to meet that threat—as well as the political decisions that have led to a continuing military imbalance on the peninsula.

It is true that the North possesses a quantitative military advantage. According to the International Institute for Strategic Studies, Pyongyang maintains an active-duty force of 1,128,000. It possesses 3,400 main battle tanks, 540 light tanks, 2,200 armored personnel carriers, 3,000 pieces of towed artillery, 4,500 pieces of self-propelled artillery, and 2,200 multiple rocket launchers. The South, in contrast, has only 633,000 active-duty soldiers, though its formal reserve is larger. It also generally lags on equipment, with 2,050 tanks, 2,460 armored personnel carriers, 3,500 towed artillery, 1,000 self-propelled artillery, and 156 multiple rocket launchers. The DPRK possesses more naval vessels, though it trails in total tonnage, and more planes, though the South's fleet is more modern.[40]

Overstated Statistics

Pyongyang's advantage, though significant, is less than its superiority at the outset of the Korean War.[41] Moreover, such dramatic statistics, in the words of military analyst Stephen Goose, "are usually overstated, almost always misleading, and often meaningless."[42] The armies of the Arab nations surrounding Israel have always been larger than Israel's but rarely successful; Germany defeated France in 1940 because its training, deployments, and strategy were superior, not because it had more troops or tanks.

Seoul, too, has its advantages. South Korea's weapons are generally more sophisticated than those of the DPRK. They are also newer and hence more reliable. Goose called that "the single most important aspect" of any ROK-DPRK military comparison.[43] Even the Pentagon has acknowledged that the ROK's aircraft, transportation system, and military-industrial capability are superior.[44] Similarly, the ROK's Ministry of National Defense observes that "South Korea can claim an increasing edge over the North in military science and technology, backed by the rapid growth of its aerospace, automobile, communication and electronic industries."[45] The North's overwhelming reliance on hydroelectric power makes its industrial base more vulnerable to air strikes than is the South's. Moreover, the ROK's soldiers, some of whom received extensive combat experience in Vietnam, are believed to be better trained and led—a significant advantage. Observes one analysis, "The North Koreans may lack the small unit skills necessary to turn military theory into practice."[46] DPRK pilots get far less flight time than do their Southern counterparts. The North has apparently never run joint-service training exercises, not even with the feared special forces. Finally, the North's forces are likely to follow a Soviet-style centralized command system, which hinders battlefield initiative, whereas South Korea's forces follow the flexible Western model.

The South would also presumably be on the defensive, which would reduce its requirements. (Traditional Soviet offensive doctrine sought a three-to-one manpower advantage, for instance, which the DPRK lacks.)[47] That advantage would be magnified by simple geography. The mountainous terrain "is such a dominant factor in assessing the Korean military balance that conventional measures of military strength do not fully apply," concluded the Congressional Budget Office.[48] There are, for instance, only three main tank attack routes, along which the ROK has erected numerous barriers. Indeed, the CBO predicted that North Korea could not use all of its tanks efficiently in an invasion and that the ROK military could use its extensive fortifications and anti-tank traps to achieve as much as a three-to-one kill ratio. Nearly a decade ago Gen. William Livsey, then the U.S. commander in Korea, pointed to "our concentration of firepower—now there's something we can talk about."[49]

Of course, the DPRK possesses a number of potential advantages—extensive tunnelling, the largest commando force in the world, a forward deployment strategy, hardened military facilities—but none of them appears to materially alter the overall military equation. The usefulness of the tunnels is limited; the commandos could not infiltrate the ROK easily; the warning time of an invasion would probably be adequate; and U.S. officers anticipate destroying the North Korean air force after the planes have been flushed from their strengthened hangers.[50] A decade ago the International Institute for Strategic Studies opined that "the opposing forces on the Korean peninsula are roughly equivalent. Neither is capable of a successful major offensive against the other without significant foreign assistance."[51]

The Friendless North

Pyongyang would not be likely to receive significant foreign assistance, since the end of the Cold War has left North Korea essentially friendless while the ROK is picking up allies. One small sign of the transformation: in its *Defense White Paper: 1991–1992*, South Korea discussed the North's relationship with both the USSR and China; those separate sections have since disappeared, and the 1994–95 volume reports growing ROK military cooperation with Russia and the exchange of military diplomatic representatives with China.[52] (Seoul has nevertheless resisted acknowledging the positive implications of that trend; in 1991 the Ministry of National Defense worried that the switch in international dance partners could push "North Korea to launch further aggression against the South.")[53]

In sum, Seoul is winning the inter-Korean competition. In 1987 the U.S. Department of Defense observed that despite the North's quantitative advantages, "any North Korean attack on the South [would be] a very difficult operation, with the outcome very much in doubt."[54] More recently Denny Roy of Singapore's National University opined, "Most credible analysts agree that the most Pyongyang's forces could hope to accomplish is to temporarily capture Seoul before being driven back into a homeland bombed to rubble by enemy aircraft."[55] Similarly, Rand researcher Bruce Bennett argues that the almost certain failure of "a North Korean major conventional attack" makes it "the least likely of the threats" faced by the ROK.[56] It is no wonder, then, that in July 1995 President Kim Young Sam stated that the North's economic decay made it almost unimaginable that Pyongyang would either start or sustain a war.[57]

Of course, it would still be foolish to be complacent, and there are critics of the ROK's military.[58] Indeed, a surprise DPRK attack would almost certainly achieve a measure of tactical success.[59] And Nye warns that while "things are better than they were last year" in Korea, Pyongyang's military threat "has not diminished."[60] Whether or not he is correct in that assessment, the South's vast economic, technological, and population advantages make an ROK triumph likely in the long term. As the Ministry of National Defense puts it, "South Korea has a comfortable edge over North Korea in terms of war sustainability."[61]

In any case, in an important sense this entire discussion should be irrelevant. When Seoul argues that further U.S. force reductions should wait until "after the security environment on the Korean peninsula has improved and South and North Korea begin to coexist peacefully," it ignores its own responsibility.[62] The only reason one has to ask whether the ROK's qualitative advantages are sufficient to match the North's quantitative edge is that Seoul has decided to accept a numerically inferior military. In short, the South's current military disadvantage is an inevitable consequence, not of geography, but of the Mutual Defense Treaty. As long as America is willing to station an army division between Seoul and the Demilitarized Zone and place its full military faith and credit on the line, the ROK would be foolish to increase its defense effort in order to attain military self-sufficiency. Indeed, fear of losing U.S. support by becoming militarily independent could prove to be a powerful incentive for Seoul to never quite match the North's forces.[63]

Promised Parity

For years ROK and American officials alike, at least when not propagandizing for higher U.S. defense outlays, have projected Seoul's imminent achievement of parity with the North. But the ROK never quite seems to get there. And it almost certainly will not, so long as it believes it can count on American military support.

For instance, in 1970, after President Richard M. Nixon announced his plan to withdraw one U.S. division, South Korea's president Park Chung Hee stated that his nation's forces would be superior to those of the North by 1975.[64] In 1975 President Park declared that in just a few more years the ROK would require no American assistance, not even air, naval, or logistical support. "We want the capability to defend ourselves, and that will take four or five years," he said.[65] Two years later his cabinet issued a report stating that "the time frame for the withdrawal of the U.S. ground forces and our plans for a self-reliant national defense have coincided, as anticipated."[66] In 1977 Kiichi Saeki, former president of the National Defense College of Japan, opined that "it should not be impossible to achieve in time a military equilibrium . . . between the two Koreas."[67] Three years later, reported Larry Niksch of the Congressional Research Service, several South Korean and U.S. officials "expressed the view that a satisfactory balance could be achieved around 1984–85 if longer range plans went according to schedule."[68] In 1982 Assistant Secretary of State James Buckley told Congress, "We have in Northeast Asia a strong and economically vital South Korea that is able to deter its northern neighbor from military advances."[69] In the same year the ROK government boasted that "the Republic's defensive power is fully capable of meeting North Korean tank assaults and aerial offensives."[70]

In 1983 South Korean leaders informed visiting congressmen that Seoul should reach military equality by 1986.[71] In 1985 Adm. William Crowe, commander in chief of the Pacific Command, stated that "if South Korea has advance warning of an impending North Korean attack, they would be capable of defending the DMZ with in-place forces and with follow-on augmentation of regular and reserve forces."[72] Also in 1985 General Livsey observed, not only that the combined U.S.-ROK forces "are now able to defeat any renewed aggression from North Korea," but that "by the early 1990s, all comparisons between South and North Korea, including the military, will favor the ROK."[73]

In 1987 the ROK defense minister told a forum at Washington's Center for Strategic and International Studies that his country expected to achieve a military balance with the DPRK within two to three years.[74] In the same year Eulkwon Kim of Korea's Ilhae Institute offered a slightly different analysis that reached a similar conclusion: "There's a maxim in military strategy that if you have only 70 percent of the enemy's objective capability, you can defend against him. And within the next one to two years, South Korea will have reached that level."[75] A South Korean officer, in residence at Washington's National Defense University, predicted that "the ROK will be capable of defending itself in the early 1990s"; thereafter "the North Koreans may lose forever the chance to unify the Korean peninsula by force."[76] At the same time, Taylor argued that

> given the continuation of current trends, there will be a cross-over point in the early 1990s between the military capabilities of the North and South. . . . After the crossover, other things being equal, a successful conventional invasion would have a very low probability of success even without a U.S. military commitment at the 1987 level of 40,000 troops.[77]

A year later Taylor, along with Amos Jordan, also of the Center for Strategic and International Studies, concluded that "the balance of military power on the peninsula is gradually shifting in favor of the South, despite enormous military efforts in North Korea. Sometime in the mid- or latter 1990s, given present trends, Seoul will be able to defend against any North Korean thrust."[78] In 1989 Gen. Louis Menetry, the U.S. commander in Korea, said that with continuation of South Korea's military modernization program, "there should be stability on the peninsula without the United States being part of the equation in the mid-1990s."[79] A year later the Pentagon acknowledged "steady improvements in ROK defense capabilities" and stated that the ROK had "the potential to play the lead in its own defense."[80] In 1991 the ROK Ministry of National Defense proclaimed that by the mid-1990s the South would eliminate the cumulative investment gap then still favoring the DPRK.[81] Indeed, in the late 1980s South Korean presidents Chun Doo Hwan and Roh Tae Woo, along with two different defense ministers, predicted that the ROK alone would be able to deter a North Korean attack by the 1990s.[82]

Still Lagging Militarily

It is now the mid-1990s, and Seoul still possesses a smaller military than does the North. Why? "While the capabilities of the ROK armed forces clearly have improved considerably as increased spending, permitted by a growing economy, has been translated into better equipment and training," stated the U.S. Department of Defense in 1987, "the exceptionally high percentage of North Korean defense spending has allowed it to keep pace with the South."[83] South Korea's explanation is similar: "North Korea adopted its 'Four-point Military Guidelines' in the early 1960s and has given top priority to building up its military."[84] True, the DPRK did significantly expand its military, surpassing Seoul in total manpower in 1978 and expanding the disparity in succeeding years.[85] Yet that is no excuse for South Korea's numerical military inferiority. With a larger population and exploding GDP, the ROK nevertheless maintained its manpower level at around 600,000, where it was during the 1960s.[86] Seoul did not, acknowledges the Ministry of National Defense, begin "its own force improvement program" until "twelve years later than North Korea," after which "the disparity between the military capabilities of South and North Korea [became] quite severe."[87] In sum, the South chose not to match Pyongyang's military build-up. And it could do so because of American protection. Seoul admits that it "concentrated on its economic and social development" while North Korea emphasized military production.[88]

However much sense that strategy may have made three and perhaps even two decades ago, it is out of sync with today's world. Indeed, the ROK admits as much when it states its objective of creating "a defense posture strong enough to deter any North Korean provocation."[89] Having concentrated on economic development in the past, Seoul now has the capability of matching the North, no matter how much the latter spends, without unduly burdening its economy.

For instance, the South has no shortage of manpower. The Central Intelligence Agency has estimated that the ROK has 8.1 million males fit for military service, more than twice the 3.5 million available to the North. The number of men turning 18 every year also greatly favors South Korea—456,000 compared to 247,000.[90] Indeed, the ROK sent small contingents of soldiers to participate in UN peacekeeping missions in Somalia and, most recently, Angola.

ROK Defense Outlays

As for spending, the latest International Institute for Strategic Studies figures show respective GDPs of $379.6 billion and $20.9 billion for the ROK and the DPRK in 1994, a South Korean advantage of about 18 to 1. That estimate matches those of other sources. In 1995 analysts at the Research Institute for National Unification estimated the South's advantage to be 18 to 1.[91] At that level the South need only spend 5.5 percent of its GDP to make its defense budget equivalent to the entire North Korean economy. If Seoul made a political decision to substantially augment its forces (assuming the North refused to engage in serious arms reduction talks), North Korea would find itself in a race that it simply could not win.

The South has not made such a decision because it does not have to. Claude Buss of the Hoover Institution explains that "the physical presence of American troops comforts and strengthens South Korea."[92] But that kind of "comfort" is counterproductive, enabling Seoul to avoid its defense responsibilities. (In the view of one South Korean analyst, pervasive reliance on the United States also discourages initiative by battlefield officers, who once tended to expect American forces to take the lead.)[93] In 1989 Defense Minister Lee Sang Hoon estimated that increasing ROK military outlays from 5 to 8 percent of GNP would offset an American withdrawal.[94] In the summer of 1995 analysts at the Korean Institute for Defense Analyses reached much the same conclusion.[95] Indeed, once when I suggested withdrawing American troops to a representative of the institute, he exclaimed, "We'd have to spend more," not "We'd be helpless." That point was recognized by the ROK Ministry of Defense when it estimated (without explaining its methodology) that the ROK would have to spend an extra $26 billion to make up "for the withdrawn portion" of the U.S. forces.[96] The South has simply refused to do more. That Seoul does not want to further increase its defense spending is understandable, given the additional tax burden that would be required. But that reluctance is no reason for the United States to maintain troops in the ROK.

However, some American officials are also determined to preserve the Mutual Defense Treaty and therefore do not want the South to become self-sufficient. At the 1989 U.S.-Korean Security Council conference in Seoul, one member of the audience asked whether the ROK could take on more responsibility within the current military structure. Yes, a Pentagon representative replied, but "it would call into question the presence of U.S. troops in Korea."[97] In short, if the Koreans did more, people in the United States might wonder why our forces were still needed. For that official, at least, the stationing of U.S. forces in Korea, once thought to be the means of preserving peace on the peninsula, had itself become the end, one that required maintaining the South's unnecessary dependence on America.

Antiquated Commitment, Transformed Peninsula

The basic problem in Korea is that America has preserved, largely unchanged, a commitment forged in a war more than four decades ago. In 1950 the DPRK achieved military superiority primarily through generous backing from the Soviet Union. As historian William Stueck puts it, "The inequality of the contest had much to do with the relative support given the two sides from beyond Korea's boundaries."[98] In a sense, U.S. intervention was simply a counterbalance to previous Soviet assistance to the North.

The ROK was equally vulnerable at the close of the war in 1953. South Korea had suffered roughly 350,000 battle casualties, more than twice the number of American dead and wounded. One million civilians were casualties, including thousands of civic leaders liquidated by DPRK forces. Seoul was devastated, having changed hands four times. Five million people were homeless. The country's GDP ran an estimated $1.35 billion, around a dismal $75 per person. The government was authoritarian and unpopular, led by an aging, unreasonable petty despot. At the same time, hundreds of thousands of Chinese soldiers remained in the North, fully capable of reigniting the conflict. In short, if there was a country that then needed defending, it was South Korea.

Even a decade later the ROK remained poor. Per capita GDP is believed by some to have been as low as $87 and probably no more than $100 in 1962. Real per capita growth was running little more than 1 percent a year; exports, primarily commodities such as animal products and silk, totaled a meager $40 million. The country was under military rule, near the beginning of the reign of the longest running dictator of all, Park Chung Hee. (Although the North was hardly prosperous, for a time it appeared to be more successful economically, in part because it benefited from the large pool of skilled labor in the northern part of the peninsula, where Japan had concentrated industry, and had more plentiful natural resources and hydroelectric power.)

Then Park, despite his political thuggery, ended up doing enough right economically to allow the ROK to soon turn into one of the world's greatest success stories.[99] From 1962 to 1993 economic growth averaged a staggering 8.5 percent annually. The South's economy regularly expanded at double-digit rates in the late 1980s and has barely slowed in the succeeding decade. For example, South Korea's real GDP jumped 7.7 percent in 1994 and was continuing to expand in 1995 at roughly 7.3 percent. In 1993, estimated the World Bank, the ROK's GDP was running about $340 billion, with per capita GDP of nearly $7,700.[100] Estimates for 1995 approach $400 billion and a $10,000 per capita GDP. As a result, the South has become an important regional economic player.[101] Moreover, Koreans who once immigrated to America in search of economic opportunity are now returning to the ROK.[102]

In contrast, the North, which during the 1960s is thought to have had a higher per capita GDP though a smaller total GDP, began to fall behind at an accelerating rate during the 1970s. Its economy appears to have started shrinking in 1989 or 1990 and is still contracting.[103] So serious is the DPRK's plight that some analysts wonder if the communist state can long survive, though so far it has proved to be surprisingly resilient.[104] Even Pyongyang has acknowledged the severity of its plight, by requesting food aid from Japan, South Korea, and the United Nations.[105]

Military Industry

With the ROK's economic growth has come industrialization; high-technology production; access to international capital markets; and, especially relevant for the South's defense, development of an indigenous arms industry. A nation that in the 1970s did not even make its own rifles was a decade later producing virtually all of its conventional arms, including F-5 fighters, helicopters, rocket launchers, self-propelled howitzers, M48 and T88 tanks, armored personnel carriers, frigates, and Hawk and Honest John missiles.[106]

In fact, by the mid-1970s, Seoul appeared to be outspending the North on defense, although estimates of the differential varied widely. (The U.S. Arms Control and Disarmament Agency later reconfigured its estimates, placing Pyongyang ahead until 1982. But the South Korean government maintains that it surpassed Pyongyang starting in 1976.)[107] Sang-Woo Rhee, a professor at the ROK's Sogang University, figures that the ROK's cumulative military spending finally matched that of the North in 1988.[108] The ROK now devotes between two and three times as much to the military as does its Northern rival, which resulted in an astounding $8 billion gap in 1994, according to the International Institute for Strategic Studies. Writes Yong-Sup Han, a professor at the Korean National Defense University, "South Korea's defense spending in 1994 amounted to $12 billion, more than twice that of the North. This gap in defense spending is expected to widen to a ratio of 2.4 to 1 by the year 2000."[109] In fact, in late 1995 Seoul announced that it intended to double its military budget by 2001.[110]

Pyongyang cannot count on any outside factors—such as large-scale Soviet aid and the return of 20,000 battle-hardened Koreans who had been serving in the Chinese military, which gave it a decided advantage over the ROK in 1950—to compensate for the gap.[111] To the contrary, as noted earlier, Seoul is beginning to cooperate militarily with the DPRK's former allies. Moscow has even begun shipping arms to Seoul to help pay off its $1.56 billion debt and has proposed joint development of high-tech weapons.[112] Analyst Vladimir Miasnikov goes so far as to argue that "the [1994] summit talks in Moscow proved once again that Russia no longer can be considered North Korea's ideological or military ally, and Russia's relations with the ROK have developed more actively than with the DPRK."[113] Thus, eliminating the remaining imbalance with the North should be only a matter of time for Seoul—even without America's help.

Politically, too, South Korea has made enormous progress. In 1987 free elections passed the presidency to a former general, Roh Tae Woo, who provided a peaceful transition to genuine democracy. In 1992 a former dissident, Kim Young Sam, became the first nongeneral in decades to serve as president. Although the country's politics remain fractious in the mid-1990s—especially after Kim Jong Pil's secession from the ruling party, Kim Dae Jung's reentry into politics, and prosecutions as a result of Roh's huge political slush fund—democracy seems firmly rooted and a return to military rule increasingly improbable.[114]

Democracy and Defense

Oddly enough, some people have suggested that democratization may prove to be a barrier to greater ROK defense efforts. In 1990 William Taylor and Michael Mazarr of the Center for Strategic and International Studies warned that "the assertive opposition in the National Assembly is likely to cut defense spending."[115] That thesis implies a rather insulting view of South Koreans—that they fail to understand the potential seriousness of war with, and conquest by, the North.[116] However, since America shields Seoul from that threat, it should come as no surprise that some politicians, along with their constituents, seek to take advantage of the superpower shield and direct more resources into nondefense programs.

When presented in the past with an obvious need to do more, however, the ROK has responded: the Nixon cutbacks, the Carter withdrawal proposal, and the conflict with America over human rights all convinced Seoul "that South Korea must move quickly to become less dependent on the United States for its defense."[117] The Korean government itself admits as much.[118] The result was a dramatic take-off in South Korean military expenditures and development of indigenous arms production. As one South Korean officer put it, "The disappointing U.S. withdrawal [under Nixon] gave the ROK government and soldiers a chance to realize the importance of self-reliance."[119] The experience of this decade, too, belies fears of South Korean appeasement. In 1990, when Taylor and Mazarr penned their warning, Seoul was spending $10.6 billion on defense; in 1995 outlays hit $14.4 billion.[120] Further increases can be expected, since in 1995 the Korean Defense Ministry noted that "we urgently need to secure a combat capability to replace the reduced U.S. forces as they pursue their reduction and role change. Since assistance from the U.S. has served as the cornerstone of our defense, [the modest Bush troop] reduction has been a major blow."[121] Indeed, Seoul was looking even further ahead, explaining that it was working on the development of a "military capability . . . adequate to meet the requirements of the united Korea and of the twenty-first century."[122]

Conclusion

America's ties with South Korea are strong, but they do not represent the sort of vital interest typically thought to warrant a threat to go to war. Even if the ROK's security were vital to America, however, a U.S. security guarantee would no longer be required. Assistant Secretary of State Richard Solomon proclaimed in 1991 that "the United States intends to maintain appropriate forces in Korea so long as our two governments agree that a U.S. presence is necessary to deter a renewed outbreak of hostilities."[123] There was a time when those forces were necessary as a deterrent, but no more. In 1991 Seoul warned against "drastic" force reductions "until the Republic gains the capability to defend itself on its own."[124] That time has come. The South has matured enough politically to graduate from the status of U.S. protectorate, and it has grown enough economically to bear the burden of its own defense.

Obviously, Seoul does not yet support that kind of shift. When asked if cultural and social conflicts, such as the subway brawl during the summer of 1995, might encourage the departure of the U.S. soldiers, Foreign Ministry spokesman Yim Sung Joon argued, "Keeping troops on the Korean peninsula is in U.S. interests."[125] However, the Ministry of National Defense has more honestly admitted to looking out for number one. According to the ministry,

> A drastic curtailment of the [U.S. presence] should be avoided to ensure the current military posture in relation with North Korea; an appropriate level of additional reduction might be considered so long as side effects against ROK military capability can be avoided, and so long as it is after the security environment on the Korean peninsula has improved and South and North Korea begin to coexist peacefully. Over the long term, it would be desirable that an appropriate size of the U.S. forces will be stationed in Korea for the support of the Korean security as well as to carry out the role as the regional balancer.[126]

In short, American forces should stay forever, or almost. At one point the ROK government spoke of "the eventual U.S. troop pullout" without quite as long a list of preconditions and acknowledged that "U.S. Forces cannot remain in Korea forever."[127] Those statements have, however, since disappeared from the Seoul's *Defense White Papers*. Ironically, as Seoul has moved closer to its goal of "self-reliant" defense, it appears to be resisting more fervently the idea of a U.S. withdrawal at any point.

But the South can, if it chooses, "ensure the current military posture in relation with North Korea," avoid "side effects against ROK military capability," and ensure the peninsula's "security environment" irrespective of the state of South and North Korean relations. All it needs to do is spend more on defense. As long as Washington guarantees South Korea's security, however, Seoul will remain dependent. Although ROK military outlays have been rising in absolute terms, they have been falling as a percentage of that government's overall budget, from 35.9 percent in 1980 to 30.4 percent in 1990 to 24.2 percent in 1994, and as a percentage of GNP, from 6.0 percent in 1980 to 4.4 percent in 1990 to 3.5 percent in 1994.[128] In 1993 a proposal was actually advanced to demobilize 100,000 soldiers to save money.[129] Simply returning to the relative defense effort of 1980 would yield an 83 percent budget increase, which would provide the kind of resources necessary to match the DPRK.

Obviously, proposals to spend more on the military may not be popular with Korean taxpayers, who would prefer to put the money to other uses. In fact, the Ministry of National Defense has worried about some Koreans' being "unduly optimistic about our security environment" and therefore has worked to build "a strong national security consensus."[130] The best way to overcome such complacency would be for Washington to announce it was phasing out its defense guarantee. East Asian expert Ralph Clough comments that President Nixon's withdrawal of the Seventh Division in 1971 came "as a shock to the South Koreans."[131] They obviously need another such shock before they will develop the truly "self-reliant defense posture" that Seoul says it seeks.[132]

What if, however unlikely, the ROK chose not to increase its efforts, as some fear, if America withdrew? There would still be no justification for maintaining the U.S. defense commitment. The Korean people may freely decide whether they feel sufficiently threatened to warrant spending more, and whether they are willing to undertake the burden of doing so. If they unexpectedly decided not to, it would make no sense to force U.S. taxpayers to pony up and place the lives of young Americans on the line. Such a South Korean decision might be foolish, but then, as Seoul argues, "A sovereign state should be able to defend itself independently without relying on foreign assistance."[133] And a sovereign state can choose not to do so. It is certainly not Washington's role to protect nations unwilling to defend themselves. And it most assuredly is not the purpose of the U.S. military to allow a country with one of the world's fastest growing economies to continue concentrating its resources on business investment, consumer goods, and social services while the American people bear its defense burdens.

ROK president Kim's trip to the United States in 1995 was intended to "cheer up" Americans, explained Prime Minister Lee Hong Koo. "This occasion celebrates what we've achieved together."[134] And, in fact, South Korea has achieved much because of Washington's protection. But the South no longer requires American aid, and the United States no longer receives sufficient benefits to counterbalance the costs of its security commitment and troop backstop. It is time to place full responsibility for the ROK's defense on the South Korean people.

5. A Strategy for Disengagement

U.S. troops have been stationed in South Korea for the past half century. Although their withdrawal would unsettle a government and people grown used to America's presence, it really should surprise neither. After all, in 1984, 4 of 10 South Koreans advocated that the United States stay only until Seoul became militarily self-sufficient.[1] With the economic gap between South and North expanding at an embarrassing rate, that time is now.

South Korea's Ministry of National Defense has acknowledged that "considering the changes in our security environment including the emerging South-North arms control question, reduction of troops will become inevitable."[2] Unfortunately, the ministry was referring to South Korean troop levels. But surely the first cuts should come in the forces of the United States, whose support has always been justified by the exceptional military circumstances on the peninsula. Only after the American troop presence has disappeared should the ROK, which obviously has both the most at stake in and the primary obligation for its own defense, downsize its army. In 1971 Prime Minister Kim Jong Pil responded to the Nixon administration's partial withdrawal: "Now is no time to survive by depending on others—U.S. troops in our country will go home sooner or later, which means that we must defend our country through our own strength."[3] Again, that time is now.

Nevertheless, disengagement would be a dramatic step. Its most important impact would probably be symbolic. Opines Claude Buss of the Hoover Institution, "In the minds of many Korean and American officials, the military role of the U.S. forces is less important than the psychological, political, and diplomatic effects of their presence. As Defense Secretary [James] Schlesinger stated in 1974, U.S. forces in Korea symbolize America's continued interest in the overall stability of that part of the world."[4] It would be important, therefore, for Washington to emphasize that placing responsibility for Korea's defense on Koreans would not mean indifference to the ROK's safety.

America should withdraw its troops and eliminate its defense guarantee as part of an orderly process that would allow the South to take whatever steps it believed necessary to secure its future.

History of Pullouts

America has had more than a little experience in withdrawing troops from Korea. In April 1948 Washington decided to remove its forces, which had occupied the southern portion of the Korean peninsula since Japan's surrender, by the end of the year (when the Soviet forces had returned home). Disagreements between the State Department, which opposed withdrawal, and the Department of Defense, which wished for a speedy pullout, delayed implementation of that decision, however.[5] Newly installed ROK president Syngman Rhee indicated that U.S. forces would not be necessary once his nation had "a sufficient military force for national defense," but he did not believe that was yet the case.[6] Nevertheless, the Truman administration began removing troops in September 1948; by June 30, 1949, only 500 advisers remained. The departing units left some $40 million worth of military equipment, ranging from small arms to trucks, with the South Korean army. Washington also provided modest shipments of war materiel and established a military training program.[7]

However, the United States refused to supply heavy weapons. The Pentagon doubted both Korea's importance and the longevity of the Rhee regime; it preferred not to waste resources on the South's military. Indeed, the Joint Chiefs argued that the South was "of little strategic value to the United States" and that any commitment "of military force in Korea would be ill-advised."[8] One reason Secretary of State Dean Acheson downplayed the importance of Korea was to minimize European concerns should the ROK be overrun.[9] Rhee also greatly exacerbated Washington's reluctance to help. His oft-repeated threat to invade the North made Washington simultaneously reluctant to provide Seoul with potentially offensive weapons and anxious to pull out its forces to avoid entanglement in any invasion of the DPRK.[10] As a result, South Korea was ill prepared for the Northern onslaught of June 25, 1950.

The war brought a return of American soldiers—360,000 at the peak—many more than necessary for even the very cold peace that descended on the peninsula in mid-1953. Thus, a second withdrawal occurred between September 1954 and May 1955. Washington pulled out a total of six divisions, matched by China's withdrawal of 200,000 troops from the North. The United States again left equipment for the ROK forces. Two U.S. infantry divisions stayed to help shield Seoul; also remaining was a smattering of artillery, air defense, logistics, service, and other units, for a total of about 60,000 soldiers.

Nevertheless, South Korea sharply criticized America for the pull-out, which was marked by public protests. Explains Lt. Col. Lee Suk Bok, "Korea remembered the first withdrawal . . . in 1949, which caused the Korean War. The relatively poor support for the Korean Armed Forces compared to Communist countries' patronage of North Korea accounted for the North Koreans feeling bold enough to invade the South. The ROK was not sure whether the United States could keep her promises."[11] Criticizing Washington for not better performing what was, after all, a charitable act of defending a distant nation with no intrinsic strategic interest to the United States took some gall. But the ROK's sensitivity demonstrates the importance of giving South Korea due warning of any policy change. In any case, the U.S. withdrawal in the mid-1950s was an obvious success: Seoul responded by adding five infantry divisions of its own.

Nixon Doctrine

Washington next drew down its forces in the South in 1971. That step reflected U.S. détente with China and what has been variously called the Nixon or Guam Doctrine, enunciated shortly after the inauguration of President Richard M. Nixon in 1969.[12] Explained the president, "We shall look to the nation directly threatened to assume the primary responsibilities for providing the manpower for its defense."[13] Nevertheless, the South Korean government was "shocked" by Nixon's decision, says Ralph Clough. As he explains, "It was not the withdrawal of the division alone that disturbed them, but the implications for Korea of the sudden change in the direction of U.S. policy. The shift to détente with China, the enunciation of the Nixon Doctrine, and the intimations that more U.S. units might be removed from Korea left Park Chung-hee troubled."[14]

South Korea resisted Washington's proposal, making all of the usual arguments: the North presented too much of a threat, U.S. credibility would suffer, Seoul and Washington would lose bargaining power, and an arms race on the peninsula might result.[15] To its credit, the Nixon administration held firm, though it offered Seoul a $1.6 billion military aid package to support the ROK's Five-Year Modernization Plan. That program initiated a major military build-up, which eventually boosted ROK defense spending far above that of the North.

However, Nixon rejected a Department of Defense proposal to pull out more troops. His successor, Gerald Ford, planned to withdraw another 15,500 soldiers in 1975, but an adverse vote in the House after the collapse of South Vietnam caused him to reverse course. Instead, Secretary of Defense James Schlesinger made a well-publicized trip to the ROK to emphasize the administration's support. He announced, "I have come here to exemplify both the high regard of the American people for their Korean ally and the continuing commitment to a common cause."[16]

The Aborted Carter Withdrawal

In the same year, however, Jimmy Carter, then a dark-horse candidate for president, questioned the presence of U.S. troops in Korea. His position reflected a number of considerations: recognition that Seoul had spurted far past the North economically, concern over the ROK's human rights record, belief that the USSR and China were willing to restrain North Korea, expectation that air and sea power were sufficient to fulfill America's defense commitment, and opposition to squandering manpower in a region he considered less important than Europe or the Middle East.[17]

President Carter announced his plan to reduce U.S. forces in Korea on March 9, 1977, and immediately ran into a storm of opposition abroad and at home. Not surprisingly, the Park regime resisted the initiative, as did Japan and other East Asian nations, which opposed any reduction in America's presence.[18] Domestically, Carter faced opposition, not only in Congress, but from officials in his own administration.[19] They argued that such a step was inappropriate when the Cold War seemed to be at its height and America appeared to be in retreat from Asia after the debacle in Vietnam. The public protests of Gen. John Singlaub, chief of staff to the U.S. Eighth Army in South Korea, also helped to galvanize opposition to the Carter initiative, and Carter fired Singlaub.[20]

For all of the surrounding furor, the Carter proposal was actually quite limited—"aseptic involvement," in the words of Georgetown

University professor Earl Ravenal.[21] Although candidate Carter apparently originally favored withdrawing all U.S. forces, President Carter merely intended to pull out the last infantry division and assorted miscellaneous ground units. He planned to leave behind some 14,000 air and logistics personnel. The administration also promised to supply Seoul with $800 million worth of equipment—including helicopters and armored personnel carriers—and $1.4 billion in credits over five years for weapons purchases; to give the ROK access to advanced technology; to conduct joint military exercises; to enhance the American air, communications, and intelligence units remaining in the ROK; and to maintain the Mutual Defense Treaty.

Why Bother?

Most important, Washington's promise to go to war would remain unchanged and the departing troops were to be redeployed, not demobilized. As Secretary of Defense Harold Brown explained to Congress in 1977, "It probably makes sense to continue approximately our current deployments in the Western Pacific, and with them, our ability to react swiftly to any aggressive moves by North Korea."[22] Administration officials talked about "restructuring" forces and denied that the plan involved a "pullout." The Joint Korean-American communiqué of July 26, 1977, even emphasized the possibility of a return of American forces, if necessary. "Operating here is the incalculable principle of 'compensation,' rather than the principle of strategic requirements," observed Ravenal, and the compensations seemed to become as expensive as the supposed savings.[23] The question really should have been, why bother?

Few, if any, asked that question, however. Rather, the president found himself involved in an extended, emotional debate over whether he was risking Korean and regional peace. The arguments were quintessential Cold War concerns: Would China and the Soviet Union really restrain North Korea? Would Pyongyang be tempted to strike at its southern neighbor, which remained militarily weaker? Would even a modified withdrawal, coming so soon after America's retreat from Vietnam, herald Asia-wide disengagement?[24]

Although the administration withdrew one small contingent, it soon postponed the next stage. After U.S. Army estimates of increased DPRK military strength surfaced in 1979, perhaps conveniently timed for the benefit of opponents of withdrawal, the administration dropped the plan.[25] Only 3,670 soldiers had been moved.

Indeed, before Carter left office, his administration actually upgraded U.S. forces by adding AWACS aircraft, enhancing naval fleet and air strength, and bolstering ground-based airpower.[26] Nevertheless, complains Lieutenant Colonel Lee, "mistrust and disappointment pervaded the traditionally cordial relationship between the two allies."[27]

Still, the Carter shock, like the Nixon shock, helped to push the South toward the "self-reliant" defense that it now claims as a goal. Writes Makoto Momoi of Japan's National Defense College,

> The Seoul government responded to the withdrawal plan by moving to consolidate the populace behind President Park ... and by taking steps to accelerate the modernization of the Korean armed forces. Not only was the ROK's Force Improvement Program stepped up, but there was a more rapid development of South Korean defense production capabilities, including substantial improvements in the capabilities for production of sophisticated arms. Equally important, the South Korean people demonstrated an increased willingness to bear sacrifice. Even opposition groups rallied to support the president on this issue. This left the South Koreans feeling stronger and more self-confident than before.[28]

Carter's successor, Ronald Reagan, assured new ROK president Chun Doo Hwan that there would be no troop withdrawal; Chun responded by lauding "the restoration of trust."[29] U.S. force levels edged upward, and for eight years Reagan, who criticized "welfare queens" at home, encouraged one abroad.

However, South Korea's economic and military progress had become impossible to ignore by the end of the decade. Therefore, the Bush administration planned, as part of its April 1990 East Asia Strategic Initiative, to implement a modest, three-stage reduction in U.S. forces.[30] The first cut, of 7,000 personnel (5,000 Army and 2,000 Air Force), was completed in 1992. The second phase, which involved restructuring the Second Division and shrinking force levels by 5,000 to 6,000 personnel, was scheduled for 1993 through 1995. However, it was canceled in November 1991 as a result of the North Korean nuclear controversy. Also set aside was the 5- to 10-year review of further cuts intended to leave merely a minimum force for deterrence.

Even those modest plans, only partially carried out, had an impact on South Korean policy. Reported Seoul's Ministry of National Defense, "South Korea has drawn up its own contingency plan, with a view to minimizing the effects of too rapid a reduction of USFK [U.S. forces in Korea] troops, easing military tension on the Korean peninsula, and achieving a more self-reliant defense posture in the long run."[31]

Lessons Learned

Several lessons emerge from those experiences. First, Washington has to decide its policy on the basis of its own interests, not South Korea's desires. The ROK may never want American troops to go home. Second, Seoul's unnatural dependence on America requires the United States to give early notice to the South and structure the withdrawal program to complement increased South Korean efforts to meet security needs. Third, America should completely withdraw its forces from Korea, rather than replicate the past game of offering expensive "compensations" in an attempt to buy ROK acquiescence to a plan that promises little real change. Fourth, the United States should set a short withdrawal time frame, one that could be implemented by one president, preferably within a single term. Fifth, Washington should eliminate the Mutual Defense Treaty, once U.S. troops are withdrawn, in order to ensure genuine disengagement. Sixth, America must stick with its plan despite the inevitable criticism from those with either a vested interest in or an emotional attachment to the status quo.

What should America do in the mid-1990s, especially with a new administration possibly taking power in early 1997? Washington should decide on a rough phase-out period of, say, four years—with the exact timetable subject to negotiation—at the end of which all U.S. forces will have been withdrawn from the peninsula and the Mutual Defense Treaty will be canceled. Washington should initiate early consultations with the ROK both to fashion a smooth disengagement program and to help ease the psychological blow to Koreans who still look to the United States for their defense, such as the cabinet minister who called the presence of American troops in Korea "natural."[32] Indeed, Seoul should be encouraged to make the formal public announcement, at which time, as argued later, it should publicly challenge Pyongyang to demonstrate the sincerity of its earlier peace proposals by pulling its troops back from their aggressive positions and engaging in meaningful arms control negotiations.

Army First

U.S. infantry units, which the South could most easily replace, should be pulled out quickly. That would have the added benefit of eliminating the tripwire intended to make American military involvement automatic, thereby allowing the president and Congress to make a reasoned decision about America's response should a conflict occur. Air and naval units should be withdrawn next and more slowly. Although some analysts favor continuing to provide air and naval cover after withdrawing the ground units, doing so would not be cheap; it is the existence of those formations, as well as those intended for potential reinforcement, not merely their deployment in Korea, that is expensive. Moreover, there is no reason why Seoul, which currently possesses a technologically superior, albeit outnumbered, air force and navy, could not quickly develop adequate air and naval power. It might even purchase U.S. equipment.

Once U.S. forces are withdrawn, Washington should sever its defense guarantee. Proposals to undertake the first step—pull out the troops—have been controversial, but not uncommon. President Carter, Rep. Robert Mrazek (D-N.Y.), William Taylor of the Center for Strategic and International Studies, Ralph Clough of the Brookings Institution, and the National Council of the Churches of Christ have all, at one time or another, proposed bringing home some or all of America's forces.[33] But the next step, eliminating the underlying defense guarantee, has rarely been mentioned, let alone seriously considered. Indeed, the Carter administration emphasized that it was making no change in the Mutual Defense Treaty. That administration even sent an aircraft carrier to South Korea after the assassination of President Park to reinforce its commitment to the country's defense.

Similarly, William Gleysteen Jr., a former ambassador to the ROK, once suggested cutting U.S. ground forces when the South's army reached parity with that of the North. But he advocated preserving the treaty because "the United States will have to ensure that no misleading signals about unwavering U.S. commitments are conveyed to any player—North, South or beyond the peninsula."[34] What then was the purpose of his proposal? Preserving the commitment requires Washington to maintain sufficient military forces to intervene in the event of war, which precludes any meaningful cost reduction. The risk of America's involvement in a Korean war would remain unchanged. And the problem of America's entanglement in internal Korean affairs would only be ameliorated, not eliminated. Finally, Seoul would remain a de facto protectorate, despite the removal of the most visible symbol of America's dominance.

Pacific Adjustments

Once American troops are out of Korea and the treaty guarantee is abolished, the Pentagon should adjust its Pacific deployments to reflect the fact that the ROK is no longer covered by the U.S. defense safety net. That would involve demobilizing some forces and perhaps repositioning others.

Washington should couple military disengagement with a commitment to sell Seoul any conventional weapons, including those of America's departing troops, that it wishes to acquire. As Makoto Momoi has observed, the primary military contribution of America's forces has been firepower, and Washington can effectively "transfer" much of it to the South.[35] If the North is serious about its numerous proposals to follow a U.S. withdrawal with large-scale reductions in ROK and DPRK forces, then a South Korean build-up would be unnecessary. If not, however, the ROK could easily afford to make some major purchases. So long as the sales were coupled with a troop withdrawal, the United States should be willing to negotiate coproduction agreements, since the resulting transfer of technology—for aircraft or other systems—would help enhance the ROK's defense capability.[36]

Equipping the South in that way would avoid the Truman administration's mistake of 1949, when it withdrew America's troops without adequately preparing the Korean army to replace them. Washington's principal reason for leaving the ROK militarily naked was understandable: the Rhee regime's bellicosity.[37] (In fact, Rhee continued to press for Washington's acquiescence in an attack north after the war and even developed an invasion plan in 1955.)[38] Unfortunately, however, the foreseeable result was a DPRK invasion. Today

91

a South Korean attack seems extremely unlikely.[39] Nevertheless, to discourage a reinvigorated Seoul from considering a strike north, Washington should make it clear that Seoul would receive no U.S. aid for such an attack, even if, say, China intervened on North Korea's behalf. To argue that the United States should occupy its allies (not just the ROK, but also Germany and Japan) or keep them weak to prevent them from undertaking aggression turns the purpose of supposedly friendly security relationships on its head.[40] It is also likely to poison relations as allies realize that America is containing rather than defending them.

Washington should also continue improving its relations with the North. The United States should move to full ambassadorial representation, eliminate the remaining barriers to trade and travel, and encourage Pyongyang to allow greater cultural and economic interchange. America should also endorse contacts between the DPRK and Japan, Taiwan, and other countries in the region. The purpose would not be to replace America's ties with the South but to bring the North into a more normal relationship with its neighbors and the overall international system.[41] The greater Pyongyang's stake in a peaceful and stable peninsula, the better.

Regional Agreement

Given the past role of the Korean peninsula as a fulcrum of conflict, the United States should forge an agreement with China, Japan, and Russia that all four countries will discourage any aggressive action by either Korea. Those nations could also work together to help mediate disputes and encourage cooperation between the two Koreas. Such an accord need not be formal, drawn up at an international conference; an informal understanding would be sufficient.[42]

That would not be the same as the South Korean proposal for a peace treaty guaranteed by America and China.[43] There is no need to formally guarantee peace on the peninsula, especially when such a step could draw all four nations more deeply into the two Koreas' still potentially volatile struggle and conceivably threaten a major-power confrontation in the unlikely event of war. Instead, a policy of nonintervention by the great powers would both make conflict less likely (since an aggressor, either North or South, could not expect outside assistance) and isolate any war that might occur.

Encouraging collaboration and consensus on Korean affairs would help promote broader regional cooperation as well. Despite the fears of some, there is no reason to believe that East Asia would explode into chaos and war without the presence of 37,000 U.S. soldiers in the ROK. There are destabilizing factors present, of course, as there are in most regions. But the incentives for nations to maintain peace are also strong. Admits Seoul's Ministry of National Defense,

> The surrounding four countries, which confronted each other in the previous Cold War structure, are moving into a state of friendly cooperative relations. Following this, they are promoting such efforts as the expansion of economic exchange and cooperation for the aggrandizement of common interests, multilateral regional security cooperation, etc. Especially, regarding the problems relating to the Korean peninsula, an international cooperative atmosphere is being formed within the context of a common understanding about its importance for regional and world peace and stability.[44]

In particular, Washington should encourage the expansion of ties between South Korea and Japan, which remain tainted by the latter's half century of colonial rule.[45] Tokyo supports America's military presence in the ROK—it vigorously opposed the Carter withdrawal plan, for instance. Observes historian Frank Baldwin, once Jimmy Carter was elected, "members of Japan's foreign affairs and defense establishment put down their cups of green tea and moved swiftly to block Carter's plans."[46] However, there is no reason why the world's second-ranking economic power, which surpasses both China and Russia, could not help fill any security vacuum left by a U.S. pullout, especially since Japan and the ROK have significant interests, including the maintenance of regional peace, in common. Col. R. Mark Bean would go further and encourage a formal Northeast Asian security coalition including China.[47]

Not that many Koreans would like to see a larger Japanese role, although some, at least, are willing to countenance increased cooperation so long as it revolves around America. Argues Ahn Byung-joon, a political science professor at Yonsei University, "South Korea, Japan and the US must deepen their partnership for common interests as well as common values beyond the Cold War alliances."[48] But fear and loathing of Tokyo are one issue that unites many Koreans in both North and South.[49] So strong have those sentiments been that serious defense consultations between the ROK and Japan began only in November 1994, and only recently has Seoul spoken favorably of potential military cooperation with Tokyo.[50] Some South Koreans bridle at the thought of Japanese support even in war. One official at the Ministry of National Defense stated that Seoul would accept such assistance "only at the last moment," if then. The people are just "not sentimentally inclined to accept" aid from Japan.[51]

However, sentimentality is no excuse for irresponsibility. The ROK can avoid exorcising the ghosts of World War II only because it believes Washington would rescue it in case of war. Washington needs to drop its defense promise and assist Seoul to refashion its relationship with Tokyo. There are, after all, many steps short of the sort of physical presence of Japanese soldiers in Korea that would reawaken far too many memories. Possibilities include shared intelligence gathering, joint naval exercises, cooperative weapons development, and even financial contributions, though the latter seem the least appropriate as Seoul's economy continues to grow so swiftly.[52]

Japan's Role

Of course, other nations in East Asia and the Pacific share the South's disquiet over the prospect of Japan's playing a larger security role in the region. But ever-expanding global economic interests and growing nationalistic feelings make it inevitable that Tokyo will someday enlarge its military. Observes former secretary of state Henry Kissinger, "With Korea and China gaining in military strength, and with the least impaired portion of Soviet military power located in Siberia, Japanese long-range planners will not indefinitely take the absolute identity of American and Japanese interests for granted."[53] Washington's military presence in the region may slow that process; it is not likely to halt it.

In any case, as discussed in more detail in chapter 7, it is unreasonable to expect the United States to forever garrison the region to avert nervousness caused by Japanese aggression more than five decades ago. The best policy for Washington would be to encourage a responsible expansion of Tokyo's armed forces—adding defense-oriented weapons, such as frigates and interceptors, for instance—and to channel Japanese efforts into nonthreatening activities, such as aiding the military programs of neighboring democratic states, including the ROK.

Asian Regionalism

At the same time, Washington should promote the strengthening and expansion of regional institutions. Seoul itself acknowledges the changing nature of its security requirements as the Northern threat fades. Observes the ROK government, "We feel that our strategic concept should change from the existing one aimed at the North to the one that promotes all-azimuth security cooperation with neighboring countries."[54]

An East Asian NATO, or Western European Union (WEU), the continental defensive system of which America is not a member, is probably some time away, given the greater disunity in this region than in Europe.[55] However, Europe, with the European Union, continentwide legislative and regulatory bodies, and the WEU, demonstrates how disparate and once divided countries can draw together and how shared economic success can promote other, powerful links. Moreover, organizations such as the Association of Southeast Asian Nations, with its Post Ministerial Conference, Regional Forum, and Free Trade Area; the Asia-Pacific Economic Cooperation; the Council on Security Cooperation in the Asia-Pacific; the Pacific Economic Cooperation Conference; and the East Asian Economic Caucus (EAEC) all provide bases for serious regional cooperation on issues ranging from economics to security.

Perhaps most important, they provide an opportunity for Japan to gradually expand its role within a regional framework. Just as NATO and the European Community (now the European Union) helped channel German power for Europe's good and lessen concerns over growing German strength, so alliances and associations in East Asia could help promote regional stability in the absence of U.S. military forces.

The best service that Washington could render would be to promote free trade throughout the region and with America, perhaps through initiatives akin to President Clinton's New Pacific Community initiative, and to encourage security consultations without the United States present, or present only as an observer. (For that reason the Malaysian-inspired EAEC moves in the wrong direction, both by limiting its activities to economics and by barring participation, not only of America, but also of Australia and New Zealand.) The most important impetus Washington could give to security cooperation would be to plan and implement a program for withdrawal from Korea and, later, elsewhere in the region. Although there is a decided bias today toward "cooperative" security built on bilateral alliances with the United States, a more serious "collective security" regime, whether regionwide or more limited, would become a necessity after an American withdrawal.[56] As Kissinger has noted, regional cooperation will come, not from "shared domestic values," but from a common concern with "equilibrium and national interests."[57] That should, however, prove to be sufficient.

Such an alternative might seem unsatisfactory to countries that prefer to rely on America. Singapore's Lee Kuan Yew, for instance, has been particularly critical of Tokyo and has voiced his preference that Washington "provide the stabilizing anchor force around which the smaller countries can cluster."[58] But that preference, however natural, is no basis for U.S. policy. Indeed, predictions that doom would follow a withdrawal of U.S. troops from Korea match those of two decades ago about the effects of a pullout from Vietnam. True, U.S. Department of Defense officials contend that calamity did not come to pass after the Vietnam episode because of America's continuing presence in Korea and elsewhere in the region.[59] But the dangerous world of 1975, with a newly triumphant communist Vietnam, still aggressively communist China and Russia, and less confident ROK and Japan, has disappeared. While the United States might be "uniquely positioned to be a constructive and enduring force for stability in the region," as the Pentagon claims, the specific threats that justified such a unique containment force are almost all gone.[60]

Measured Withdrawal

As compelling as the changes in the world over the past 45 years make the case for disengagement, it would obviously be best not to initiate a precipitous withdrawal. The South has asked for "the close consultation of both sides" before any "additional reductions in the US forces."[61] That is a reasonable request, so long as the discussion is over timing of the withdrawal rather than the decision to withdraw, which must be based on American interests. Only the United States can make that decision.

However, planning a pullout warrants serious input from the ROK. Although Seoul's military strength may be sufficient to both deter the DPRK and rebuff any invasion, the South has relied on the U.S. defense guarantee and therefore should be given time to augment its military forces and develop security arrangements with its neighbors to counterbalance an American withdrawal. Washington also needs to inform Japan and other interested nations of any plan before they read about it in the *New York Times* or the *Washington Post*. Doing so will better enable them to work with Seoul and each other to plan for a future without American protection.

Washington should emphasize that the ties between nations, in contrast to governments, would remain as strong as ever. South Koreans remain very sensitive to what ROK president Kim Young Sam calls "wedge-driving" by the North.[62] Indeed, one analyst at the Research Institute for National Unification fears a time when "the DPRK and the US establish a full diplomatic relationship and the bilateral relations become as good as that of Seoul and Washington."[63] However, equivalent relations between the United States and the two Koreas are as close to an impossibility as exists in international affairs. Pyongyang remains a Stalinist-style dictatorship, which makes it simultaneously bizarre, unpleasant, and unpredictable. Trade with North Korea, even after it abandons communism, is likely to remain modest for years, in contrast to the widespread and profitable economic links with the ROK. Moreover, there is no pro-DPRK lobby in the United States, unlike in Japan; almost all Americans of Korean extraction are from the South. Finally, as President Kim has rightly noted, the United States and the ROK "are truly blood allies."[64] All of those ties ensure a stronger relationship with South Korea than might develop with the DPRK.[65] Nevertheless, the United States should be cognizant of ROK concerns and attempt to allay them.

The skill with which Washington disentangled itself from its Korean commitment would obviously affect its international reputation. President Carter's withdrawal proposal died amidst sustained foreign and domestic criticism; a new initiative needs to be carefully designed and implemented, with the United States indicating its continued interest in East Asia and its willingness to facilitate increased regional economic, political, and military cooperation. In particular, diplomatic efforts would be needed to help assuage the concern of friendly Pacific states over the likelihood of increased Japanese influence, a logical, if unsettling, result of an American pullout. Serious consultations with Seoul and its neighbors before implementing a withdrawal program would ensure a more orderly process and help preserve America's international credibility. An accomplished pullout would also provide a model for disengaging elsewhere in the world.

Setting a Deadline

Nevertheless, it is important for the United States to set a deadline, or the ROK will have an incentive to delay fully augmenting its military as long as possible to maintain the U.S. security guarantee. Most Koreans, other than a minority of students whose leftist ideology blinds them to the threat from the North, would prefer to keep the American defense shield.[66] Even leading opposition figure Kim Dae Jung says he supports a troop drawdown only as part of détente with the North. Moreover, the fallback position adopted by opponents of disengagement will be to seek a postponement rather than a cancellation, since the former usually turns into the latter, as it did with President Carter's plan. In the view of supporters of the ROK defense subsidy, the timing of a U.S. withdrawal will never be right, just as the point when Seoul is to reach military parity with the North always seems to be a few more years in the future. Therefore, Washington must insist that only the timing and details of the pullout, not the denouement itself, are subject to negotiation.

The United States should encourage the South to use an American phase-out as a bargaining chip with North Korea. Seoul should announce the withdrawal and give the DPRK two choices. One is to engage in serious negotiations over adoption of confidence-building measures and arms reduction. The other is to watch South Korea build up its military to match that of the North.

Although it is impossible to predict how North Korea would respond, giving Pyongyang a choice would provide a useful test of the DPRK's intentions. Some analysts, such as the Carnegie Endowment's Selig Harrison, believe that the North has long been serious in its desire for arms reduction.[67] In fact, when Harrison visited Pyongyang in late 1995, North Korean officials told him that they were "not opposed to the continued presence of American forces in South Korea."[68] Past experience makes it difficult to give much credence to anything emanating from Pyongyang, but the DPRK's ongoing economic difficulties and what seems to be genuinely more responsive attitude suggest at least a reasonable possibility that it is prepared to change course.[69] That North Korea might now be willing to accept (or even to encourage) U.S. force deployments is, of course, no reason to maintain them. But if Pyongyang is genuinely concerned about the possibility of South Korean aggression, it would have an especially powerful incentive to reach an accommodation with the ROK. Even if the North was lying to Harrison, it would still have strong reason to negotiate, since the alternative would probably be a South Korean program to spend its adversary into the ground. In fact, the Seoul government predicted as much in 1993:

> From a mid- and long-term perspective, the probability of peaceful coexistence between South and North Korea is predicted to increase. It is very likely that international cross-recognition of the two Koreas will come about as the worldwide conciliatory atmosphere warms after the Cold War era and as the four major regional powers come to increasingly desire stability on the Korean peninsula. When North Korea takes into account the considerable gap between the two Koreas in terms of national power, the predicted loss of their military supremacy and the expected limit of Kim Jong Il's charisma after Kim Il Sung dies, they are predicted inevitably to renounce their strategy of communizing the South by force and to embrace a pragmatic opening and reforming of their society.[70]

Starting Point

The two sides could start by implementing the Agreement on Reconciliation, Nonaggression and Exchanges and Cooperation between the South and the North, which envisions a direct military hot line and crisis management system, as well as many other steps.[71] Soon thereafter should come more serious forms of arms control. Over the years there have been many disarmament proposals, including a border pullback, large-scale troop demobilization, and freezes on new weaponry.[72] Intermixed with those actions could be a formal peace treaty, family visits, food assistance, business investment, and the like. Economic cooperation could prove to be a particularly effective means of bringing the two nations together.[73] The long-term result of that course should be genuine détente and a "peace regime" of some sort.[74] Ultimately, reunification could follow, though melding two such disparate systems will never be easy, even if the communist regime in the North eventually implodes.[75]

However, if North Korea refuses to negotiate—seriously—then the ROK government will need no additional evidence to generate public support for an arms build-up.[76] (Phasing out rather than immediately canceling the U.S. security guarantee would deter a DPRK attempt to preempt Southern military expansion.) Indeed, experience indicates that Seoul has always responded to U.S. withdrawals with increased military expenditures. South Korea's Ministry of National Defense itself speaks of having its efforts "stimulated" by the Nixon troop reductions.[77] In 1975, for instance, the government imposed a special 15-year defense tax.[78] Similar was the experience after the announcement of the Carter initiative. Observes Japan's Makoto Momoi,

> The South Koreans adapted extremely well to the withdrawal decision. The decision had actually been anticipated for some time, though the manner of its announcement came as a surprise. The Seoul government responded to the withdrawal plan by moving to consolidate the populace behind President Park and . . . by taking steps to accelerate the modernization of the Korean armed forces. Not only was the R.O.K.'s Force Improvement Program stepped up, but there was a more rapid development of South Korean defense production capabilities for production of sophisticated arms. Equally important, the South Korean people demonstrated an increased willingness to bear sacrifice.[79]

The fact that South Korea is now a democracy rather than a military dictatorship does not make a defense build-up less likely. Even the minor Bush troop withdrawal caused the ROK to respond constructively. Explained Seoul's Ministry of National Defense, after the announcement of Washington's East Asia Strategic Initiative in 1990, with its plan for a three-step reduction in American forces, "South Korea has drawn up its own contingency plan, with a view to minimizing the effects of too rapid a reduction of USFK troops, easing military tension on the Korean peninsula, and achieving a more self-reliant defense posture in the long run."[80] The shock of a full U.S. pullout would create an even greater impetus for action.

Indeed, Israel provides an example of a democracy willing to undertake enormous efforts for its own defense even in peacetime. Tel Aviv has regularly spent 10 percent of its GNP on the military. During the 1970s and early 1980s Israeli defense outlays regularly exceeded a quarter and once broke a third of GNP.[81] Democracies can make prudent provisions for defense—if there is sufficient incentive to do so.

Conclusion

Four decades of American withdrawal plans and proposals have been generally half-hearted, mismanaged, and interrupted. Washington needs to adopt a new approach, based on South Korea's declining security value to America and increasing ability to defend itself. The United States should therefore make a firm decision to pull out all of its troops, while negotiating with Seoul over the length and sequence of the withdrawal. The disengagement decision needs to be final, with demobilization of the troops and cancellation of the Mutual Defense Treaty to follow. Only then will the American people be free of a commitment that costs far more than it is worth and the Korean people be free of a dependent relationship that insults their nationhood.

6. The Nuclear Complication

For 40 years the Korean peninsula, though volatile, presented a threat limited to conventional war. Neither Korea possessed nuclear weapons; although Washington stationed tactical warheads in the South, Pyongyang's nuclear-armed allies seemed unlikely to risk a nuclear confrontation with America.

However, the Cold War on the peninsula grew dramatically more complicated during the late 1980s and early 1990s with the increasing threat of a North Korean nuclear capability. Although a signatory to the Nuclear Non-Proliferation Treaty (NPT), Pyongyang had not concluded a safeguards agreement with the International Atomic Energy Agency (IAEA). Evidence of an active nuclear program combined with the imminent refueling of one of the North's nuclear reactors, which would allow the extraction of weapons-grade plutonium, and construction of another, even larger, reactor created a crisis atmosphere punctuated by brinkmanship and threats of war by both sides. The issue quickly surged to the fore of regional politics.

Along with the threat of war came negotiations, and an apparent settlement was reached in 1994—providing for allied construction of two light-water reactors to replace Pyongyang's older, graphite facilities in return for a halt in a weapons program that the DPRK continues to say does not exist. The crisis is "defused," in the words of Robert Manning of the Progressive Policy Institute, not resolved.[1] Hardly a month goes by without a reminder that the North Korean government remains, if no longer quite an outlaw regime, a highly bizarre and unpredictable one. Even the best case for the years ahead probably involves a continuing stream of obstructions, prevarications, and ultimatums from a government that believes international diplomacy is like dealing at a Mideast bazaar.

Although the potential of a nuclear North Korea greatly complicates America's involvement in East Asia, it does not create a new justification for the now-obsolete U.S. security guarantee to South Korea. To the contrary, the potential for a nuclear confrontation on the peninsula exponentially increases the risks of U.S. involvement, and thus makes disengagement even more imperative.

The North Korean Nuclear Program

The DPRK began its nuclear effort in the mid-1950s and was originally assisted by the Soviet Union, which helped establish an atomic energy research center in 1962, and China, which aided the North's uranium-mining effort.[2] North Korea joined the IAEA in 1974, giving Pyongyang access to technical assistance in the peaceful use of nuclear energy. Over the years the DPRK constructed a 5-megawatt and a 50-megawatt reactor, and Pyongyang began building a 200-megawatt reactor in 1985.

For all of the furor generated by the nuclear issue, we actually know relatively little about the North's activities. In 1989 satellite photos first revealed what appeared to be a nuclear reprocessing plant. The available evidence indicates that the DPRK's program is centered at Yongbyon, 60 miles north of Pyongyang, and has three reactors, two reprocessing plants, two waste disposal tanks, a radio-chemistry laboratory, and other facilities and equipment. Another reactor and reprocessing plant, as well as other facilities, are located elsewhere.[3] North Korea could have additional, secret installations. Defense analyst Joseph Bermudez has warned, "The problem is that you can't tell what's inside the buildings and what's underground."[4] In September 1991 Ko Young Hwan, a North Korean defector, claimed that the DPRK had an entire facility below ground at Bakchon, also near Pyongyang.[5] Defectors' reports are often discounted—among other things, they are thought to tell South Korean intelligence agents what the latter want to hear—but the possibility of a nuclear facility at Bakchon makes it harder for the allies to enforce nonproliferation. All told, as *Jane's Intelligence Review* puts it, "There is little doubt that the primary objective of North Korea's nuclear programme has been, and continues to be, the production of nuclear weapons."[6]

Naturally, the North denies the existence of any nuclear weapons program. And experts have disagreed for years about the imminence of any weapon. Some analysts believe that the DPRK may already possess one; most assume that the North is as least a couple of years away from creating a deliverable bomb. Indeed, all we really know is that, as a result of its 1989 nuclear refueling, Pyongyang possesses sufficient plutonium to make one or possibly two weapons if it has the technical capability and will to do so.

Potentially, the most fearsome aspect of Pyongyang's program is its construction of a 200-megawatt reactor. The 50-megawatt facility could produce enough plutonium to make at least one bomb a year; once operational, the larger plant could generate enough fuel to make 7 to 10 bombs annually. Pyongyang's underdeveloped economy hardly justified even the 50-megawatt reactor to generate power, which led to the fear that the North hoped to use the larger facility to create either a sizable arsenal or an export product for other would-be nuclear weapons powers.

International Soap Opera

The North's behavior has only exacerbated concern about its intentions.[7] Although the DPRK signed the NPT in 1985, it took seven years to accept a safeguards agreement, a process that normally takes about 18 months.[8] Since then the issue has taken on all of the attributes of an international soap opera, with the North acting like a woman who accepts a marriage proposal one day, only to act like a woman scorned the next.

Initially, the North's program received little attention. Then in 1989 the Central Intelligence Agency believed that the DPRK first unloaded weapons-grade plutonium from its 50-megawatt reactor. The following year the North tested bomb components, opened a plutonium-processing plant, and inaugurated a new uranium-processing plant.

As calls for international inspections rose, North Korea denied that it had a program and resisted any oversight, rejecting a Japanese offer of diplomatic recognition in return. When evidence of an atomic research complex seemed irrefutable, the issue loomed as the most important on the peninsula. Northern intransigence soon led to proposals for more than negotiations. Among the options discussed at the annual U.S.–South Korean security talks in November 1991 were economic sanctions and a naval blockade. More ominous, officials began to discuss potential military remedies. On October 30, 1991, the ROK Defense Ministry released a white paper that stated that the DPRK effort "must be stopped at any cost."[9] Possible measures for doing so included a preemptive air or commando strike to destroy the North's facilities, suggested on two occasions by ROK defense minister Lee Jong Koo. (Minister Lee later moderated his tone, stating that "military and other sanctions against the North might be made by the United Nations, but we cannot go so far as to run the risk of another Korean War.")[10]

American Would-Be Bombers

There was strong support for the military option in America. The Bush administration suggested as much when it issued a statement jointly with Seoul saying that North Korea's "nuclear arms program must be stopped in advance without fail."[11] A number of analysts pushed for the "Israeli solution," named after Israel's strike on Iraq's Osirak reactor in 1981. Said *Chicago Tribune* columnist Stephen Chapman, "An air attack on the nuclear complex at Yongbyon would shut down North Korea's program by destroying its reactors and the reprocessing plant needed to produce fuel for bombs—just as Israel's attack delayed Iraq's nuclear plans by at least two years."[12] (He later reversed course to oppose military action.)[13]

The DPRK originally used the alleged presence of American tactical nuclear weapons in the South to justify its refusal to allow IAEA inspections.[14] In October 1991 DPRK foreign minister Kim Yong Nam stated that inspections would be allowed "if such a nuclear threat is removed."[15] However, after Washington announced its intention to withdraw the bombs, Pyongyang quickly added new conditions— that the ROK renounce nuclear protection by the United States and forbid the overflight of planes and docking of ships carrying nuclear weapons. Yet in December 1991 the North concluded an agreement with South Korea providing for even more intrusive inspections than those typically carried out by the IAEA, which itself reached an accord with Pyongyang two months later. Hope of a real détente between the two bitter enemies blossomed.

Unfortunately, the two Koreas almost immediately deadlocked over implementation of their agreement. As is so often the case with North Korea, it is hard to separate genuine objections and implausible excuses. During my visit to Pyongyang in August 1992, DPRK officials complained that the South Koreans sought to include inspections of conventional military installations, a matter to be handled by a separate negotiating committee, and were unable to grant the right to visit U.S. bases, which the North Koreans believed to be necessary since America had introduced nuclear weapons to the peninsula.

Although the two Koreas subsequently deadlocked on bilateral inspection procedures, the IAEA made its first inspection in May 1992 and by the end of the year had conducted six examinations of North Korean nuclear facilities. The agency's conclusions were positive if not definitive: the DPRK appeared to have produced more than the 90 grams of plutonium that it admitted possessing, but it had generally been cooperative. Although the IAEA was skeptical of some of Pyongyang's explanations of the purpose of its apparent reprocessing facility, the North took IAEA investigators to sites not on the formal inspection list and offered to allow the agency to make additional special visits on demand. As a result, in November 1992 Ronald Lehman, head of the U.S. Arms Control and Disarmament Agency, reversed his earlier pessimistic assessment of the North's nuclear efforts, stating that international efforts had "stopped" the DPRK's program and "blocked" its ability to amass "a sizable number of nuclear weapons over time."[16] Pyongyang seemed to have moved further in 2 years than in the previous 40, and hope for genuine détente grew.

Northern Obstructionism

But in January 1993 the DPRK refused the IAEA access to two suspected nuclear waste depositories, and tests showed that the North had lied about how much plutonium it had extracted.[17] Pyongyang tied its refusal to the ongoing Team Spirit military exercises in the South. When the IAEA made an unprecedented demand for a special inspection of the two sites, North Korea denounced the agency for fronting for the United States. Pyongyang then announced that it was refusing to allow any further IAEA visits, withdrawing from the NPT (no other nation had ever done so), and abrogating the inspection agreement. The IAEA declared the North out of compliance, and the international crisis flared again.

It remains unclear why the North acted when and as it did. Presumably, it feared that the IAEA inspectors would discover further evidence that it had lied about its production of plutonium; it may also have underestimated the intrusiveness and effectiveness of the IAEA. Or Pyongyang may simply have decided to test the new governments in both the ROK and the United States. Another possibility is that the regime decided it had received too few tangible benefits from its decision to forgo nuclear weapons. (The principal international reaction seemed to be demands for yet more inspections.) The joint U.S.-ROK military exercises, long a sore point with the North, may have triggered an internal political battle. Or perhaps the decision reflected the perceived need by designated successor Kim Jong Il, reputedly in charge of the nuclear program, to demonstrate his commitment to the military. Perhaps the regime simply decided the time was right to play the nuclear card yet again.

Naturally, Pyongyang's official explanation was that it was forced onto its controversial course by the United States.

> A grave situation has been created today in our country, which threatens its national sovereignty and security of our state.
>
> The United States and south Korean authorities have defiantly resumed the "Team spirit" joint military exercises, a nuclear war rehearsal against the Democratic People's Republic of Korea, and, in coincidence with this, some officials of the Secretariat of the International Atomic Energy Agency (IAEA) and certain member nations following the lead of the United States had a "resolution" adopted at the February 25 meeting of the IAEA Board of Governors, demanding a special inspection of our military sites unrelated to nuclear activities.
>
> This is an encroachment on the sovereignty of the Democratic People's Republic of Korea, an interference in its internal affairs and a hostile act aimed at stifling our socialism.[18]

Private Arguments

In private conversations, Northern diplomats argued that the facilities at issue were conventional military, not nuclear, installations and therefore were exempt from the inspection regime, and that in making its demands the IAEA was yielding to Washington's pressure. Would America have opened up its bases under similar circumstances, they asked. The DPRK government, they said, remained committed to three-way talks with the United States and the ROK over nuclear inspections on the peninsula and was willing to return to the NPT if such talks got under way. They also said that they were ready to discuss the two sites with the IAEA if it acted independently and not under U.S. pressure, though they did not guarantee that Pyongyang would ultimately allow inspection of those facilities.[19] The North put particular emphasis on ending military exercises in the South, an issue that clearly agitated Northern officials whom I met in Pyongyang in August 1992.

In any case, fears of a North Korean nuclear bomb rose to a fever pitch, especially in the United States. The CIA warned that the North might already have enough plutonium to build at least one nuclear weapon. The ROK suspended economic activities in the DPRK, and Japan backed away from discussions about improving relations with Pyongyang.

Although the Clinton administration generally reacted with circumspection, as the IAEA's March 31 deadline approached, Secretary of State Warren Christopher told a House appropriations subcommittee that "there will be enforcement action taken within the U.N. Security Council."[20] He focused on economic sanctions, even though there was no guarantee that such measures would have much effect on the DPRK's already isolated economy. That course was complicated by the fact that UN action required the acquiescence of China—long the North's closest ally—that said that it would not penalize Pyongyang. "We support patient consultations to reach an appropriate solution," explained Chinese foreign minister Qian Qichen. "If the matter goes before the Security Council, that will only complicate things."[21] Moreover, Pyongyang warned that sanctions could mean war.

Advocates of War

Advocates of military action again came to the fore in the United States. Columnist Paul Greenberg argued that "America and its allies should be readying an Israel-style strike against North Korean facilities now."[22] Similar was the analysis of Frank Gaffney of the Center for Security Policy, who contended that "the choice—as with Iraq two-and-a-half years ago—is not between possibly going to war with North Korea and not going to war. Rather, it is a question of risking going to war *now*, when U.S. military capabilities are relatively strong and North Korean nuclear forces are minimal (or not yet completed), rather than later when such advantageous conditions will almost surely not exist."[23] House Defense Appropriations Subcommittee chairman John Murtha (D-Pa.) called for destroying the North Korean facilities even though, he admitted, "there is no question we would have to be prepared to go to war."[24] Over the following year Sen. John McCain (R-Ariz.), former secretary of state Henry Kissinger, and former National Security Council adviser Brent Scowcroft, along with columnists Charles Krauthammer, Lally Weymouth, and William Safire, among others, argued for a similarly belligerent response.[25]

Administration officials refused to rule out that possibility. At one point Secretary of Defense Les Aspin stated bluntly, "We will not allow the North Koreans to develop a nuclear bomb."[26] But the North "suspended" its withdrawal from the NPT and talks continued; the United States and the ROK agreed to suspend their Team Spirit exercises later in the year, and the DPRK accepted restricted IAEA visits to maintain the continuity of safeguards by replacing batteries and film in the North's nuclear facilities. The ensuing months were dominated by painful negotiations, broken agreements, recriminations, frustrated inspections, threats (from Washington as well as Pyongyang), reports that the North had already constructed one or more bombs, and ultimately a breakdown in the IAEA monitoring process.[27] At one point the DPRK appeared to be speeding up construction of its 200-megawatt reactor. After the IAEA found its seals on the suspected reprocessing plant broken and could not certify compliance, the United States broke off bilateral talks. In May 1994 Pyongyang indicated that it had begun removing the 8,000 fuel rods from its 5-megawatt nuclear reactor without allowing international inspectors to take test samples.

Imminent Showdown

Again, a showdown seemed imminent as the IAEA accused the DPRK of eliminating evidence of its potential nuclear capability and the North announced its intention to leave the agency. The U.S. administration halted further force reductions in South Korea, enhanced regional air and naval power, began upgrading military readiness, and shipped several Patriot missile batteries to the ROK. Washington and its allies also moved toward sanctions—first a ban on North Korean arms exports and UN development aid, to be followed, if necessary, by a prohibition on trade and other financial flows. Moreover, talk of war again filled the air, and not just from armchair warriors. For instance, Gen. John Shalikashvili, chairman of the Joint Chiefs of Staff, complained that the "culprits" running

North Korea "do not lend themselves to the kind of deterrent action that we were able to apply to the Soviet Union during the Cold War." Thus, he warned, the Pentagon required new thinking on how to "deal with these capabilities with the least possible collateral damage."[28]

The political leadership seemed even more bellicose. Senate Minority Leader Robert Dole (R-Kans.) argued that "the military option must be kept open."[29] Aspin's successor as secretary of defense, William Perry, acknowledged that sanctions "might provoke the North Koreans into unleashing a war" but indicated that the United States might propose them anyway.[30] Moreover, he refused to rule out preemptive military strikes, later calling that option an "open possibility."[31] The defense secretary went on to echo Frank Gaffney's argument of the previous year: "I'd rather face that risk [of war] than face the risk of even greater catastrophe two or three years from now" if the North continues its nuclear program.[32] Although President Clinton refused to say whether he would consider attacking the North's nuclear facilities, he emphasized that "North Korea cannot be allowed to develop a nuclear bomb. We have to be very firm about it."[33] In fact, the administration consciously began preparing the public for the worst. Perry explained that he wanted to ensure that Americans were aware of "what the national security issues are" since "sanctions do increase the risk of a military confrontation."[34]

That official jingoism went over far less well in South Korea and Japan than in America. Although concerned about the North's nuclear program, the East Asian countries were not so alarmed that they were willing to embrace high-risk policies. As James Fallows of the *Atlantic Monthly* pointed out, "The closer you got to Ground Zero of the North Korea nuclear threat, the less panicked the mood became."[35] He added,

> Relatively few [of the American commentators] had been to Korea; almost none could have named a member of the North Korean government apart from Kim Il Sung and his son Kim Jong Il, or have explained where Yongybyon was relative either to Seoul or Pyongyang. Yet these American arguments proceeded with the tone of absolute certainty that typifies talk-show discourse these days. The whole spectacle, as viewed from the Korean peninsula, was perfectly bizarre.[36]

Indeed, the East Asian countries began to worry more about the danger of a rash American initiative than about Pyongyang's program.

Compromise Accord

Then came an unpublicized trip by Selig Harrison of the Carnegie Endowment for International Peace and the better known visit by President Jimmy Carter to Pyongyang and Kim Il Sung's offer to freeze the North's nuclear program.[37] In return, the United States halted its campaign for sanctions. More negotiations followed. The U.S.-DPRK talks, though not the agreed-upon South-North summit, continued despite the death of Kim Il Sung on July 8, 1994. The result, signed on October 21, was the so-called framework agreement.

The agreement committed the DPRK to remain within the NPT and freeze operations at its 5-megawatt reactor, radio-chemistry laboratory, and fuel fabrication plant, as well as halt construction of the 50- and 200-megawatt reactors. The IAEA was to resume inspections, including ad hoc visits to other sites. Pyongyang was to satisfy "IAEA needs for access to data and sites to resolve discrepancies concerning the DPRK's production of plutonium" (i.e., the two waste disposal facilities) within 5 years, begin shipping abroad the 8,000 spent fuel rods now stored in cooling ponds within 7 years, and dismantle its old nuclear plants within 10 years. North Korea also promised to participate in bilateral talks with the ROK on economic and political relations, as well as on implementation of the 1991 North-South Joint Declaration on the Denuclearization of the Korean Peninsula.

In return, the United States, representing a new entity, the Korea Peninsula Energy Development Organization, to be largely funded by South Korea and Japan, was to provide the North with 500,000 tons of heavy oil annually, to make up for its loss of electrical-power-generating capacity, as well as two light-water reactors, to replace the older gas-graphite models under construction. Washington also promised to not use nuclear weapons against North Korea as long as the latter remained a member of the NPT, to eliminate economic sanctions against Pyongyang, and to move toward the establishment of diplomatic relations.[38] The reactors alone could run $4 billion (though that estimate is based on the cost of building a comparable unit in the ROK), of which $2.8 billion is to come from the ROK, $800 million from Japan, and the rest from the United States and other nations.

The accord was a compromise: in essence, it put aside questions about the North's past activities in order to prevent the expansion of Pyongyang's atomic capabilities and create an environment in which regional relations can improve. Then, perhaps five years from now, the issue of inspection of the disputed sites will come to the fore. The administration has proclaimed the agreement a success; Perry argued that it "is a good deal for the United States and the world community. It deserves a chance to work."[39]

Not surprisingly, the framework has come under sharp criticism, some of it overwrought if not hysterical. For instance, Frank Gaffney called it an act of "appeasement" ranking with Neville Chamberlain's abandonment of Czechoslovakia in 1938.[40] Columnist Greenberg said it amounted to giving "a devious dictator bent on wielding nuclear weapons" what he wanted and then declaring "victory."[41] Senator Dole complained that the accord "shows it is always possible to get an agreement when you give enough away."[42] His sentiments were echoed by a number of GOP House and Senate members, especially after the Republicans won control of Congress in the 1994 elections. For instance, Sen. Craig Thomas (R-Wy.) contended that the agreement made it appear that "if you misbehave, if you're the child that doesn't behave, you're the one that gets the biggest presents."[43] Sen. Hank Brown (R-Colo.) said he found it very difficult "to think that it makes much sense to signal to the world that there is any reward for breaking your word."[44] Senator McCain worried that "an impression has taken hold abroad that the United States has become much easier to intimidate" and that the nuclear agreement had helped squander American prestige after the Persian Gulf War.[45] However, none of them suggested any alternative—except for Gaffney, who had long wanted to send in the bombers and hope for the best—let alone a better alternative.

So far the North has left its nuclear program in deep freeze, the Korean Peninsula Energy Development Organization has succeeded in its first round of negotiations, the initial load of equipment has been shipped from South to North (on a Chinese ship), and Washington and Pyongyang have discussed opening consular relations. But the future is, of course, unclear. North Korea has continued to bargain—objecting to South Korea's being the source of the light-water reactor, requesting an extra $500 million to $1 billion in economic and technical assistance, issuing new threats, and demanding new talks.[46] As one U.S. diplomat told the *Washington Post*, "The baby's healthy, but also prone to a lot of infections."[47] Even seemingly simple collateral issues, such as rice aid from the South to the North, have been marred by Pyongyang's obnoxious behavior (forcing the ROK ship to fly the North Korean flag), and other provocations continue (the seizure of a South Korean fishing boat and the dispatch of several armed infiltrators to the South). The accord could collapse at a number of points during the next decade.

Possible Northern Intentions

One of the problems in developing policy toward the North is that there is an information vacuum. Very little is known about the North, its government, and the regime's decisionmaking processes. The lengthy transition following the death of Kim Il Sung only exacerbates the problem. It would appear that Kim Jong Il is in charge and remains committed to the flexible policies approved by his father shortly before his death. But that is only an assumption, albeit a reasonable one.

Unfortunately, the consequences of a mistake could be significant. An unstable North Korean regime could end up with nuclear weapons, or, even worse, precipitous action by Washington could spark a new war, endangering not only the 37,000 American service personnel now stationed on the Korean peninsula but literally millions of South Koreans as well.

It would help if the West could divine the DPRK's intentions. What is really going on in Pyongyang? CIA director R. James Woolsey argued in early 1993 that "an obvious reason for the standoff is that North Korea has something significant to hide."[48] But that is not the only conceivable interpretation. There are at least five possible reasons for Pyongyang's nuclearized course. The first, and most threatening, is the Woolsey thesis, that the North has a nuclear development program under way *and* has always been committed to building a bomb. That scenario assumes that the regime underestimated the IAEA's technical expertise and thought that it could gain the benefit of accepting international inspections while shielding its efforts from IAEA scrutiny. When the inspectors got too close, Pyongyang threatened to quit the NPT. The October 1994 agreement is a mere sham that has not halted North Korea's program (or, at least, the accord will soon be violated).

That is a reasonable hypothesis, but not one compelled by the facts. What do we really know? Various agencies of the American government conducted a not-so-secret debate during late 1993 and early 1994 about whether or not the North had constructed a bomb.[49] All then–defense secretary Les Aspin would say was that "there is a range of uncertainty" that included "the possibility that they do."[50] On the other hand, South Korean president Kim Young Sam stated that he did not believe that Pyongyang had constructed one.[51] Later in 1994 a North Korean defector claimed that the North had produced five bombs, but his claims were dismissed by both the IAEA and South Korea.[52] In the autumn of 1995 the ROK Ministry of National Defense concluded that North Korea had not constructed a bomb.[53] Reports a U.S. Institute of Peace working group, "What all this adds up to is a nuclear program whose only purpose seems to be to produce weapons-grade plutonium but which, to date, may not have succeeded in producing substantial amounts of such plutonium or weaponized nuclear devices."[54] We don't even have any evidence that the North has reprocessed its plutonium, let alone tested a weapon or created an effective delivery system.[55]

Thus, we should consider the other possibilities. For instance, the DPRK may have had a nuclear program under way but decided in late 1991 to drop it in exchange for the expected benefits: diplomatic recognition by Japan and the United States, aid from the ROK and Japan, and investment from and trade with Seoul and the United States. One analyst has suggested that Pyongyang may view its nuclear program (and the continuance of the armistice regime, which North Korea made an issue in 1995) "more as instruments to build ties to the United States than as goals in themselves."[56] In a move perhaps triggered by the Team Spirit exercises, however, more hard-line elements may have pounced, contending that all the DPRK had received for its more conciliatory course were ever-escalating demands, and therefore the regime should "just say no" to more inspections. Some North Korean diplomats and officials have apparently hinted at just such a policy struggle in conversations with Westerners.[57] (One variant is that Pyongyang perceived vacillation and weakness in Washington, which encouraged it to renege on its promises.)[58] That scenario differs significantly from the first in that it suggests that the North may intend to live up to the framework's conditions, though undoubtedly all the while attempting to squeeze ever more benefits out of Washington.

Possibility number three is that a frustrated North has been sporadically playing the "nuclear card," irrespective of the actual state of its program, in an attempt to wring more concessions from the United States, the ROK, and Japan. Since those nations have shown that nothing else gets their attention, the DPRK may believe that it has to revive the nuclear threat from time to time. That could also be the reason for the dispute over South Korea's participation in the reactor project.

The fourth scenario is that North Korea's intransigence in 1993 reflected an effort by then–heir apparent Kim Jong Il to shore up his rather thin military credentials by proving that he would protect the defense establishment's, and his nation's, interests. His father's decision to negotiate a settlement cleared the way for a peaceful accord, and economic desperation as well as foreign concessions allowed the younger Kim to return to the NPT process in a strengthened political position.

Finally, the fifth possibility is that the DPRK has little or no program but has brilliantly exploited the West's fears as part of a blackmail campaign. It would be foolish to base U.S. policy on such an assumption, but the possibility remains.

Worst-Case Scenario Is Still No Crisis

Unfortunately, it is impossible to know which of the possible scenarios is accurate. Many private analysts and government officials alike have been surprised by the North's inconsistent course.[59] The critical point, however, is that only the first scenario represents a serious problem to which there is no diplomatic solution. The other four are susceptible to negotiation, however hated that course may be by students of the "start bombing" school.

And even the worst case—that North Korea has, or remains committed to building, an atomic weapon—does not necessarily mean that the DPRK is intent on aggressive war. There are, of course, some who seem to see no difference between the North's possession of one or two nuclear weapons and a world in flames. Columnist Charles Krauthammer, for instance, said in mid-1994 that the administration's "appeasement" of Pyongyang had brought us to a "time of acute danger."[60] Robert Manning said that the possibility of a North Korean nuclear capability "poses an intolerable threat to U.S. interests."[61] Even worse, Richard Fisher of the Heritage Foundation worried that it might so unsettle the international nonproliferation regime as to require "repeated military confrontations to stop would-be proliferators" lest America and its allies face "possible attacks by future nuclear-armed rogue states."[62]

Of course, we would prefer that the North not acquire nuclear weapons. The regime's previous criminality suggests that it is fully capable of inaugurating another conflict, but one or two crude bombs with questionable deliverability would not dramatically change the peninsula's balance of power.[63] The simple desire for a nuclear capability is not itself evidence that Pyongyang plans to acquire one. Consider: A recent Asia Society study group implicitly defended India's and Pakistan's nuclear weapons programs, explaining that, unlike North Korea, those two countries were not "proliferation sharks." The report went on to say, "Indians and Pakistanis view their security threats as all too real, and some regard American rhetoric on nuclear proliferation as hypocritical and a cover for hegemonic ambitions."[64] Yet Pyongyang makes much the same argument, and while its contentions may be self-serving, they cannot be dismissed out of hand. Observes the International Institute for Strategic Studies, "It can be argued that North Korea had good cause to embark on a nuclear weapons programme."[65]

Bitter Competition

Since their creation, the two Koreas have competed bitterly in the economic, military, and political arenas. In the early years Pyongyang held the advantage on almost all fronts. But the DPRK's economic edge disappeared during the 1960s; in the following decade Seoul was outstripping its rival in terms of international recognition. By the 1980s the contest between the two states was essentially over: the South was twice as populous, dramatically more prosperous, a serious player in international economic and technological markets, and one of the globe's leading trading nations. Only on the military side did Pyongyang retain a lead, one largely reflecting the fact that America's security guarantee, then backed by a 43,000-man tripwire, made additional defense spending by the ROK unnecessary. (Thus, even then there was little justification for maintaining the so-called Mutual Defense Treaty.)

Today the gap between the two nations is even greater. The South possesses a GDP estimated to be 18 times that of its northern rival.[66] North Korea would have to devote its entire national production to defense to meet Seoul's expenditure of just 5.5 percent of its GDP. Pyongyang lacks the hard currency necessary to buy spare parts for its plentiful tanks and other weapons, which probably contributes to the large number of broken-down military trucks evident throughout the capital city as well as its environs when I visited in 1992. The readiness and training of the DPRK forces are questionable: the regime gives its pilots little time in the air, for instance. The domestic transportation infrastructure is primitive and in disrepair; many military personnel spend their time performing domestic civilian tasks; and the DPRK has apparently never conducted a combined-forces exercise. Although, a sudden onslaught by the North's million-man military might succeed in capturing or destroying Seoul, which lies just 30 miles south of the border, even many South Korean analysts now discount the likelihood of a Northern invasion.

Thus, the North's only potential edge is the development of a nuclear weapon. And, in fact, Pyongyang's original objective in pursuing a nuclear program may have been honestly defensive: Over the last two decades it has been steadily losing its military advantage. That decline has accelerated with the end of the Cold War—the collapse of the Soviet Union and China's steady move toward rapprochement with the ROK. By the early 1990s the DPRK found itself at a particular disadvantage, given the presence of tactical American nuclear weapons (since withdrawn) in the South and the defection of its allies. In short, in the DPRK's view, there may be little, other than continuing American restraint, to prevent an invasion backed by U.S. nuclear weapons.

North Korean Insecurity

Although we understandably view North Korean fears as paranoid, they are not completely irrational. After all, Washington explicitly threatened to use nuclear weapons to halt a North Korean invasion in 1955. Moreover, North Korean officials allegedly cited the potential U.S. threat when they sought Soviet assistance to build a bomb in 1963.[67]

And conceivably U.S. moderation would not be enough. Before the Korean War, ROK president Syngman Rhee threatened to march north to recover what he called the "lost territories." Former president Chun Doo Hwan considered a military strike on the DPRK in retaliation for the North Korean bomb attack on him and his cabinet in Rangoon in 1983. Indeed, some opponents of an American military withdrawal are privately uneasy about the possibility of South Korean aggression in the absence of Washington's restraining hand.[68]

The potential threat would be even greater if the South developed atomic weapons. Only under U.S. pressure did Seoul abandon its program in the 1970s (Washington pressed South Korea and such nations as Belgium, Canada, and France to drop sales of fuel-fabrication facilities, heavy-water reactors, and reprocessing systems).[69] In fact, recent unverified reports suggest that the ROK came quite close to developing an atomic weapon.[70] Moreover, reports Peter Hayes of the University of Sydney, "There is little doubt that South Korea now has a near-nuclear option."[71] The North has raised a similar alarm over Japan. "Japan is going against the trend in the world toward nonnuclearization and peace after the end of the cold war and is actively stepping up its attempts to become a nuclear power," states one official publication.[72] Those fears seem genuine, if misguided. After all, South Korean officials have raised some of the same concerns about Tokyo.[73] Moreover, Japan admits that it has the ability to quickly create a nuclear arsenal if it desires and has informally raised the possibility of making nuclear weapons in response to the DPRK's initiative.[74]

In this already unsettling environment, the North finds itself with a shrinking economy as it faces an adversary whose economic lead grows hourly. In time Pyongyang's conventional military capabilities are going to be severely degraded, and its ability to defend itself, let alone threaten the South, will be concomitantly reduced. For that reason, concluded *Jane's Intelligence Review*,

> Nuclear weapons are also a relatively cheap form of deterrent and the cost of deterrence became an important consideration in the 1980s as the North Korean economy began to collapse. . . . North Korea is increasingly incapable of supporting its massive conventional forces. The logic of nuclear weapons as an ultimate deterrent has never been more clear.[75]

Under those circumstances Kim Il Sung and son Kim Jong Il may have come to view an atomic bomb as a, and perhaps the only, means of ensuring the regime's survival, whether against a military attack or more general external political pressure. Explained defector Ko Young Hwan in 1991, an atomic bomb was viewed by officials in the North "as the last means they can resort to [to] protect their system."[76] (In fact, that is a more widely understood lesson than some might think. After the Persian Gulf War, the chief of staff of India's military reportedly observed, "Never fight the U.S. without nuclear weapons.")[77]

Along the way North Korea undoubtedly has also recognized the potential political and economic value of a nuclear weapon. After all, only the threat of a North Korean bomb has caused Japan and the United States, in particular, to treat the DPRK seriously. Merely the whisper of its atomic project, however limited, has allowed the North to manipulate not only its antagonists but its allies, including China, that also do not want Pyongyang to build a bomb. In that way, the well-publicized fear of the North's nuclear efforts has probably encouraged the regime to push ahead. Development of a nuclear capacity would allow either international sale of the technology or further shakedown of Western nations to prevent such sales. Observes Joseph Bermudez, "The nuclear arsenal is North Korea's only bargaining chip, and one it can be expected to continue to use both skillfully and effectively."[78]

Groping toward a Peaceful Solution

None of this is to suggest that the DPRK's possession of nuclear weapons would be a good thing. But it probably would not be cataclysmic. It is for that reason that many South Koreans and Japanese view the possibility with so much greater equanimity than do many American analysts. Lee Chung Min of the Sejong Institute, for instance, argues that "as important as the nuclear issue is, the fundamental security threat to South Korea over the next few years is likely to stem from a number of other developments," such as North Korea's potential political instability and economic decline.[79] Thus, the United States should exercise care in the risks that it runs in order to attempt to prevent the North from developing or possessing a nuclear weapon.

But some action is clearly warranted. The prospect of a nuclear-armed DPRK is obviously not pleasant. As Arnold Kanter, former under secretary of state for political affairs, put it, "North Korea is not Pakistan."[80] The regime in Pyongyang launched the Korean War, which resulted in 1 million Korean deaths some four and a half decades ago, and used terrorism in succeeding years. The problem is not that those running the North are literally crazy; if they were, it is hard to believe that they would not have started a war sometime during the past 40 years. The problem is that, in the past, at least, the regime has been calculatingly brutal. As Denny Roy of the National University of Singapore puts it, "There is method in Pyongyang's alleged madness. North Korea's domestic and foreign policies are in fact quite rational—given the leadership's goals and constraints."[81] And their nuclear strategy, however frustrating to Western nations, so far appears to have been quite successful.[82]

Unsettling Arms Race

Even if Pyongyang did not start a new conflict, it could use an atomic bomb to pressure South Korea and possibly Japan. (That makes the North's attempts to develop ballistic missiles particularly disconcerting.)[83] Such an effort at political blackmail could spark an unsettling regional nuclear arms race; in fact, there are some reports that both the ROK and Japan appear to be laying the basis for moving ahead with a nuclear option if they believe it to be necessary.[84] Not without some reason did former South Korean president Roh Tae Woo call the prospect of a North Korean bomb "dangerous and destabilizing."[85] He exaggerated, however, when he said it "could in an instant shatter the peace in Northeast Asia and the world."[86] Could, but probably wouldn't, since the price of breaking the peace would also rise exponentially. Although regional relations would be more complicated and the risks of conflict greater, in practice the most serious actual consequences might turn out to be "roiled stockmarkets around the globe."[87] No one knows for sure.

Thus, Washington should develop a strategy for simultaneously promoting DPRK compliance with the framework and détente with the South.[88] The first step is to fulfill the terms of the accord. As of early 1996, Congress has not yet appropriated sufficient funds to pay for the promised fuel oil. Second, the United States should continue to rely on diplomacy. Despite sharp criticism of the Clinton administration by advocates of a confrontational strategy, so far the policy of restraint seems to have worked. Pyongyang may be exceedingly difficult to deal with, but the DPRK does appear to respond to positive incentives. The North's ratification of the safe-guards agreement, acceptance of IAEA inspections, cancellation of its threatened withdrawal from the NPT, and agreement to the framework were all achieved diplomatically. Observes one group of experts, "While cause and effect are hard to assess with assurance, this pattern of behavior suggests that U.S actions can have at least limited effect on the decisions of a North Korean leadership that may be uncertain about how to deal with its parlous condition."[89]

It is widely accepted that North Korea has frozen its nuclear program. That resolves, today at least, the gravest threat: that Pyong-yang would either generate a large nuclear arsenal or promote prolif-eration among other outlaw states. Explains South Korean president Kim Young Sam, "It is a very good result that we have somehow stopped North Korea from going on to develop nuclear weapons. The balance sheet is positive."[90] And the pact does not depend on trust. Should the North fail to allow IAEA inspections, or reactivate its nuclear program, the United States can cut off oil shipments, work on the light-water reactors, and moves toward diplomatic recognition.

Real Costs

Of course, the accord's costs are real. The framework leaves the DPRK in possession of enough plutonium to possibly produce a bomb or two. There is, however, no credible evidence that the regime currently possesses a workable bomb—it has tested no device, for instance—and the danger posed by one or two weapons pales in comparison with the potential of producing several a year after construction of a larger reactor.[91] Building a light-water nuclear reac-tor and providing oil shipments could cost the West $4.5 billion, more if it helps update the North's electrical grid, and will help strengthen a regime that continues to pose a military threat to its southern neighbor. Nevertheless, those costs are minor compared to the costs that would be occasioned by a new war. Critics of the accord will argue that once the United States establishes diplomatic relations and allows trade with the North, Washington will be hesi-tant to break those ties, even if the DPRK regresses. But those mea-sures are long overdue and should continue, irrespective of the state of Pyongyang's nuclear program.

The framework includes no mechanism to force North Korea to talk with Seoul, a promise that Pyongyang has made and broken in the past.[92] Even if talks occur, there is no way to ensure that they will be meaningful. Rewarding a potential proliferator creates an incentive for other nations to attempt to acquire, or to threaten to acquire, atomic weapons. Few, however, are sufficiently threatening to extract the concessions given to the DPRK. Some South Korean analysts have additional worries, including the potential impact on U.S. security guarantees.[93] Yet, as argued throughout this volume, Washington's commitment itself is outmoded. Finally, there are innumerable points over which the agreement could founder during the coming decade, including U.S. failure to fulfill promises.[94] Or Pyongyang could simply change its mind, deciding that the risks of liberalization, however modest, are too high. So far, however, the accord has remained on track, and any settlement worked out with the North, short of military conquest, faces potential repudiation.

Thus, the benefits of the framework—forestalling additional plutonium production and promoting a dialogue among the DPRK, the United States, the ROK, and Japan—make it worthwhile.[95] In December 1994 Thomas Hubbard, deputy assistant secretary of state for East Asian and Pacific affairs, observed that the IAEA "has indicated substantial satisfaction with the way the talks have gone between North Korea and the IAEA [and] has indicated that they have resolved most of the issues involved in setting up their system for monitoring the freeze."[96] And should the accord fail, the result would simply be to return us to the situation of mid-1994. That's not good, but it's hardly comparable to "appeasement," as were the irrevocable remilitarization of the Rhineland and the dismemberment of Czechoslovakia, for instance.

Nothing Better

Moreover, even the pact's severest critics have offered nothing better. That is because they have nothing to offer. Congressional refusal to fund the framework, for instance, would probably cause the North to repudiate the entire agreement. That would plunge East Asia back into the crisis atmosphere of 1994, something that would hardly encourage resolution of the problem.

Not that the framework is likely to bring utopia overnight. Columnist Georgie Anne Geyer complains that the agreement "has had no discernible behavioral effects on the closed communist state. Pyongyang is as obdurate as ever, in fact, in many ways even more."[97] Evidence of North Korean recalcitrance is, and forever may be, with us.[98] Nevertheless, the presence of U.S. diplomats and telephone executives, among others, in the DPRK is a striking break with the past. Pyongyang obviously faces serious problems in attracting outside investment, but it is trying.[99] A growing number of foreign businessmen are traveling to the DPRK.[100] And the admittedly modest contacts between North and South, especially economic, are nevertheless broader than ever before.[101] The mere fact that North Korea went begging to Japan and then South Korea for rice is a dramatic concession, even if the DPRK hid the fact from its own people. Even more stunning is Pyongyang's statement to Harrison that it no longer opposes the presence of U.S. forces on the peninsula.

Anyway, the most important purpose of the framework was to freeze the North's nuclear program. Before, North Korea appeared to be moving toward production of a bomb, and the allies were moving toward a confrontation with the DPRK and possibly China. Both of those ominous trends have stopped. It is hard to imagine any policy other than engagement that is likely to moderate the North's actions. The alternatives—economic sanctions and military action—offer no guarantee of success and are far riskier.

To enhance fulfillment of the accord, Washington should continue the process of establishing diplomatic ties with the DPRK and allowing the North to promote investment and trade. Despite the accord, the Clinton administration has so far lifted few restrictions on contacts with the North. In fact, humanitarian groups even now cannot legally provide food relief. Dropping those barriers would provide the North with a continuing, positive reason to abide by the agreement.

Of course, that is a "concession," something some hard-line Western analysts don't want to give to North Korea, but it is a minimal one that offers some small benefits to the United States as well— access to DPRK mineral exports, for instance, as well as a larger window on the secretive "hermit kingdom." Anyway, other nuclear states, such as Kazakhstan and Ukraine, received aid tied to their compliance with the NPT, and the North has agreed to do more than usual through the planned IAEA special inspections (never carried out elsewhere) and separate nuclear agreement with Seoul.[102]

Surely it is wise to offer some cheap carrots to reduce the chance of a confrontation that might plunge the Korean peninsula and its more than 60 million people into war.

The South's Role

South Korea's role is equally significant. Although Pyongyang's reputation for recalcitrance is well earned, Seoul has also impeded meaningful dialogue at times. Thus, Seoul must choose, suggests Robert Manning, "whether it is retribution or conciliation that is ultimately in the best interest of the Korean people."[103] However tempting the former, the latter course is more likely to lead to the sort of "soft landing" that most South Koreans believe to be in their interest. And that probably requires a relaxed attitude toward aid to, investment in, and trade with the North.[104]

More significant, the diplomatic option should include a commitment to three-way talks to implement the two Koreas' independent nuclear inspection agreement signed in late 1991.[105] South Korean and American officials argue that that would allow the DPRK to divide the allies, but Pyongyang has little leverage with which to promote a split. (Anyway, Washington and the ROK shouldn't paper over the gap when they find that their interests diverge.) Another complaint is that agreeing to such talks would be yielding to Northern extortion, but negotiations are a very cheap price to pay for the possibility of finding a way to both avoid war and denuclearize the peninsula. As the nation that first introduced nuclear weapons to the peninsula, the United States should willingly join discussions about a nuclear inspection regime that would satisfy both North and South.

The ultimate objective of three-way talks should be willingness on all sides to allow investigation of any suspected facility. But the initial inspections could be more modest: for instance, Washington could offer to open several American bases where it once deployed nuclear weapons in return for IAEA access to the two waste facilities and South Korean examination of Yongbyon. Additional bases and facilities could be opened to view over time.

The United States should also offer to help jump-start, through the Joint Military Committee, talks between South and North to promote inspections of conventional facilities. As part of that process, America and the ROK should announce a permanent cancellation of joint exercises, a phased withdrawal of Washington's 37,000

125

soldiers, a willingness to consider pledging no first use (by America) of nuclear weapons, and replacement of the armistice with a peace treaty.[106] The two nations should then invite the North to respond by entering into three-way talks and demobilizing some of its forces and pulling other units back from their advanced, threatening positions near the Demilitarized Zone. (Advocates of mutual reductions and withdrawals are many, but all assume that the United States will maintain its defense guarantee, even though, as argued earlier, the original justification for it is long past.)[107]

Confidence-Building Measures

A variety of confidence-building measures is possible, including establishment of hotlines, advance notifications of troop movements, nonaggression declarations, an expanded demilitarized zone, exchange visits of military officers, and mutual information disclosure, many of which are contained in the Basic Agreement on Reconciliation, Nonaggression, and Exchanges and Cooperation between the South and North signed by both Koreas on December 13, 1991. If Pyongyang refuses to respond positively, that will provide evidence of its aggressive intentions and should cause the South to engage in a serious military build-up.

The basic objective is to convince the North that it will gain more by staying within the engagement process. Observes Kim Kyung-won, president of the Institute of Social Sciences, "While we cannot count on the Pyongyang leadership's conscience, we can assume that it will not act against what it considers its own best interests."[108]

If the framework agreement survives, the crisis will be defused and détente may flourish on the Korean peninsula. But assuming that outcome is inevitable would be extraordinarily dangerous. North Korea's behavior is predictable only in the sense that it is likely to be unpredictable. Says one South Korean expert, the North's "traditional negotiation tactics" involve the "detailing of a new agenda while negotiating over the current agenda."[109] The DPRK's objection to South Korean participation in construction of the nuclear reactor demonstrates that Pyongyang apparently doesn't believe any deal is ever set in concrete. Thus, North Korea is almost certain to test both the United States and the ROK—as it did the latter by forcing one of Seoul's rice-laden relief ships to hoist the DPRK flag and accusing the crew of another of spying, for instance—even if it adheres to the framework. A whole array of demands is possible, including the withdrawal of U.S. forces from the South, full diplomatic recognition, foreign aid contributions, and the signing of a peace treaty.[110] Washington and Seoul should respond with a difficult combination of firmness and patience, as they did regarding ROK provision of the reactors. Simple desperation (why else would North Korea beg for rice from hated Japan?) seems likely to keep the North close to fulfillment of its promises.

However, what if the accord appears to break down and Pyongyang threatens to resume its nuclear effort? Although the North has so far fulfilled its major nuclear-related commitments, it has apparently improperly transferred some of the oil shipments to the military. That is not terribly significant, since oil is fungible. Probably of greater concern is whether the North may rethink the bargain if it finds that the inevitable stream of foreign visitors—businessmen, engineers, construction workers, IAEA inspectors, journalists, diplomats, scholars, international bankers, aid officials, and others— begins to "infect" the communist system. William Taylor, a frequent visitor to the North, also asks whether, in the end, North Korea will allow inspections of the two waste depositories, given the strength of the regime's previous refusal.[111] Internal CIA assessments are reportedly even more negative.[112]

If Pyongyang balks, the West should nevertheless avoid taking precipitous action and look for evidence of why the North acted as it did—essentially to decide whether the regime of Kim Jong Il is irrevocably committed to the acquisition of nuclear weapons or is opening yet another round of negotiations. So long as the latter might be the case, and negotiation could prove fruitful, Washington should pursue a diplomatic option.

Even if the former seemed more likely, however, restraint would remain a virtue, especially if Pyongyang did not appear to be attempting to construct a large arsenal. In the long term, the DPRK is likely to find a nuclear capability more useful in guaranteeing the survival of the North Korean state and as political leverage than as offensive weapons for use against the ROK, especially as economic ties between Seoul and China, Pyongyang's closest remaining friend, increase. The most important impact of a North Korean bomb ultimately might be to drive the South and Japan to obtain their own nuclear arsenals, not to inaugurate war.

The Risks of Coercive Nonproliferation

The prospect of a North Korean bomb is an unpleasant example of proliferation, certainly, but not unprecedented. In the 1960s Washington faced the likelihood of Maoist China—secretive and factious, unpredictable and irrational, belligerent and threatening—gaining nuclear weapons. The Johnson administration seriously debated preemption, a step advocated publicly by some politicians and journalists. For instance, in 1968 New York's James Buckley, the soon-to-be-elected conservative candidate for the U.S. Senate, argued that bombing China's nuclear facilities would "have been a prudent" idea because it would have eliminated "an atomic capability which is now increasingly threatening."[113] Three years before, the *National Review*, edited by his brother, William F. Buckley Jr., had observed,

> There is something to do, now. We can destroy—destroy literally, physically—the present Chinese nuclear capability, and thereby guarantee, since their underlying industrial recovery power is meager, that they cannot become a nuclear power for a good many years ahead. We can do so without undue risk or loss; without, even, very great loss to China other than to the nuclear installations themselves.[114]

Cooler heads prevailed, and almost certainly for the best. It seems like nothing has changed, however. William F. Buckley Jr. wrote in 1993, "That we are obliged to abort [North Korea's] nuclear bomb is axiomatic."[115] But the potential of a North Korean nuclear bomb no more warrants war than did that of a Chinese bomb.

The Illusory Solution: Economic Sanctions

The favorite and supposedly more moderate form of coercive nonproliferation, economic sanctions, still involves a serious risk of provoking war. Even if that worst-case scenario could be avoided, there is little evidence that sanctions would achieve the desired result. Trade restrictions have had only limited efficacy throughout history—generally the poorer the country, the more strategic the product, and the more isolated the regime, the greater the chance of success. But even the best cases are dubious: Sanctions against Iraq have helped enforce UN weapons inspections and restrictions, though Baghdad continues to resist at almost every step. Sanctions against other outlaw regimes, like those of Iran and Libya, have proved less successful. North Korea is poor, vulnerable, and alone, and its economy is probably already the most isolated on earth. Whether the additional pressure of sanctions would be sufficient to force compliance is unknowable.

The threat of hardship alone is not likely to be enough. As Clark Sorensen of the University of Washington puts it, "Despite the fact that North Korea has recently undergone three years of economic contraction and a wrenching redirection of their trade from the former Soviet Union to China in the wake of Russian demands for payment in hard currency, repression has prevented serious unrest, and there is no known organized opposition."[116] North Korea's repressive government has long survived with very little; presumably it can survive with less for at least some time.

And it won't even have to do with less if sanctions are not supported by Iran, a major oil supplier already operating under an American embargo, and China, which supplies Pyongyang with both food and oil and could veto any UN measure. Although Beijing has typically abstained on sanctions votes, Premier Li Peng has explicitly denounced Washington's proposal to target the DPRK.[117] Throughout the entire controversy, Chinese officials at all levels have pressed for a peaceful resolution, suggesting that China would at least moderate any attempt to isolate the North.[118] Even if Beijing allowed sanctions to take effect—perhaps with promises from the United States to drop pressure on human rights and from Seoul to increase investment—it would also have to be willing, and able, to suppress the widespread informal border trade between Koreans and neighboring Chinese of Korean heritage.

Similarly, Japan, home to some 800,000 residents of Korean descent, about 250,000 of whom are active in the pro–North Korean Chosen Soren, would have to end trade and financial transfers worth as much as $4 billion annually. Particularly hard to stop would be the $500 million to $1.8 billion, much of it transported in cash, provided by the 7,000 Korean-Japanese who visit North Korea every year.[119] Enforcing UN sanctions, as well as allowing Washington to use Japanese bases to enforce an embargo, would raise complicated political questions for the Japanese government, especially for one supported by the Socialist Party, which has traditionally maintained close ties with the North.[120] Moreover, Tokyo, shaken by the 1995 gas attack in its subway, also fears that its enforcement of sanctions might touch off terrorism by some pro-Pyongyang Korean-Japanese.

Even Russia, which has had strained relations with the North ever since the USSR recognized South Korea in 1990, has been reluctant to press for sanctions. President Boris Yeltsin says sanctions must be an "ultimate" act, undertaken only after other options have been exhausted.[121] Increasing nationalist pressure may further harden Moscow's stance.

Ironically, if sanctions against the DPRK did work, the outcome might be war or chaos rather than capitulation. If China and Japan seriously enforced an embargo and the United States interdicted Iranian oil shipments, pressure on the North, which is already suffering from famine, could be significantly increased. As a result, however, the DPRK might simply implode, a possibility that scares South Koreans who fear the cost, estimated at anywhere between $200 billion and $1 trillion (the latter being more than twice the South's annual GDP), of a West German–like takeover of a chaotic postcommunist North. The South is not as wealthy as West Germany, and North Korea is proportionately larger than East Germany, making the burden of absorption dramatically greater.[122] The prospect of millions of refugees fleeing political turmoil, civil war, and famine also frightens Seoul.

Even worse, if the economic controls threatened to bring down Pyongyang's regime, it might strike out rather than surrender. Recent history offers a sobering reminder of that danger. Although obviously complex, Japan's decision for war against America in 1941 was triggered in part by U.S. sanctions against the sale of petroleum and other critical products, as well as the freezing of Japanese assets. That Japan perceived those steps as a serious threat is reflected in the fact that one Japanese proposal offered to trade the withdrawal of troops from southern Indochina for the sale of a million tons of aviation fuel.[123] In particular, the Japanese military feared that sanctions would degrade its ability to fight.[124] Thus, Tokyo took what many officials even then recognized as a wild gamble, but the Japanese viewed the risk as preferable to succumbing to U.S. economic pressure. Observed East Asian expert Nathaniel Peffer, "When the President ordered the freezing of the Japanese assets in this country in 1941, he was decreeing a state of war with Japan."[125]

Although communist North Korea differs substantially from imperial Japan, the former is paranoid, possesses an oversized military, and could see sanctions as threatening its ability to act as a nation and even to defend itself. Pyongyang might therefore choose to react much as Japan did.[126] And past coercion of the DPRK has generally proved to be counterproductive. Observes Robert Manning, "The history of North Korean international behavior suggests that when squeezed into a corner it will not make concessions but will lash out."[127]

Pyongyang might therefore decide to risk everything immediately rather than accept what looked like inevitable collapse. For what it is worth, the North warned both the United States and Japan that sanctions would be considered a "declaration of war" and that "sanctions mean outright war." Pyongyang also informed Japan that it "would be unable to evade a deserving [sic] punishment."[128] North Korea also moved additional military units closer to the DMZ and deployed some 300 anti-aircraft guns around its Yongbyon nuclear complex in January 1994 in preparation for possible sanctions.[129] And American officials appeared to take the DPRK's threats seriously, with Secretary Perry acknowledging that there would be "some increase in the risk of war if we go to a sanction regime."[130]

A substantial U.S. military build-up in the South might help deter a military response from the North; indeed, it probably would be necessary to win Seoul's acquiescence in the imposition of sanctions. William Taylor argues that "it would be reckless and irresponsible to go back to sanctions without simultaneous reinforcement of the South.[131] Even *New York Times* columnist Anthony Lewis, long considered a dove, argued that "the best way to show firmness is to beef up the U.S. military force in South Korea" and that "sanctions must be accompanied by a strengthened deterrent."[132] But building up U.S. forces in the South would not be cheap. Moreover, if Pyongyang misinterpreted the build-up as a prelude to an allied invasion, it might attack first.

Military Foolhardiness

Proposals to destroy North Korea's nuclear facilities are even more foolhardy. What makes such saber rattling so disturbing is that military action is likely to be neither effective nor safe. First, it is not clear that such a strike would obliterate the North's nuclear program, even if there is no underground nuclear site. True, an attack could eliminate the DPRK's reactors, preventing any accumulation of additional plutonium, but the two sites from which Pyongyang has

131

barred outside inspectors are suspected waste sites, not production facilities. If the latter exist, and we don't know that they do, they, along with North Korea's existing supply of plutonium, are probably buried deep underground somewhere, which limits our ability to destroy them. Says one administration official, "Even if we wiped out everything we see, we would never know if we got it all."[133]

The only other option would be to use nuclear weapons, as advocated by Mark Helprin of the Hudson Institute, though perhaps no one else.[134] In contrast, while Secretary Perry is willing to consider military strikes, he says that he can't envision any circumstance in which using nuclear weapons "would be reasonable or prudent military action."[135] There would be more than a little irony in using nuclear weapons for only the second time in history to divest another nation of a possible nuclear capability. However, an unsuccessful strike, nuclear or nonnuclear, would actually encourage the regime to persevere—rebuilding its reactors, if necessary, as did Iraq after Israel's 1981 raid on the Osirak reactor—since such a raid would prove that only an atomic bomb would allow the North to effectively defend itself.

That is not all. Destruction of the North's reactors could also lead to radioactive releases over China, Japan, Russia, and South Korea. True, Senator McCain argues that "precision targeting could effectively damage the capabilities of [the DPRK's nuclear] facilities without requiring that they be reduced to rubble, and with little or no radiation release."[136] Others are far less sure, however. And while such a prospect might seem a modest risk to policymakers in Washington, residents of the region are likely to hold a different view.

And one strike would not necessarily be enough. Japanese diplomat Hisahiko Okazaki argues, "It was learned from the experience of the Iraqi nuclear development that 'pinpoint attacks' on nuclear facilities will not be effective unless they are repeated at certain intervals. If not actually repeated, then a threat of renewed strikes has to be maintained, which would mean a continuous state of war between North Korea and the outside world."[137] Similarly, Richard McCormack, under secretary of state for economic affairs under President Bush, worries that "even a large-scale bombing would not prevent the country from developing its nuclear weapons. Only an actual invasion and occupation could produce that result."[138]

Trigger for War

Although proponents of military action may be right in believing both that Washington and Seoul could successfully take out unknown facilities at unknown locations and that Pyongyang, long considered one of the most bizarre regimes on earth, would quietly acquiesce to such devastating, and very public, international humiliation, the odds are against that result. Indeed, the people arguing the most vehemently that the North would sit idly by while being pounded by American aircraft are often the same ones who have long insisted that U.S. troops need to remain in the South to deter possible Northern adventurism. Pyongyang is crazy enough to attack the well-defended ROK if America withdraws its troops from South Korea, according to their argument, but is rational enough not to retaliate if America attacks North Korea.

At a minimum, the North would probably resume its terror campaign, apparently dormant since 1987, that once blew airline passengers out of the sky and massacred South Korean cabinet members. This time, however, Americans, too, would almost certainly become targets.

Far worse is the possibility of armed conflict. More than a million DPRK soldiers are poised within a short drive of Seoul, which has a population of 16 million people. An attack on the North's nuclear installations could easily goad Pyongyang into launching a full-scale invasion of the ROK.

The consequences of a new Korean war would be ruinous to all concerned. There is no doubt that the United States and the ROK would prevail, but at what price?[139] It is worth pausing to consider the destruction wreaked by the first conflict. "In the three years' internecine war, more than 1.5 million lives were lost, including about 800,000 civilians and 36,813 American soldiers who fought under the flag of the United Nations. Also, about 3.6 million were wounded and 1.2 million were reported missing in action. Altogether, more than 6.3 million were either killed, wounded, or missing in action. To this figure one has to add approximately 10 million who were separated from their families as they fled to the south, or to the north."[140]

It is commonly thought—with good reason, since China would be unlikely to again intervene on the North's behalf and Russia might cooperate with the ROK—that the war would be more likely to last three months than three years.[141] But the consequences would still be grave. One analyst warns that the start of the war would be "very bloody, with high casualties on both sides."[142] Even if the allies were able to stop North Korean infantry and armor from overrunning Seoul, the South's capital could be devastated by artillery and possibly missiles and chemical weapons. A scholar at the Rand Corporation estimates that even limited artillery barrages could kill tens of thousands of people, and chemical weapons could generate over a million casualties.[143] The destruction of Seoul alone would be a high price to pay for eliminating the North's nuclear potential. Even the hawkish Heritage Foundation acknowledges that "war against North Korea would devastate the Korean peninsula and must be avoided at every reasonable cost."[144]

Rational Calculations

Of course, given the cost of war to the DPRK, any rational calculation by the North's leadership would result in restraint. In fact, just such an assessment has kept the peace for 40 years. As columnist Stephen Chapman once argued, "One fear is the North would respond by attacking the South. But the regime will almost certainly be deterred, as it has been before, by the knowledge that it would be defeated and probably toppled in such a war. More likely, Kim will do what Saddam Hussein did after the Israeli raid—nothing."[145]

But Iraq had no effective means of striking Israel, and Israel has nuclear weapons, which would have made Iraqi aggression suicidal.[146] North Korea, in contrast, has placed missiles and artillery within range of Seoul and massed two-thirds of its army troops within 50 or 60 miles of the border. Even small-scale reprisals by the DPRK—for instance, Scud missile attacks against ROK cities and nuclear power plants—could lead to counterattacks by Seoul and soon escalate out of control.

Not surprisingly, North Korean officials have responded sharply to the allies' military threats; in 1991 Prime Minister Yong Hyung Muk warned that "these words reflect the very dangerous attitudes present in the South, and they could drive the Korean Peninsula into a state of war."[147] Three years later North Korean officials were promising to turn Seoul "into a sea of fire."[148] Contends William Taylor, who has held frequent conversations with high-level DPRK officials, including Kim Il Sung shortly before the latter's death,

The leadership in Pyongyang is not comparable to Iraq's Saddam Hussein in 1981. There is a very high probability that the DPRK would attack south immediately; many of their leaders have told me so, and there is no reason not to believe them. The North Korean leadership will not allow its system and the *juche* ideology to be discredited by an act of "aggression" from the West. The DPRK would perceive that if it did not take any action, it would also encourage further preemptive measures by Seoul or Washington. Thus, it would risk escalating any attack south, hoping to intimidate the West into [ending] the conflict quickly.[149]

Air strikes by the United States, or a commando operation by the South, would be an act of war that Kim Jong Il could not easily ignore, even if he is committed to maintaining an opening to the West, as suggested by recently released tapes of his conversations with two defectors.[150] It would prove particularly difficult for him to face down the military if it has gained influence since the death of Kim Il Sung, as theorized by some.[151] After all, for the Kim regime not to respond to a military strike would appear to hard-line factions to be precisely the sort of appeasement for which Western hawks say the United States could never stand. Indeed, the ruling elite might adopt William Perry's analysis as its own: if the United States and the ROK appear to be dedicated to the regime's destruction, then it might be better to have war now rather than later, when the DPRK will be weaker and the South stronger. Adm. Richard Macke, then commander in chief of the U.S. Pacific Command, implicitly acknowledged that possibility when he warned a Senate committee, "We must be careful not to give them the perception that their survival is threatened—if that happens, they might lash out."[152]

Some Americans seem unconcerned about the prospect of many Korean deaths, South and North. Lest that judgment seem unduly harsh, one South Korean told journalist James Fallows that he asked Brent Scowcroft "whether Americans had thought about the effects of [a preemptive strike] on the 60 million people living on the peninsula. I had the feeling that it was an afterthought."[153] Some ROK policy analysts complain that their nation was treated merely as an "interested party" by Washington during the nuclear negotiations.[154]

Risk to America

Even if the impact on Koreans were irrelevant, and it most certainly is not, Washington should consider the cost to America. So long as the United States retains its security commitment to the ROK and places 37,000 soldiers as a tripwire to ensure American involvement in any war, the threat of coercive nonproliferation measures extends the risk of war to the United States. Some 34,000 Americans died in battle in the last conflict on the peninsula; military strikes would risk a second Korean war. That possibility does seem to bother some analysts who largely ignore the danger to South Korea. For instance, *Wall Street Journal* columnist George Melloan asked, why not just destroy the North's reactor? His answer was, not the risk of widespread ROK civilian casualties, but "that the U.S. has 36,000 troops in South Korea who would be vulnerable to Scud missile retaliation in the absence of any effective defense."[155]

In the end, patience is a virtue. It worked with the Chinese nuclear program. It worked with the Soviet empire. And it has so far worked with North Korea. Instead of using coercion, Washington should seek to generate a new package of carrots and sticks, while limiting the amount of public pressure it brings to bear, which may very well encourage the status-conscious North Koreans to be more recalcitrant. Time is on the allies' side. Although it is foolish to count on North Korea's collapse, it is also irresponsible to make policy on the assumption that the present system will last forever. And the longer Washington is able to keep the North talking, the greater is the chance that internal changes in the DPRK will alleviate the problem.

The United States should emphasize that stronger diplomatic and cultural relations, growing trade, and increased participation in international organizations all depend on resolving the nuclear issue. The ROK needs to emphasize that investment and trade, emergency assistance, and improved relations are all predicated on Pyongyang's fulfilling the framework agreement.

The Role of Regional Powers

Washington and South Korea should continue to work with other regional powers, particularly China, though relations between Washington and Beijing are currently strained. Beijing appears genuinely opposed to the DPRK's acquisition of a bomb. Explained Chinese foreign minister Qian Qichen, "We do not want to see the existence of nuclear weapons on the Korean Peninsula."[156] And Beijing has played a moderating role so far.[157] China remains reluctant, however, to place significant pressure on the North, given the historic ties between the two nations and North Korea's status as one of the few remaining communist states. To increase Chinese willingness to cooperate, Washington might point to the risk of North Korean, and possibly South Korean, bombs leading to a Japanese bomb, something Beijing, which has opposed virtually any Japanese rearmament, surely would not welcome. The United States should also note the possible difficulty of restraining a fearful ROK leadership from launching a preemptive strike, which could humiliate the DPRK, disrupt the region's economic and political relations, and possibly reignite military conflict on the peninsula—none of which would benefit China, which has greater economic relations with the South than with the North.

Japan is also an important player. The North wants diplomatic recognition from and trade with Tokyo, as well as reparations for the latter's colonial misrule earlier this century. The two countries initiated discussions on normalization of relations in 1992, but less than two years later the talks collapsed over Japanese insistence that the DPRK end its nuclear program and account for a Japanese citizen believed to have been kidnapped by Pyongyang. In 1995 official contacts began again, and the DPRK made an extraordinary appeal for emergency shipments of rice. Tokyo offered to expand the discussions to the question of normalization of relations.[158] Ultimately, the North hopes for significant aid to relieve economic difficulties, which officials now admit exist.[159] (Even Kim Jong Il was captured on tape stating that "after 30 years of socialism, to feed people we have to penetrate into the Western world. Now, we are far behind the Western world.")[160] South Korean analyst Kim Kook Chin even argues that "Japan is the only real option" as leverage with the DPRK.[161] Although he probably overstates the case, since the South's contacts with Pyongyang have been growing—the ROK, not Japan, ended up providing rice to North Korea, for instance—Tokyo seems to be the only likely source of large-scale financial transfers.

The United States should encourage the regional powers, who have most at stake in achieving a nuclear-free peninsula, to take the lead in negotiations with the DPRK. Self-aggrandizement tends to be an American weakness: officials in both Seoul and Tokyo state that they felt they were informed, rather than consulted, about the framework negotiations and were simply handed a bill at the end.[162] Still, Washington's junior partners like being coddled. Observes columnist Georgie Anne Geyer, "The South Koreans, so long dependent upon American might to defend the peninsula, basically want the United States to 'take care of it' even while they resent that fact."[163] Regional consultations should occur between interested parties without American leadership or even necessarily participation.

Further, Washington should be prepared to brandish the "stick" of a regional nuclear arms race. If Pyongyang moves ahead and develops an atomic bomb, it will be because Kim Jong Il believes that his nation or his political dynasty, or both, will be more secure as a result. (The underlying assumption would be that a nuclear capability would allow the North to deter any military attack and cause surrounding states to treat it with respect and perhaps offer economic bribes for good behavior.) Washington might help disabuse him of that notion by warning the North that if it develops a nuclear capability, the United States will no longer discourage the South, which under American pressure dropped its nuclear weapons program in the mid-1970s, from acquiring a countervailing weapon. Indeed, if necessary, the United States could threaten to provide the South with a small nuclear inventory, sufficient to cancel the DPRK's advantage, as well as whatever anti-missile technology is available.[164] Washington should also point out that Japan would be likely to follow suit. Thus, the DPRK would end up less, rather than more, secure. (Obviously, such a spread of weapons would be undesirable, but it might be the lesser of evils. Moreover, Washington could always change its mind; the threat of an arms race, communicated privately to the DPRK leadership, might help make such a decision unnecessary.)

The Dangerous Desert Shield Model

What of the U.S. presence if the North refuses to choose peace? Under no circumstances should Washington begin a conventional build-up in South Korea, as proposed by some. A number of policy-makers and analysts want to use the nuclear controversy as an excuse for increasing America's troop presence. Senator McCain, for instance, proposed a Desert Shield–style build-up in the summer of 1994. Columnist Stefan Halper called for almost trebling force levels to 100,000, "the number at which the U.S. military optimizes its capabilities, and the North knows it."[165] Frank Gaffney advocated halting the departure of the nearly 14,000 soldiers flown in as part of the Team Spirit exercises and augmenting American forces "with airborne, naval and air force elements sufficient to contend with near-term contingencies."[166] William Perry testified before the Senate Foreign Relations Committee that the administration had intended to add more than 10,000 soldiers to America's forces in the ROK before the breakthrough that led to an agreement with the North.[167] The *Washington Times* simply editorialized in favor of "adding troops, planes and equipment."[168] Other proposals include military exercises, airlifts, and naval movements, as well as mundane conventional increases.[169]

Such steps are unnecessary, given the South's ability to supplement its own defenses. Richard Fisher of the Heritage Foundation declares, "South Korea must be defended."[170] Certainly. But why not by the South Koreans?

Moreover, an American build-up would be dangerous, since it might convince Pyongyang that war was coming—that Desert Shield was about to be followed by Desert Storm. America's shipment of Patriot missiles to the ROK caused one Northern newspaper to comment that "we cannot but take a serious view of such military steps . . . a very dangerous act which can be seen only on the eve of the outbreak of war."[171] That could be merely hot air, of course, but the Persian Gulf War may very well have taught the DPRK that its only hope in a conflict is to attack before Washington is ready. As one U.S. official puts it, the lesson for the North was, "Don't let the Americans build up their forces; don't let them put in air power; don't let them take the initiative; don't let them fight a war with low U.S. casualties."[172] If North Korea comes to view a conflict as inevitable, it is likely to strike preemptively.

Although the administration hasn't undertaken a major build-up, it has gone out of its way to reassure the South of its commitment. Coincident with the signing of the framework, American lawmakers and administration figures were in Seoul informing ROK officials that the U.S.–South Korean alliance was more important than ever.[173] That is precisely the wrong strategy, however. It simultaneously encourages Seoul to remain dependent and maintains an unnecessary burden on America. In fact, the United States shouldn't leave any troops on the peninsula, especially if the North acquires a bomb. America's original security commitment grew out of guilt at having left Seoul militarily unprepared for the DPRK onslaught in 1950; during the Cold War South Korea was also viewed as an important surrogate in the strategy of containment. The world has changed, however. Not only has the USSR disappeared, but the ROK now vastly outstrips its rival. American troops remain in the South out of habit, not need.

Dangerously Entangled

It is bad enough that today many of America's 37,000 soldiers continue to act as a living tripwire between the DMZ and Seoul. To leave them as nuclear hostages in the event that the North acquires an atomic bomb would be unforgivable. Nowhere else on earth would so many Americans be so at risk.

If the North forges ahead with its nuclear program, the United States should not retain, let alone strengthen, its nuclear guarantees to Korea and Japan, and possibly other nations in the region.[174] America's past conventional intervention on behalf of tangential interests, in Vietnam, for instance, proved costly, but the risks from the fighting that would accompany a nuclear contest between American allies and their antagonists would be far worse.

Admittedly, an inter-Korean nuclear exchange involving America would probably not spread to our homeland, as it might have during the Cold War when the Soviet Union was allied with the North. Nevertheless, American involvement would still entail very real risks. At the very least, it would create dangerous tensions in U.S.-Chinese relations, and it might even cause Beijing to lash out against small pro-U.S. states, particularly Taiwan, in the region. More probably, North Korea would attempt to hit Japan or begin a terrorist campaign in the United States. Although the United States is the world's dominant military power, it cannot act with impunity.

For years the United States used its nuclear umbrella to protect its European and East Asian allies from potential attack by the Soviet Union. But adopting the same strategy to deter nonhegenomic powers that pose no threat to America's vital interests—risking the safety of U.S. soldiers and perhaps even cities to prevent attacks on allied states by regional rivals—would move America into dangerous and uncharted waters. The Soviet Union's communist leadership, for all its brutality, was always rational and calculating, not reckless. Acting as guarantor against smaller states would risk conflict with potentially more unstable and unpredictable middling powers in order to protect otherwise self-sufficient states.

140

Washington already finds itself dangerously entangled in the affairs of India and Pakistan, which have fought conventional wars against each other and possess at least threshold nuclear capabilities.[175] There are even disturbing reports, albeit disputed by some U.S. officials, that those two states approached the nuclear brink over Kashmir.[176] Moreover, Washington risks entanglement on Russia's doorstep as a result of the pressure the United States has put on Ukraine to dismantle its nuclear arsenal (inherited from the USSR). The Clinton administration has promised to mediate any Russian-Ukrainian disputes and offered Ukraine the prospect of some association with NATO, which could bring a security guarantee. Further, the administration appears to have made some sort of security commitment to Ukraine to induce Kiev to abandon its nuclear deterrent.[177] When asked if the United States now ensured Ukraine's borders, Secretary Christopher stated, "The security guarantees do relate to that subject and provide assurance in that connection."[178] Indeed, the Clinton administration signed a secret protocol, denying American citizens knowledge of the new burdens they may be undertaking in the context of the tense relationship between Russia and Ukraine.[179] Those connections are dangerous enough. There is no reason for the United States to risk nuclear exposure in East Asia as well.

South Korea understandably would be reluctant to sit atomically naked if it had no American umbrella while the North possessed the bomb; thus, Seoul would be likely to revive its nuclear weapons program. Japan and even Taiwan would also have potential cause for concern. North Korea is now developing the Scud-D, with a range of 1,100 kilometers, that could reach Japan. Further advances could put the Republic of China within range.[180] And Taiwan's president Lee Teng-hui has stated publicly that his nation has the capability to build a nuclear weapon.[181]

Japan would find it especially hard to eschew nuclear weapons if both Koreas developed them. Relations among the three countries remain difficult because of Japan's brutal colonial rule in the first half of this century. While Tokyo has little to fear from the two Korean states (or even an aggressive united Korea) armed with conventional weapons, a Korean government with nuclear weapons, even if it never intended to use them, could place enormous pressure on Japan. Japanese acquisition of nuclear weapons in response would unsettle the entire region, however, and could spur other neighboring nations to try to develop their own nuclear capabilities.[182]

The possibility of such rampant proliferation would be unpleasant, to be sure, but not necessarily catastrophic, since it would also increase the price of aggression by any regional power. In fact, some analysts seem to fear proliferation precisely because it would decrease the need for U.S. defense guarantees in East Asia. Richard Fisher warns that "American public opinion may turn against our present military commitments to South Korea and Japan" if the two develop independent nuclear deterrents.[183] Yet preserving allied nuclear dependence to retain a justification for protecting nations capable of defending themselves is a poor reason to oppose proliferation.

Proliferation Dilemmas

For a variety of reasons, an increasing number of nations in East Asia and elsewhere are likely to acquire atomic weapons in the years ahead, despite the NPT. In fact, in time both South Korea and Japan may very well decide that their national interests require acquisition of nuclear weapons irrespective of the present U.S. guarantee, especially if they begin to doubt Washington's willingness to risk nuclear retaliation and terrorism to defend distant allies that lie next door to such major, nuclear-armed powers as China and Russia.[184]

Obviously, Tokyo is concerned. In the summer of 1995 Japan froze grant aid to the PRC over the latter's nuclear tests, amid calls for even broader economic sanctions.[185] At some point Tokyo may feel the need to respond more directly. Indeed, for years Japanese officials have talked about preserving the option of developing nuclear weapons, albeit usually in whispers to one another.[186] In turn, Japan's nuclear potential is a concern for many Koreans. Writes Taewoo Kim of the Korean Institute of Defense Analyses, "Probably the most fundamental dilemma facing South Korea will be that it ends up without nuclear weapons anyway but with nuclear weapons in the hands of the surrounding states, outward-looking Chinese military modernization, and Japan's growing nuclear potential, not to mention the nuclear suspicion in North Korea."[187] During the summer of 1994 a best-selling book in the ROK argued that a united Korea would need nuclear weapons to counter China and Japan.[188]

For purposes of negotiation, the threat that Seoul and Tokyo might acquire nuclear weapons would probably have a far greater deterrent impact on the North than would the threat of a permanent extension of the American nuclear umbrella. Not only will the credibility of the U.S. commitment inevitably decline as Washington withdraws or reduces its military forces abroad, but any continuing U.S. nuclear presence, however limited, in the region will encourage Pyongyang to create its own countervailing weapon. The DPRK needs to be convinced that acquisition of an atomic bomb would leave it less, rather than more, secure. Even Kim Jong Il might pause at the prospect of both South Korea and Japan developing their own nuclear forces.

In addition to the particular consequences of proliferation in East Asia, some observers fear the broader impact on the nonproliferation regime. Argues Arnold Kanter, "Even if Japan and South Korea continue to resist pressures to develop their own nuclear weapons, the entire global nonproliferation regime nevertheless could unravel if countries from Ukraine to Iran conclude that the international community is prepared to stand by while North Korea pursues a nuclear weapons program."[189] Senator McCain puts it more dramatically: "The eventual outcome of North Korea's pursuit of nuclear status will be a world where the proliferation of weapons of mass destruction explodes exponentially."[190] The normally sober-minded Stefan Halper goes even further, contending that "anything less" than full North Korean compliance with the NPT "would bring the rapid, uncontrolled spread of nuclear weapons and the almost certain use of them."[191]

Yet proliferation occurs case by case. Ukraine has nuclear weapons because of the breakup of the Soviet Union and will ultimately yield them only if it believes it can still protect its security; North Korea's actions will have little or no influence. Similarly, India and Pakistan acquired nuclear weapons capabilities because of geographic and military factors peculiar to South Asia; international precedent had little to do with it. And possession of nuclear weapons obviously does not inevitably lead to their use, else Britain, China, France, India, Israel, Kazakhstan, Pakistan, Russia, South Africa, the Soviet Union, Ukraine, and the United States would all have been lobbing atomic bombs at one another or neighboring states over the last 50 years. Although the risk that the bombs will be used rises, so does the risk of using them.

In fact, in coming years the United States is likely to face a number of challenges to its preference for nonproliferation. Unfortunately, to the extent that the NPT works, it is a little like gun control statutes: the law abiding submit and the criminals arm themselves. As a result, more analysts are proposing coercive nonproliferation, particularly the use of military force. But the problems of such a course are manifold, ranging from the difficulty of destroying the most important sites, to the danger of radioactive leaks to nearby states as well as local civilian populations, to the threat of terrorist retaliation and significant political difficulties in mounting Osirak-type operations. The case of North Korea presents all of those problems, as well as the possibility of full-scale war.[192]

As a result, it would be better to begin discussing how the United States can best adjust to a world in which nuclear weapons *do* proliferate. That does not mean that there is no value in attempting to slow some programs and stop other states (especially those with aggressive or erratic regimes) from acquiring nuclear weapons. But Washington should replace today's all-or-nothing approach—America either prevents a state from acquiring weapons, by war, if necessary, or extends America's nuclear umbrella—with a mixture of strategies, including development of anti-missile technologies, expansion of anti-aircraft capabilities, maintenance of a sufficient U.S. nuclear deterrent, and judicious provision of deterrent forces to friendly states.[193] Observes the Cato Institute's Ted Galen Carpenter, "Without the threat posed by a would-be hegemon, it is difficult to imagine what interest could be important enough for the United States to risk the consequences of a nuclear war to defend NATO member Turkey from a nuclear-armed Iran or to defend South Korea from a nuclearized North Korea."[194]

Conclusion

With the demise of the USSR, Pyongyang is left as perhaps the most unstable and potentially threatening actor on the world stage. The possibility of North Korea's acquiring nuclear weapons rightly unsettles, not only its neighbors, but also the United States. Nevertheless, even if the current framework agreement should fail, there would be no imminent crisis, let alone one that justified turning the possibility of future conflict into the far greater likelihood of war today. Replacing an unpleasant Korean cold war with a very hot war by launching a preemptive military strike against the North's nuclear facilities would be particularly foolish.

Instead, the United States and the ROK should continue to pursue diplomatic options to reinforce Pyongyang's apparent decision to forgo its nuclear course. If the DPRK is firmly committed to acquiring an atomic bomb, the best way to expose that intent is to make an attractive offer that begs acceptance. If that offer is not accepted, the best response will then be for the South to develop a strong conventional deterrent backed by a small nuclear arsenal. In any case, the U.S. troops should come home—they are not necessary to defend Seoul, and America has no interest in the region that warrants holding them hostage in a game of nuclear chicken on the potentially unstable Korean peninsula.

There are no good options and plenty of bad ones for dealing with North Korea if it eventually develops an atomic bomb. But that is also the case with Iran, Pakistan, and other countries around the globe. All we may be able to do is choose a second best option. That, however, is the right course despite the temptation to adopt a more vigorous—but ultimately more dangerous—response.

7. The Asian Context

South Korea is not America's only security commitment in East Asia. Even more important is the U.S. link to Japan, a larger and wealthier nation—and one with the potential of becoming a major military player as well. That is not all. Only recently did Washington abandon its bases in the Philippines, and it still maintains a defense treaty with that nation. America has long had military ties with Thailand and remains formally allied with Australia and New Zealand. The United States is developing a security relationship with Singapore by using its port facilities. More than 100,000 U.S. troops remain stationed on land and ship throughout East Asia and the Pacific. The Cold War may be over, but little has changed in terms of U.S. defense policy.

Korea: One Piece in a Puzzle

Washington could choose to dismantle its Korean commitment without adjusting its other security relations. American defense promises to other nations might look less secure, but the ROK does present a special case. The American commitment is to go to war on the Asian mainland on behalf of a once-destitute country now able to defend itself. The relationship was originally forged during the Cold War, when the security of a small, distant nation was plausibly related to America's global struggle with the Soviet Union. Now that conflict is over.

For that reason, the ROK has, especially in recent years, attempted to justify Washington's commitment on broader grounds. Explains Seoul, "As the region still shows an uncertain security picture, the role of the USFK [U.S. forces in Korea] will continue to be important for the security of the Korean peninsula and regional stability."[1] Good try, but no cigar: 37,000 soldiers in Korea provide an insignificant war-fighting capacity in a region where China, Japan, and Russia collectively possess roughly 3.8 million soldiers, 3,600 aircraft, and 2,800 ships.[2] Assistant Secretary of Defense Joseph Nye contends that the prepositioning of equipment in the South is "a terrific force multiplier."[3] But Nye's logic is flawed even if one grants the premise that it might be in America's interest to fight a land war in Asia. The prepositioning of military hardware does not require troops on-site. Moreover, forward basing makes less sense in the modern era when the Department of Defense can quickly transport manpower and materiel around the world; one estimate is that force deployments to East Asia could begin within 10 hours.[4] Yet the U.S. security guarantee and troop presence thrust Washington into the middle of a potential struggle in a region of far greater interest to the surrounding three great powers. By almost any measure, the Mutual Defense Treaty with South Korea is a bad deal for America.

Moreover, to devolve defense responsibility for the ROK to the ROK would not prevent America from retaining aircraft, bases, fleets, and troops elsewhere in the region. Ronald McLaurin, president of Abbott Associates in Washington, D.C., has argued that "a loss of the base of cooperation with Korea could therefore prejudice the American presence in all of northeast and east Asia, pushing U.S. presence all the way back to Hawaii."[5] Neighboring states might be displeased by the U.S. decision, but they would undoubtedly recognize its logic. Over the long term there would be no serious loss of American "credibility," the all-purpose criticism of any proposed change in the status quo. Credibility is lost when expectations are not met; expectations can be changed, however. And one of those changes could be the reduction of Washington's list of client states by one.

Japan would have little choice but to go along, since it would presumably prefer to preserve its own relationship with Washington irrespective of the state of America's ties with Seoul. True, James Kelly, president of Pacific Forum/CSIS, worries about "erosion" of America's position simply as a result of drift by the Clinton administration.[6] But the tangible effect of such "erosion" is hard to detect. Defense commitments in East Asia survived the fall of Cambodia and Vietnam, partial withdrawals from Korea, and departure from the Philippines. They would survive a pullout from Korea.

However, it makes little sense to stop a military policy review with Korea. While Seoul provides a dramatic example of an antiquated commitment kept alive only by the artificial life support of political elites in their respective nations' capitals, obsolete U.S. security guarantees litter East Asia. Indeed, the Pentagon's formal strategy statement seems to envision American military involvement in the region forever. According to the Department of Defense,

> America has pledged its commitment to the security of the Asia-Pacific region and has spent its resources and blood fulfilling that pledge. The United States has sent military forces to major wars against aggression in Asia during this century—World War II, the Korean War, and the Vietnam War, as well as a number of smaller conflicts. As these experiences have proven, America's interests in the region must be protected and America's commitments will be honored. They also provide a lesson: Asian tensions have the potential to erupt in conflict, with dire consequences for global security.[7]

As a result, Washington has sprinkled the region with defense treaties, bases, and troops. As part of the Pacific Command, the Pentagon stations forces in Alaska, Australia, Diego Garcia, Guam, Hawaii, Japan, Singapore, and South Korea; and more are afloat.[8] The largest amounts of materiel and numbers of personnel are based in Japan and the ROK, with whom the United States has formal treaties. America maintains a treaty with, but no forces in, the Philippines. The Department of Defense also cites *defense ties* (including visits, talks, and exercises) with Brunei, Cambodia, Fiji, French Polynesia, Indonesia, Kiribati, Laos, Micronesia, Mongolia, Nauri, Niue, Papua New Guinea, Tonga, Tuvalu, and Vanuatu, among other nations.[9] America's informal duties may be almost as great. There is, for instance, a general expectation that Washington would protect Taiwan from Chinese aggression and back the Philippines against Beijing in any violent confrontation over the Spratly Islands, and Vietnam's relationship with the United States could eventually evolve in the same direction.[10]

Mired in the Past

There is no doubt that East Asia and the Pacific are important for America, but the Pentagon appears to be living in the past, prepared to fight the last war, or wars. Indeed, U.S. policy is variously mired in World War II and the Cold War, with officials fixated on fears of old enemies mixed with anxiety over potential danger posed by

149

supposed friends. Thus, even as the global military balance has dramatically changed, American commitments and deployments in East Asia have remained essentially the same. Washington has gone so far as to proclaim that all of its Asia-Pacific security commitments, including those to the Marshall Islands, Micronesia, and Palau, "remain inviolable" because "the end of the Cold War has not diminished their importance."[11] Washington policymakers will be making the same argument after the second coming of Christ.

America's troop deployments, too, seem set in concrete. Many Korean officials, from former president Roh Tae Woo to past and probable future presidential candidate Kim Dae Jung, have suggested that some U.S. forces should stay after the two Koreas are reunited. Explains Chang-Il Ohn, a professor at the Korean Military Academy, "Even after Korean unity is restored in the future, however, this defense alliance relationship between Korea and the United States may be necessary to deter Korea's neighbors."[12] One American military officer has written about the possible configuration of a postunification force.[13] In fact, Secretary of Defense William Perry has said that "we anticipate a permanent presence for U.S. troops in Korea and Japan as long as our troops are welcome in those two countries."[14] What we see is the public-choice school of economics at work, with policymakers desperately seeking new excuses for old organizations and treaties.[15] Whereas U.S. forces in East Asia were once intended to contain a specific security threat, now, explains the Department of Defense, "America clearly has a stake in maintaining the alliance structure in Asia as a foundation of regional stability and a means of promoting American influence on key Asian issues."[16]

The failure to adjust the U.S. stance is particularly striking because, in one sense, American policy in the Far East has been a notable success. Behind the U.S. defense shield, noncommunist governments throughout the region have become economic tigers and moved toward democracy. Indeed, Japan is now the world's second-ranking economic power, and South Korea vastly outstrips its northern antagonist on virtually every measure of national power. Taiwan's dramatic success helped force Beijing to begin its reform course and currently unnerves the People's Republic of China because it demonstrates Taipei's ability to survive as an independent nation. Members of the Association of Southeast Asian Nations (ASEAN) such as Thailand and the Philippines also seem to be moving forward on the path toward strong, self-sustaining economic growth. Even Vietnam, scarcely two decades away from war with America, is eagerly seeking political and economic relations with the United States. Australia and New Zealand enjoy splendid isolation. The only thing Singapore has to fear is fear—its fear of freedom at home and of Japan abroad.

The ability of Washington's allies to care for themselves would suggest rethinking America's promises to defend, alliances with, troop dispositions in, and other potential military involvement with all of those nations. Equally important are the reduced potential threats to America's interests. Obviously, the past was messy. "To see the need for visible American power, look to the Far East, where America went to war three times in 25 years," argues columnist George Will.[17] However, the adversaries of the United States in those three wars have either vanished or imploded. The Empire of the Rising Sun has been replaced by the almighty yen; post-Mao China is dramatically different from the one that went to war for North Korea, itself an economic wreck; and Vietnam wants American investment and trade. More important, the global struggle that caused the United States to intervene, rather than remain aloof as it had during the earlier Russo-Japanese conflict and Japan's war against China, has vanished. Neither Japanese nor communist imperialism survives to tie mundane regional antagonisms to U.S. security interests. Today, as Richard Scalapino notes, the most serious threat "lies *within*, not outside," individual countries.[18]

Internal problems are generally not susceptible to solution by use of U.S. military power. Moreover, it is hard to see what hegemonic threats, with a serious potential effect on America, might, let alone are likely to, arise out of those more nebulous difficulties. If they don't, then there is no obvious reason for U.S. involvement. The mere existence of conflicts—a score currently rage from Africa to the Balkans to Southeast Asia to the Transcaucasus—does not require American action. Even the possibility of future U.S. intervention in a worst-case scenario does not require maintenance of an antiquated strategy of forward deployment. The Pentagon opines that it does not view "responsibility sharing as a substitute for American leadership or for our overseas United States military presence."[19] But leadership, or at least influence, comes in many forms, most of which do not require an ongoing overseas military presence—especially when troops in, say, Okinawa are ill suited for resolving the most likely problems, such as a naval firefight over the Spratly Islands.[20]

What might be the new threats, supposedly serious enough to require a U.S. military presence in East Asia? Threats so dangerous that, as McLaurin argues, "Forward deployment of U.S. forces in East Asia is an important element in a strategy designed to keep conflict away from American shores. A fallback to Hawaii would mean that the first line of American defense is at the national boundary of the United States."[21] Several threats have been proposed, but none deserves to be chosen.

Threatening Specter One: Revitalized Russia

The greatest theoretical menace to regional peace is Russia, which still possesses the most potent military in the area. But Moscow today is very different from Moscow during the Cold War, which appeared to be so threatening.[22] The USSR has collapsed. A much smaller Russia is suffering from severe economic distress, ethnic unrest, and military problems. Total Russian defense outlays are running about $63 billion, down dramatically from those of just a few years ago.[23] Moscow is selling off its aircraft carriers, dividing its Black Sea fleet with Ukraine, and letting its Pacific fleet rust away.[24] In short, explains Hyon-Sik Yon, a research fellow at the Korean Institute for Defense Analyses, "The Asian balance of military power thus does not favor Russia and will probably remain that way."[25] Moscow's policy reflects the changing balance. Concludes the ROK Ministry of Defense:

> Discarding the expansionist policy backed up by powerful military capability pursued by the Soviet Union, Russia has adopted a purely defensive strategy to safeguard its territory. It has been making efforts to ease tension and implant stability in the Far East through gradually reducing its Far Eastern troops, refraining from intervention in regional military disputes, reducing military operation drills, opening military bases to foreign observers, and promoting military exchanges with other countries in the region and the establishment of a new regional collective security system.[26]

The fear that Russia might attack any of its East Asian neighbors is little more than a paranoid fantasy. More likely would seem to be economic implosion and domestic disintegration, with consequences that would be more chaotic than dangerous to surrounding states. Those possibilities are best combatted by regional economic investment and trade, not the forward deployment of American forces.

Obviously, nothing is forever, and Moscow's future course is not guaranteed. However, even should a more authoritarian or military-dominated regime take power, it is not likely to act aggressively in East Asia in the foreseeable future. Russia would still have to focus on achieving economic revival and combatting internal challenges, such as the one it faces in Chechnya. Beyond that, Moscow's attention seems focused on the "near abroad," the former constituent parts of the USSR, as well as the question of NATO expansion. Matters of dispute in the Asia-Pacific region do exist—the Kurils, or "northern territories," seized from Tokyo at the end of World War II, for instance—but none seems likely to lead to war. In such cases Washington could attempt to mediate, which, again, does not require forward deployed U.S. troops.[27] Should serious frictions develop, there would probably be abundant time, not only for America but for other powers in the region, to adopt countermeasures.

Threatening Specter Two: Marauding Mandarins

Russia is not the only country where communism has steadily weakened. Something similar is occurring in the People's Republic of China. Beijing is growing economically but is entering an uncertain political transition: the central authorities face increasing pressure to yield additional power to provincial governments. In the near term, at least, the PRC's faction-ridden gerontocracy has neither the ability nor the will to seriously threaten neighboring countries, despite its recent saber rattling over the Spratly Islands and Taiwan. That the regime is brutal and undemocratic does not mean that it poses the sort of global threat that cannot be contained by its neighbors and therefore warrants U.S. intervention.

Nevertheless, in the minds of some, Beijing is the new potential hegemon that needs to be contained by America.[28] (Chinese officials, who are not stupid, are aware of those sentiments; they have sharply criticized what they see as U.S. attempts at containment.)[29] University of California professor A. James Gregor argues that "the history of the People's Republic of China has been characterized by irregularity, instability, and violence."[30] So, too, may it be in the future, he warns. George Will has put it even more vividly:

China, a regime in crisis, is trying to use naked intimidation to control, if not eliminate, Taiwan's freedom of movement on the international stage. The disruption of air and sea traffic by missile tests conducted provocatively near Taiwan was a notably crude attempt to deter Taiwan from trying to raise its international profile, as it did with its President's visit to Cornell University in May. The CIA says China is involved in territorial or maritime disputes with Russia, India, North Korea, Tajikistan, Taiwan, Japan, Vietnam, Malaysia, Brunei, and the Philippines. The influence of China's military, which includes the world's largest army and a rapidly growing blue-water Navy, may wax during the coming post-Deng succession crisis.[31]

Columnist Jeffrey Hart even writes of potential war between America and China by the year 2015.[32] Yet there is less here than meets the eye.

Predictions about Beijing's future course are as risky as those about Russia. In recent years official Washington, at least, has generally thought of the PRC as an ally. The United States even began arming that communist nation that had fought a bloody war against America between 1950 and 1953.[33] Now the PRC is increasingly seen as a likely enemy.

An Exaggerated Threat. China has, however, consistently proved wrong those most inclined to associate doom with its growth. For instance, three decades ago, as Beijing acquired a nuclear capability, the *National Review* warned, "We therefore confront a major and perhaps catastrophic shift against us in the world power balance; indeed, the shift is already under way. All the western Pacific region will become hostage to Peking. The West will be driven out. The indirect threat to our interests will evolve into a direct threat to our national security."[34] The conservative publication therefore advocated military preemption. Yet none of its apocalyptic predictions came to pass. That suggests the importance of not assuming the inevitability of war.

There are several reasons why Gregor, Will, and friends are likely to be wrong, just as the *National Review* was wrong before them. First, since the PRC's ascent from Maoism and the Cultural Revolution, Chinese foreign policy has emphasized moderation and stability.[35] That is reflected most obviously in Beijing's rapprochement with

America, but it is also evident in its economic ties with Japan, attempted improvement in relations with Vietnam, expanding relationship with South Korea, and even increased trade with Taiwan.[36] William Clark of the Center for Strategic and International Studies points to China's participation in the Asia-Pacific Economic Cooperation forum, desire to join the World Trade Organization, and recognition of Israel as further evidence of the PRC's "drive for political maturity."[37]

True, Chinese defense expenditures are growing, but that is not surprising, since the People's Republic suffers from serious military deficiencies. It is nonaligned but surrounded by nations that it has battled in decades past. Observed one analyst,

> The country's long frontiers, both land and maritime, are virtually as vulnerable as ever. Beijing is worried about what it sees as an American attempt to contain it. China's economy, though making significant strides, remains fragile in terms of the population/agricultural balance, and backward in its industrial and technological base. Educational levels, even among the governing elites, are low.[38]

During its brief 1979 war with Vietnam, Beijing found that its equipment was inferior and employed human-wave attacks.[39] Other problems included low morale, lack of popular support, and outdated battle tactics.[40] Moreover, in terms of military spending, Beijing is starting from a very small base. The International Institute for Strategic Studies estimated Beijing's military spending at $28.5 billion in 1994—a third less than Japan's and only twice that of South Korea.[41] High nominal growth rates have been undercut by inflation. The U.S. Arms Control and Disarmament Agency figures the total real increase between 1983 and 1993 at about 5.9 percent, or half a percent a year.[42] Other estimates show a steady decline in real military spending in the 1980s.[43] Such data hardly suggest plans for regional conquest. Furthermore, China is sacrificing quantity as it attempts to improve the quality of its forces. Although it has been importing a few score Su-27 aircraft, it is phasing out thousands of MIG-19 and Q5 planes. "The result is an effective cut in air power," argues Shunji Taoka, a defense writer for *Asahi Shimbun.*[44]

Moreover, there are domestic limits to China's modernization.[45] In particular, Beijing's economic situation restricts the resources that the government can devote to the military. Observes Japan's Defense

Agency, "As China's current top priority is its economic construction, it is unlikely that the ratio of defense spending to total fiscal spending will drastically increase in the future. In addition, the national defense modernization is expected to gradually proceed at a moderate rate because the country faces a difficult situation with its economy showing inflationary trends and budgetary deficits."[46]

It has been pointed out, with trepidation by some, that the Chinese military has developed alternative revenue sources through extensive business dealings. However, those activities are more likely to undercut than promote Chinese military power. They focus the attention of officers on commercial profits, divert soldiers from defense duties and military training, and create financial temptations likely to corrupt the country's military ethic. Some soldiers have already become cosmetics salesmen.[47]

Of course, in the end George Will's worst fears could be realized. Perhaps, for instance, the military will be able to assert much greater political influence during an extended and fractious leadership struggle.[48] However, while militaries usually want large arms budgets, they don't necessarily want conflict. Perhaps civilian leaders "will be tempted to employ or test" their nation's new power, as Thomas Robinson of the American Enterprise Institute worries.[49] However, other analysts believe that China would prefer to follow Sun-Tzu's dictum and achieve its objectives without using force.[50] Even if the PRC proves to be more aggressive, it still is not clear what America should do. Surely Russia doesn't need defending.[51] Presumably the United States would not intervene on behalf of the DPRK in a conflict. Washington has eschewed involvement in earlier wars between China and both India and Vietnam.[52] Tajikistan's relevance to the security of the Pacific is not obvious.

More important is Japan. However, despite obvious tensions in its relations with China, Tokyo viewed Beijing with little fear even when the latter's communist doctrines were more dominant.[53] Observed A. Doak Barnett of the Brookings Institution almost two decades ago, "Tokyo has recognized that a large expanse of water separates China from Japan [and] that the Chinese have lacked strong naval or amphibious forces."[54] Japan's attitude seems much the same today—the PRC is expanding its military but poses no serious threat.[55] Chinese hostility toward Tokyo is real, but it is balanced by the desire for economic assistance. Moreover, Beijing's ill will primarily reflects the past—Japanese aggression earlier this century—as opposed to the present. Over the years the relationship between the two countries has evolved pragmatically, if cooly.[56]

Chinese Fears. Indeed, far from acting belligerently toward Tokyo, Beijing apparently fears Japan. Any hint of even modest Japanese rearmament sends Chinese officials into paroxysms of anger.[57] At the PRC's official National Day celebrations, Prime Minister Li Peng emphasized that his nation must not forget Japan's World War II aggression and must "go all-out to build China into a stronger nation so as to prevent past tragedy from repeating itself."[58] Argues Professor Toshiyuki Shikata of Teikyo University, "From a short- and intermediate-term viewpoint, China's conventional forces are unlikely to become a direct threat to Japan's territorial waters and Sea Lines of Communication."[59] If Beijing ever does acquire a greater interventionist capacity and evinces an intent to use it, Japan certainly possesses the resources to defend itself.[60]

The PRC could not easily conquer Taiwan, and moving beyond intimidation would be economically and politically expensive, as well as militarily risky.[61] Of course, there is no doubt that the issue of Taiwanese independence is important to China's rulers.[62] Despite recent attempts at intimidation, which have muted calls for independence on the island, Beijing's general policy has been to improve relations with Taiwan and expand economic ties.[63] Indeed, the PRC seems willing to accept de facto independence—a Taiwan with its own army and no officials from the mainland—so long as the appearance of one China is maintained.[64]

Moreover, PRC officials privately estimate that an invasion of Taiwan would cost 100,000 or more casualties and recognize that military action would poison economic ties with virtually every important industrialized and industrializing state. True, Robinson warns that long-term military trends are moving in the PRC's favor, which is inevitable given the incredible disparity in size between the two states.[65] But the cost of conquest would remain very high, especially if the ROC chose to make nuclear weapons, as threatened by President Lee Teng-hui, which means that anything short of a declaration of independence by Taipei seems unlikely to put war on Beijing's agenda, and even then it would not be certain, though the danger would be real.[66]

In any case, it is not obvious why Washington should prepare to go to war over Taiwan. Arnold Beichman of the Hoover Institution argues that the United States should "have done something" about the PRC's missile tests near Taiwan but doesn't say what.[67] Destroy Chinese ships? Launch missiles at the mainland or airstrikes on Beijing? As much as Washington should work to discourage a conflict between the two Chinas, it has no serious security interests at stake in the potential struggle within what America formally recognizes as one country.[68]

The Philippines and Vietnam (along with Brunei, Malaysia, and Taiwan) are outgunned by China in their dispute over the Spratly Islands, but Beijing has so far failed to settle the issue militarily.[69] Indeed, argues Robinson, "The last thing China wants is a war"—especially over such modest stakes and when war would counteract attempts to improve relations with Southeast Asian nations, including Vietnam.[70] That could change, of course, but what interest does the United States have in attempting to forcibly settle territorial disputes to which there is no clearly right answer? Both China and the Philippines have been pressing their conflicting claims with some vigor.[71] Is Washington prepared to make Americans die for the Spratlys? If not, why are U.S. forces stationed in the region? If so, policymakers are prepared to sacrifice American lives for an interest that is not just limited but frivolous.

Today, at least, the U.S. Department of Defense emphasizes that it is encouraging a peaceful settlement of the dispute.[72] Indeed, the department argues more generally that "the United States is trusted in Asia, partly because we send our sons and daughters to stand as guarantors of peace and security in Asia," giving Washington "the capability, credibility, and even-handedness to play the 'honest broker.'"[73] But the ability to play honest broker comes from both distance and disinterestedness, not nearby military deployments. Which presumably is why Canada, with no forces in the region, is helping to mediate the dispute over the Spratlys by holding talks with all six claimants. Moreover, when the issues involve formal allies versus former enemies—South and North Korea, Japan and Russia—Washington's military presence suggests that, far from being disinterested, the United States is a potential party to the dispute. That perception, which is growing in China today, makes mediation more difficult.[74]

Moreover, it is disingenuous to suggest that America's forces are on the ground in South Korea or elsewhere to promote negotiations. The Spratlys are the most commonly cited example of the alleged Chinese threat to which Washington must respond, and friendly nations are not shy in expressing their opinion that the United States should be prepared to intervene militarily. Nor are the Spratlys the only disputed territory in the region. There are also the Paracel Islands, Natuna Island, Pratas Island, Pulau Sipadan and Pulau Ligitan, the Senkaku Islands, Sipidan Island, Rulau Batu Puteh, the Kuril Islands, and other territories.[75] Naturally, some American analysts want Washington "to pay much closer attention to this high-stakes strategic game" in the South China Sea.[76] But none of the disputes in that area—or more generally in East Asia—involves a vital interest of the disputants, let alone of the United States.

Wary Watchfulness. In sum, developments in China bear watching but do not require an American military response. Washington is likely to achieve better results by encouraging economic ties and avoiding treating Beijing as a quasi-enemy. That will give China, an increasingly important trading nation, a greater stake in peace. Nevertheless, Michael Lind of the *New Republic* may be right in warning that, in the longer term, "China may be the greatest threat to our interests," with a GDP and military that could outstrip those of America.[77] But many, many things could, and, indeed, are likely to, happen between now and then. Even the Department of Defense acknowledges that it is impossible to "be certain of China's intentions" and that its ultimate military "goals are unclear."[78] A 1994 Pentagon study group concluded that disintegration was the most likely outcome of the post-Deng leadership struggle.[79] Next was the status quo, and least likely was liberal reform.[80] Perhaps the most serious result of political turmoil would be a nationalist dictatorship, but even that wouldn't guarantee instability severe enough to affect American interests, let alone trigger conflict. Why, asks Edward Olsen of the Naval Postgraduate School, must we "seek an enemy?"[81]

Better than maintaining its existing commitments to nations throughout East Asia would be for the United States to encourage Beijing's neighbors to cooperate with China when possible, accommodate it when reasonable, and balance against it when necessary.[82] Although the PRC looms large over its neighbors, the latter are not without resources. For instance, Malaysia and Singapore have conducted joint air and naval exercises with Australia, Great Britain, and New Zealand to meet a simulated air attack. Thailand appears intent on creating a serious navy.[83] Moreover, Chinese belligerency would be likely to encourage neighboring states to organize in response. The ASEAN countries, recently joined by Vietnam, protested Chinese occupation of the aptly named Mischief Reef in the Spratly Islands.[84] Regional displeasure over Beijing's threatening stance toward Taiwan caused China to moderate its tone in mid-1995.[85] In the end, Washington needs to distinguish between understandable if bothersome nationalism, which could be exacerbated by the perception of Western attempts at containment, and aggression.[86] If the PRC begins to move down a more threatening path, there will be plenty of time for America to discuss appropriate responses—diplomatic, economic, military, and political. If truly serious threats emerged, an Army division in Korea and a Marine Expeditionary Force in Japan would prove to be of little use.

Threatening Specter Three: Japanese Imperial Redux

The only other potentially serious threat to regional peace is, of course, Japan, judged by some to have a double dose of original sin and still feared by other nations in the region. Many American policymakers feel the same way, though most are reluctant to voice their opinions publicly. Unusually candid was Gen. E. C. Meyer, former Army chief of staff, when he called Japan one of "the two biggest threats" (along with Germany) facing the United States after the collapse of the USSR.[87] Such sentiments are rarely far below the surface. The original purpose of the U.S.-Japanese alliance was as much to "smother" Tokyo, preventing it from again threatening the region, as to protect the war-torn nation from the USSR.[88] Today the Pentagon politely observes that Japan's concentration on home defense rather than overseas power projection has contributed to "overall regional security" and helped maintain the "peace and stability of the entire international community."[89] But without the United States as a "central, visible, stabilizing force in the Asia and Pacific region," warns the Department of Defense, "it is quite possible that another nation" might play that role.[90] The identity of that other country is not hard to guess.

Much of the suspicion of Japan reflects a long-standing racist undercurrent of American culture and politics. Adm. Matthew Perry's forcible "opening" of Japan in 1853 was hardly the way to start a beautiful friendship. Discrimination against Chinese and Japanese immigrants goes back a century.[91] In the 1930s Washington responded to Japanese but not German and Italian aggression and brutality, thereby initiating a truculent policy that one State Department analyst accurately predicted would, "if pursued consistently and determinedly, almost inevitably mean war with Japan."[92] The conflict, once entered, was fought on explicitly racial lines, unlike America's struggle with Nazi Germany. "The core imagery" of the Japanese, writes John Dower, was "of apes, lesser men, primitives, children, madmen, and beings who possessed special powers."[93] That bias also animated policy at home, where more than 110,000 Japanese-Americans were rounded up and incarcerated.[94] During the war, one author argued,

> In a sense, militarism and aggression are only the tactical objectives of our war against Japan. The strategic and true objectives are the ideas, the attitudes, the historical currents, the social institutions, and the economic structure that have given rise to militarism and aggression. We can bring a temporary end to Japanese aggression by driving her out of her conquests. We can bring a temporary end to Japanese militarism by eliminating her present Army and Navy. We must strike much deeper to exterminate them once and for all.[95]

Rooting Out Militarism. The belief that militarism was deeply rooted and had to be dug out served as the basis for the American occupation after the war. Various policymakers in Washington had other goals as well, of course, but Washington imposed on Japan a new constitution with article 9, which renounced war and forbade maintenance of a military.[96] The threat of communism, however, soon caused the United States to modify its policy and press Tokyo to create a small, though potent, military.[97] Washington's policy, explains one analyst, "aimed at containment of the Soviet Union and China at arms length and of Japan with an embrace."[98] Remilitarization was not uncontroversial in Japan—the Japan Socialist Party long argued that even the small Self-Defense Force was unconstitutional, a stance abandoned only recently for political reasons.[99] Nevertheless, neopacifist sentiment remains strong, with sharp popular resistance to participation in international peacekeeping missions and the provision of unarmed medics as part of the Gulf war.[100] In

May 1994 Tokyo even refused to send a military plane to evacuate Japanese nationals stranded by Yemen's civil war. So "deep is pacifist sentiment" in the electorate that Tetsuya Kataoka of Saitama University worries that his nation might collapse in the face of "a serious threat to her security."[101] Only very recently has a potential popular majority emerged that favors revising the constitution to allow greater participation in multilateral undertakings.[102]

Persistent Suspicions of Japan. Japan's cautious military rebirth has generated responses verging on the hysterical. China virulently attacked Tokyo for "the revival of militarism" and preparation "for an aggressive war."[103] The Soviet Union, rather more cynically, joined the critical chorus. Moscow, of course, did not have a significant portion of its territory overrun by Japan in World War II; indeed, the USSR attacked Japan in the conflict's waning days in order to acquire territory and influence. Yet Russia today continues to oppose an increased Japanese military role.[104]

Opposition elsewhere in the region, particularly Korea (both South and North), the Philippines, and Singapore (though not Malaysia), was and continues to be equally strident. For example, South Korea's Ministry of National Defense referred to Japan's "massive military build-up" and "massive spending."[105] Although the ministry later conceded that Tokyo "is not trying to become a militaristic superpower," defense officials are not so sanguine in private and sometimes even in public.[106] Cha Young Koo, then of the Korean Institute for Defense Analyses and now at the Ministry for National Defense, said that Japan is potentially more dangerous than China, which dominated the peninsula before Japan won control at the end of the last century.[107] Similar attitudes are evident in North Korea. When I visited Pyongyang in 1992, one analyst proposed that the United States, which, other officials regularly pointed out with some acerbity, had leveled the capital city during the Korean War, should cooperate with the DPRK to contain a potential revival of Japanese militarism. Singapore strongman Lee Kuan Yew, noting the Japanese people's past prowess as warriors, said, "I do not think they have lost those qualities" and advocated that America pressure Tokyo to abide by its so-called peace constitution.[108]

Similar fears were frequently expressed in America as well, even as the U.S. government was pressing Japan to up its military outlays. In 1970 Reps. Lester Wolff (D-N.Y.) and J. Herbert Burke (R-Fla.)

worried that "there seems to be a readiness to commit a substantial portion of Japan's vast wealth to the reestablishment of a major international military force."[109] A year later a book warned that war with Tokyo "will happen again—not immediately—perhaps 40 years from now."[110] (That is only four years earlier than Jeffrey Hart's predicted war with China—it could be a busy decade for America!) Later volumes decried the alleged rise of Japanese militarism.[111] In 1991 another book prophesied that "inexorably, the economic conflict will become a political conflict and the political conflict will become military."[112]

Nevertheless, Washington has remained officially committed to Japan's sharing the region's defense burden. The result is a modest, though significant Japanese military: 239,500 personnel, 450 combat aircraft, 63 surface vessels, and 18 submarines.[113] That puts the quantity (though not the quality) of Japanese manpower and materiel well behind that possessed by America, China, and Russia and roughly equal to that held by Britain, France, and Germany.[114] Tokyo's 1995 defense outlays came to about $54 billion.[115] Japan is in third place, behind the United States and Russia, though spending by Britain, China, France, and Germany is of the same order of magnitude and the exact ranking is sensitive to exchange rate variations. For example, in the early 1990s Japan came in seventh, behind all of those nations.[116] Tokyo's outlays look less impressive when viewed in another light, however—$54 billion is only a little more than America alone spends to defend East Asia every year. Moreover, Japanese military spending has settled at about 1 percent of GDP, lower than that of any other major nation.[117] (Japan breached that level, which had been treated as an almost sacred barrier, in 1987 but has since fallen back below it. Outlays and force levels continue to drop in the mid-1990s, and in late 1995 Japanese officials announced further cuts, particularly in ground troops.)[118]

Cheap Rider. As a result, Tokyo is what Edward Olsen calls a "cheap rider."[119] While its security contribution is large compared to those of its neighbors, it is small set against both America's spending and what Japan could provide. Argues Olsen, "Japan's defense contributions remain decidedly minimalist, parsimonious, and inordinately cautious," making the U.S.-Japanese defense relationship "patently inequitable."[120]

163

There should be no doubt about the magnitude of America's defense subsidy for Japan. Officials in Tokyo and Washington alike point to Japan's host-nation support, admittedly generous compared to that of most countries.[121] But that support, estimated at $5 billion by the U.S. Department of Defense and at $5.4 billion by the Japanese Defense Agency, is inflated in the same way as is Korea's.[122] Moreover, as noted in chapter 5, the principal cost to Washington is not unit deployment but unit creation. Were it not for the security guarantee, there would be no reason to maintain the forces used to backstop the treaty.

Even $5 billion pales in comparison to the benefit being received by Japan.[123] A savings of, say, one-half percent of gross domestic product alone is worth over $20 billion to the Japanese. Carpenter figures that Washington's security guarantee has saved Tokyo more than $900 billion (in 1995 dollars) since 1951. As he puts it, "From the standpoint of minimizing military expenditures, being a U.S. dependent has been very good indeed for Japan."[124] Even Japanese officials acknowledge that point. Although strongly supportive of the Mutual Security Treaty, Kazuyoshi Umemoto, director of the Japan-U.S. Security Treaty Division at the Foreign Ministry, admits that there "is a ring of truth" to the feeling on the part of many Americans that the defense relationship "gives Japan breathing space where it can rest and not make an effort to increase its international role."[125] It certainly does. Carpenter points out that just five days after the release of the Pentagon's official strategy paper promising to maintain 100,000 troops in the region essentially forever, reports surfaced that Tokyo hoped to cut military outlays and force levels by one-fifth over the next five years.[126]

The Pentagon also implicitly acknowledges the subsidy in its attempt to show that America's security guarantees to East Asia are in this nation's economic interest. Argues the Department of Defense, "Much of Asia's economic growth has a direct relationship to its security environment. As an example, Asia's demand for oil from outside the region makes the security of access routes imperative. . . . United States and Asian interests are clearly served by the maintenance of the sea lines of communication that support worldwide trade in oil and other goods."[127] What that cleverly written paragraph attempts to obscure is the fact that the largest Asian consumer of oil is Japan, and that it is therefore primarily Japanese, not American, interests that are served by the U.S. Navy's guarding tanker-laden sea lanes.[128] As Olsen puts it, "Japan remains far behind in relative safety, taking advantage of U.S. strategic largesse."[129]

Japan's reliance on Washington is almost total. When asked about America's potential role in the Spratly Islands, one Japanese military official indicated that Tokyo would expect the United States to intervene should conflict break out. Queried about possible Japanese military assistance in such an operation, he said no—although Tokyo might provide logistics support if asked to do so by the Southeast Asian nations. Japanese participants in a Japanese-American study group urged Washington to "remain attuned to regional perspectives and concerns generated by continued PRC military mobilization.[130]

Even worse, Tokyo seems to believe that Korea, an area of far greater interest to Japan than to America, is almost solely Washington's responsibility. In April 1994 Tokyo turned down a U.S. request to provide minesweepers and anti-submarine aircraft in the event of war with North Korea.[131] Even noncombat assistance might be in doubt, since Japanese officials publicly worry about the "painful" decisions that would be necessary to simply provide base support for U.S. operations in Korea.[132] Here, as elsewhere, America is protecting predominantly foreign interests for allies that are capable of taking care of themselves. Yet official Tokyo whines about how difficult it would be to provide even the most modest backing for Washington in the event of a regional crisis.

America receives precious few benefits from the alliance in return for its trouble. Shinichi Ogawa, of Tokyo's National Institute for Defense Studies, cites U.S. access to bases for use in defending Korea, but as argued throughout this book, that commitment is outmoded. Another supposed plus is Tokyo's host-nation financial support.[133] But military units are created to perform a military role, not to attract payments for their overseas deployment.

Even more embarrassing, Ogawa suggests as another American "security benefit" the "side effect of containing any full-scale development of Japanese military capability."[134] Similarly, one Tokyo official asked me if I would really want the imperial navy roaming the Pacific.[135] Japanese attempts to demonize themselves to preserve U.S. defense subsidies are a rather sad spectacle. In any case, relative Japanese disarmament is a benefit to America only if the reincarnation of the Empire of the Rising Sun seems likely and could be halted by America's current presence. But Japan is a very different country today than it was in the 1940s. Moreover, if the enormous domestic social and political changes necessary for a return of rampant militarism occurred, they would sweep away the Mutual Security Treaty.

Indeed, that may happen anyway if Japanese citizens come to believe that the purpose of America's military presence is more to monitor than to defend them. As a Japanese newspaper columnist put it in March 1990, the Japanese people "cannot feel good about paying for a watchdog that watches them."[136] That observation suggests that tensions could rise and ultimately end the alliance in a far more acrimonious fashion than would a gradual, measured American withdrawal. Already, economic and political brawls are erupting between the two nations with disquieting regularity, and polls find rising popular anger in both countries.[137] Washington's apparent spying on its erstwhile ally in an effort to uncover economic secrets did not go over well in Tokyo.[138] Proposals are being seriously advanced in America to use the security ties as leverage on other issues.[139] At the same time, the Okinawa rape case has created surprisingly powerful popular pressure on the Japanese government to demand adjustment, not only of the status of forces agreement, but also of the magnitude of U.S. troop deployments.[140] Such frictions—January 1996 alone saw the rape of an American girl and a car accident that killed three Okinawans—suggest that the alliance is likely to survive only as long as it is not seriously challenged or tested—a sanguine scenario that seems increasingly unlikely.

"Now More Than Ever": Clinging to the Status Quo. Nevertheless, a recent study mission made up of the usual American suspects held extensive discussions with the usual Japanese suspects and reported—surprise!—that "defense cooperation between the United States and Japan is seen as more important than ever."[141] Mission members viewed "the U.S.-Japan Security Treaty as the bedrock of Japanese security" and believed that "Japan remains the linchpin of the U.S. forward deployed strategy in the Western Pacific."[142] Those people are not alone in favoring the status quo "more than ever."[143] Another group proclaimed that the alliance "remains in the vital national security interests of both signatories."[144] The Clinton administration insists that "nowhere . . . is the need for continued U.S. engagement more evident."[145] A conference of American and Japanese officials held in July 1995 came to the same conclusion.[146]

Former defense secretary Caspar Weinberger writes simply that "most of us who served in WWII would prefer Japan to remain as it is."[147] And Assistant Secretary Nye says, "We're here to stay, and we're going to stay."[148] In sum, no matter how much the world has changed, no matter how much Japan has changed, no matter how East Asia has changed, no matter how the interests of Americans have changed, U.S. policy cannot change.

But the current relationship is outdated, not worth sustaining, and no longer sustainable. Queries Edward Olsen, "Why not simply enjoy the peace and accept the fact that the U.S.-Japan alliance has completed its tasks globally and regionally? Why invent new rationales to prop it up?"[149] The solution, then, is a gradual American disengagement combined with a modest, defense-oriented Japanese military build-up.

Numerous are American proposals for Japan to take on increased responsibility within the existing treaty framework.[150] A number of Japanese officials also endorse that approach. Washington's "interest is best preserved" through its alliance with Japan, argues former ambassador Hisahiko Okazaki. "All that is necessary is for Japan to be a real partner," and the United States should prod Tokyo to do so, he adds.[151]

However simple that approach might seem, pressure for "burden sharing" often engenders acrimonious debate and disagreement.[152] It also would not change the basic incentive structure that discourages significant Japanese defense efforts. "Maybe we have overrelied on the U.S. for security," admits one Japanese defense official.[153] Discussions won't change that, however. Moreover, sharing responsibility, when the interest to be defended is primarily Japanese and Japan is capable of defending it, is not enough. Rather, the goal should be to shift responsibility, or shed burdens, within a larger regional cooperative system. Such an approach is both more fair to the United States and more likely to work, since an American military presence means continuing Washington's defense subsidies for well-heeled allies and continuing disincentives for Japan to do more. As in South Korea, the United States should phase out its troop presence in Japan and terminate its treaty guarantee.[154]

Already there is evidence that the Japanese government is, in Carpenter's words, "hedging its bets."[155] Some people outside the government are forthright: America's military presence in the Far

East "is outdated," explains Shunji Taoka of *AERA* magazine. "Japan believes in continuity. America's Pentagon is the same way, resisting any change."[156] Yet some Japanese military officers, too, seem receptive to the idea of Japan's undertaking a role more commensurate with that nation's status as a great power. "We agree that it is time to rethink and reevaluate the security alliance," explained one military officer responsible for defense planning.[157] Ambassador Okazaki, though a supporter of the American defense guarantee, envisions an extra $100 billion in Japanese spending over a 5- to 10-year period for Theater Missile Defense, AWACS aircraft, Aegis cruisers, and the like.[158] Former army corps commander and scholar Toshiyuki Shikata and Motoo Shiina, a member of the House of Councilors, suggest Japanese defense outlays of between 1.5 percent and 2 percent of GDP.[159] (Participation in UN peacekeeping missions, in contrast, is a worrisome distraction from addressing real security issues of concern to Japan. Even worse, Washington has agreed to divert some of its own resources by lending U.S. air- and sea-lift capability to Tokyo for use in UN operations.)[160]

Misplaced Fears of an Aggressive Japan. Such an increase in defense outlays would undoubtedly unnerve some of Japan's neighbors. But surely Washington should not risk the lives of American airmen, soldiers, and sailors because Singapore, say, would prefer not to deal with the ghosts of World War II. Of course, anger about Japan's conduct in that conflict is understandable. Mass murder in Nanking, mistreatment of allied prisoners during the Bataan Death March, imperialism in the name of liberation in Manchuria, impressment of "comfort women" in Korea, and brutality most everywhere were just a few of the crimes committed.[161] But Europe has gotten past Napoleonic France's aggression in the early 1800s and is moving beyond Nazi Germany's atrocities earlier this century. South Korea seems to have forgiven China for its imperial past. It is time for the East Asian nations to recognize that Tokyo seems less inclined toward aggression than does the PRC, for instance, which Japan could help counterbalance.

Most important, the 1990s are not the 1930s. First, Japan and its political system are very different. Democracy seems firmly rooted, and there is no serious popular support for an imperialistic course today. Of course, a few Japanese, the governor of Hiroshima, for instance, still defend their nation's conduct in World War II, and the issue of Japan's formally "apologizing" for its actions has received much ink.[162] But actions speak louder than words. Virtually all of those who committed and planned the attacks are dead. Divisive internal debates over sending even unarmed soldiers abroad and authorizing military participation in civilian rescues suggest that neither Japan's politicians nor its citizens have the stomach for aggression.[163] That could, of course, change, but the circumstances are difficult to imagine and the forces loosed thereby would sweep away America's presence, not be contained by it.

Second, the regional economic and political climates are very different today. Tokyo has gained all of the influence and wealth through peace that it once hoped to attain through the Greater East Asia Co-Prosperity Sphere. Although it has interests to protect from the depredations of others—access to Mideastern oil, for instance—it has nothing to gain, and everything to lose, from aggressive war. Indeed, hostility to Japan among its neighbors is not unanimous. Some countries, such as Malaysia, welcome Japanese involvement in regional affairs.[164] South Korea appears to be by far the most hostile.[165] Nevertheless, even South Koreans are not unanimous; opinions in the ROK seem to divide along generational lines, with younger defense scholars less apprehensive about Tokyo's potential ambitions.[166] Similarly, writes East Asian scholar Ivan Hall, "Professed attitudes toward Japan depend a great deal on whether one has been talking to customers and economic planners eager for goods and investment, to politicians still playing the old 'aggression card,' to an elder generation with bitter memories, or to younger intellectuals."[167]

Third, Japan could moderate concerns about an increased regional defense role. Its military build-up should be modest. After all, Tokyo faces no immediate and serious security threats. Relations with Russia are strained over Moscow's retention of the Kuril Islands, but that quarrel presages no armed conflict. China perhaps poses a more plausible future peril, but only barely. Thus, a series of small, gradual increases in defense outlays would be sufficient. (Japan's reaction to a phased withdrawal of U.S. forces in the post–Cold War world would probably be more restrained than it would have been had the United States precipitously pulled out when the communist threat was still real.)

Moreover, Japan should tailor its military enhancements to defense—particularly to protecting against missile attack along with air and naval power projection capabilities to guarantee sea lanes. It should avoid creating a large army capable of conquering and occupying other nations. Japan would probably follow that course because, as Carpenter notes, "Japanese leaders are mindful of the continuing suspicions harbored by their neighbors."[168] In fact, Tokyo explicitly acknowledges the problem. "The way Japan is perceived by its Asian neighbors is different than the way the U.S. is perceived," states Keiji Omori, deputy director general of the Bureau of Defense Policy of the National Defense Agency.[169] He views that as a reason for America to maintain its East Asian protectorate, but it also suggests that his government would be cautious in responding to a U.S. withdrawal.

Regional Cooperation. Tokyo should also explore means of assisting friendly nations in their defense efforts. Professor Kataoka advocates "cooperation that includes dispatching Japanese combat troops" to the ROK in the event of war.[170] Michael Nacht of the U.S. Arms Control and Disarmament Agency suggests a trilateral U.S.–Japanese–South Korean agreement.[171] Those steps would probably not go over well today in Seoul, to put it mildly. Although younger South Koreans may be more inclined to consider formal military ties, leading ROK officials feel differently. One Korean defense ministry aide imagined South Korean acceptance of Japanese help in the event of a North Korean invasion "only at the last moment."[172] Still, the countries have exchanged intelligence information and navy visits; they have also begun broader defense discussions, all of which could form the basis for increased and more official ties.[173]

One less controversial possibility would be multilateral naval maneuvers, which the United States could initiate and host, eventually turning them over to the other parties as part of its disengagement program.[174] Japanese financial assistance to allied partners faced with specific military threats, such as the ROK, is another possibility.[175] Admittedly, even that course would not be easy, as evidenced by the torturous loan negotiations between the ROK and Japan in the early 1980s.[176] However, some of the issues that earlier bedeviled the relationship—Seoul's kidnapping of Kim Dae Jung in Japan, for instance—are long past and unlikely to recur in today's democratic South Korea. Moreover, the North's unnatural influence on Tokyo appears to be fading.[177] And the pressure created by a prospective American departure would probably cause both governments to be more cooperative, since they would no longer have the easy out of relying on Washington for their security needs.

Finally, as argued in chapter 5, Japan, backed by the United States, should promote regional discussions though such organizations as the Asia-Pacific Economic Cooperation (APEC) and ASEAN.[178] In that way America could shift defense responsibilities to Tokyo without raising the specter of renewed Japanese imperialism. That would also help to avoid the "vacuum" that Singapore's Lee Kuan Yew foresees after a U.S. withdrawal.[179] A Pacific alliance treaty organization was once proposed but rejected in Washington. More recently has come a suggestion for an Asian-Pacific treaty organization. However, forging a serious and effective regionwide system will be difficult and take time, for, as Robert Scalapino has noted, Asia is a region "where differences in developmental stage, historic traditions, geopolitical circumstances, and cultural-political values are extensive."[180] Moreover, those problems vary geographically and are more acute in Northeast Asia. Given the difficulties, nations in the region should take the lead, taking small steps and then building upon them.

A good place to begin is economics, given the growing regional interdependence.[181] Indeed, a number of countries and organizations are attempting to create institutions that could ultimately turn into serious consultative and decisionmaking bodies.[182] ASEAN's decision to include Vietnam, once a feared adversary, obviously reflects, in part, concern about China.[183] Burma, Cambodia, and Laos also seem destined to join in time. The ROK has suggested that ASEAN consider Korean issues, and Japan has also warmed to the idea of cooperating with the organization.[184] India hopes to open a regular dialogue with ASEAN and join APEC. Although not originally envisioned as a security organization, ASEAN has spawned both the ASEAN Regional Forum and the ASEAN Post Ministerial Conference, at which political and security topics have been discussed. Years ago, Ralph Clough of the Brookings Institution argued that ASEAN could "become one of the principal means by which Southeast Asian states protect their collective interests."[185] Moreover, new organizations could be created; two analysts have suggested a Northeast Asian security group composed of the two Koreas, the three major surrounding powers, and the United States.[186]

Tokyo seems to have become more receptive to regional arrangements as its economic ties have grown.[187] The potential for expanded collaboration also has been enhanced by greater U.S. interest in such arrangements. For instance, the Clinton administration reversed Washington's prior obstruction of regional arrangements not under U.S. control.[188]

None of that means that an East Asian collective security system is imminent. However, it is difficult to overestimate the importance of incentives. For five decades Washington has helped to arrest East Asia's political maturity by providing a superpower security guarantee, which allows neighboring countries to harbor grudges, refuse to cooperate, and ignore regional solutions. Now almost every nation in the region points to lack of unity as a reason for America's continuing military presence. Even Japanese analysts argue that the lack of regional institutions means Washington cannot withdraw— presumably ever.[189] However, only U.S. disengagement will lead to the creation of serious multilateral security ties among the regional powers. Rather like a hanging, an American pullout would help concentrate the minds of East Asia's leaders and reshape the region's current counterproductive incentive structure.

The Hard Issues. Even in such an environment, difficult issues would remain. Some people willing to countenance a conventionally armed Japan might quail at the possibility of Tokyo as a nuclear power. Worries James Lasswell, in the Office of the Deputy Chief of Staff for Plans at Marine Corps headquarters, "Faced with a nuclear-armed China, Japan would likely seek a nuclear arsenal if our presence was retracted. If Japan went nuclear, so could most of East Asia."[190] He may be right. Japan first discussed the acquisition of a nuclear capability more than two decades ago.[191] Moreover, Tokyo has suggested that a DPRK bomb would force it to reconsider its current position.[192]

A Japanese bomb would not be inevitable, however, especially since Tokyo is technically capable of delaying the decision until the last possible moment.[193] Nevertheless, American disengagement does raise that possibility, which would not be the worst outcome. American involvement in an East Asian nuclear war would be. As argued in chapter 6, the United States has insufficient security interests at stake to warrant taking that risk. And in the long term it is hard to deny to Japan a weapon possessed by two of its neighbors, nations that would seem to be less trustworthy.

Finally, some people fear driving Japan away from America, making political division and war more likely. Richard Holbrooke, President Carter's assistant secretary of state for East Asian and Pacific affairs, later complained that successive administrations had given little thought to the possibility that burden-sharing pressure could result in an increased "Japanese military capability [that] might, over time, lead to an aggressive foreign policy from Tokyo that might even eventually be at odds with America's."[194] In 1987 Meirion and Susie Harries warned that ending the defense guarantee "would precipitate Japan away from the western alliance and into the nonaligned movement among countries whose anti-Americanism is running high—or, further still, into the Chinese, even the Soviet, orbit."[195]

Although concerns about Japanese-U.S. estrangement should not be ignored, they also should not be exaggerated. Russia and the nonaligned nations offer few of the economic opportunities of America, and China is hardly ready to embrace its old adversary. Nor is Japan, poised to take a leading role in international affairs, likely to want to be a junior partner to demonstrably weaker nations. What is critical is for America to not use the threat of withdrawal as part of what the Harrieses term "aggressive posturing," which could cause serious friction, to force Tokyo to go along with Washington's wishes. At times current U.S. strategy (involving trade, at least) seems dangerously close to such posturing. Rather, Washington should implement overall disengagement without rancor.

Above all, the United States should not assume that Japan is likely to become the next "great enemy." An example of such an apocalyptic scenario was the book by George Friedman and Meredith Lebard, who in 1991 predicted that growing economic competition between the United States and Japan would result in heightened protectionist pressures, which would lead to greater political friction and eventually war.[196] Although trade frictions remain serious, the two nations seem no closer to hostility and war today than they were when the book was published. (In fact, the authors predicted that by 1992 Washington would be limiting Japanese imports, which has not occurred.) Moreover, the most effective way to head off such a confrontation would be to increase avenues of economic cooperation; eschew economic sanctions and warfare; and eliminate America's defense subsidy for Japan, which gives the island nation such an unfair economic advantage.[197] If the sort of hostility that could lead to war ever developed, the Mutual Security Treaty would hardly be an effective barrier—any more than the British-Japanese alliance forestalled fighting between those two countries in World War II.

Miscellaneous Instability

Some analysts point to potential territorial conflicts between Japan and Russia over the Kuril Islands, between Japan and South Korea over Liancourt Rock in the Sea of Japan, and between Japan and China over the Diaoyudao Islands in the East China Sea.[198] But war is plausible in none of those cases, unless the world changes dramatically—so dramatically that a few thousand U.S. soldiers on station in the region would be irrelevant.

Robinson worries that "without U.S. leadership, there will be no way to avoid eventual war."[199] Such pessimism seems unwarranted, however, since the bitterest antagonisms—those between the two Koreas and between China and Vietnam—are limited. And the latter has softened some in recent years; the two nations have held talks about their contested border and the Spratly Islands. Few disputes affect anything approaching the involved nations' vital interests; all of the countries have a stake in regional peace; and local conflicts (shooting over the Spratlys, for instance) would probably not spread (China has already endured the high cost of trying to "punish" Vietnam, so it probably wouldn't mount a punitive expedition to Manila and Luzon).

Other problems are even less likely to seriously impair either regional or American security. Many regimes have struggled with insurgencies and rebellions, but most have also remained in power and at peace with their neighbors. For instance, Cambodia's chaotic struggle against the Khmer Rouge is tragic but threatens no other nation. Burma's ruling junta turned hostile toward Thailand in mid-1995, but war seems unlikely. Vietnam, though still formally communist, is enthusiastically seeking American investment, trade, and tourism.

Tokyo, however, worries that "many Southeast Asian countries, taking into account their economic growth and changing security environment, are increasing defense spending and introducing new weapons," which in its view increases the need for a U.S. presence.[200] But the creation of a local barrier to Chinese (and Japanese) expansion southward is a good thing; multiple power centers are most likely to generate a vibrant regional balance of power. If such a balance were to break down, there would still be little cause for alarm in Washington: a conflict between Southeast Asian neighbors would not affect America's security.

The Clinton administration has expressed its desire to improve military ties with New Zealand as well as through the tricornered Australia–New Zealand–United States (ANZUS) organization.[201] Indeed, the Pentagon argues that America's alliance with Australia "makes a major contribution to regional stability."[202] The basis for that singular judgment is, however, unclear. Although military cooperation, especially on intelligence gathering, is in all three nations' interest, there is no need for a military alliance. Indeed, it is hard to think of a pact with less relevance for the future than ANZUS.[203]

Only North Korea remains a serious potential threat to other nations in East Asia, but it is no replacement for the Soviet Union. Pyongyang is desperately poor, possesses no reliable allies, and has been reduced to waving the threat of an atomic bomb to gain respect. And, as argued earlier, its chief antagonist, the ROK, is fully capable of deterring Northern adventurism.

Changes Ignored

The Clinton administration, like its predecessor, hasn't seemed to notice the dramatic changes in East Asia. To the contrary, the president's concern over his weak military image has apparently caused him to offer categorical promises to maintain American forces in the region for as long as U.S. allies desire their presence. Explains the Pentagon,

> The Clinton Administration is fully aware of the need for a strong continued forward United States military presence in the Asia-Pacific region to protect vital American interests there. As this report has stated, reductions resulting from the end of the Cold War have been accomplished; no further changes in warfighting capability are currently planned; the United States will maintain a force structure requiring approximately 100,000 personnel in Asia. The United States will also pursue modernization initiatives to improve the

> capability, flexibility and lethality of all our forces, including those in the region, and ensure that our forces will be able to deploy more quickly in a crisis.[204]

In the end, however, the administration never really explains the alleged need for a continuing and, indeed, expanding U.S. military presence in East Asia. The Pentagon cites three "vital national interests" that are supposedly served by America's regional security commitments: "preserve the survival of the United States," "advance a healthy and growing United States economy," and "promote a stable and secure world."[205] The first is vital, but it is not at risk in East Asia, given the demise of hegemonic communism. The second is important, not vital (economic prosperity is a good thing, but not the same thing as America's survival as a free and independent society), and faces only the most indirect of threats (an unlikely daisy-chain scenario disrupting U.S. trade with the entire region). In fact, a far greater threat to American prosperity is posed by the continuing expense of subsidizing the security of tough economic competitors.

The third is more a worthy goal than a vital interest. After all, the international system has never been the peaceful and stable utopia that some see as justifying Washington's scattering defense promises and troop commitments around the globe. Equally important, disorder, when it breaks out, can be exceedingly difficult to quell, especially by a distant power with a plethora of other commitments. Ensuring a "secure world" is simply beyond America's power, as we should have learned in Vietnam at the cost of more than 58,000 lives.

There is also the symbolic role allegedly played by U.S. deployments, which, argues the Department of Defense, proves that "we are engaged and consulting closely with our allies and friends, vigilant to protect our shared interests."[206] However, consultation does not require bases, and vigilance in protecting American interests does not require underwriting what are primarily allied interests. Then there's the supposed symbolism for America. Contends James Kelly, "The entire U.S. strategic mind-set is conditioned by forward deployments. The frontiers of the United States are not at its continental coastline, but far to its east or west. This fact feeds a psychology that is critical, in itself, to successfully balanced economic and political policies."[207] That psychological conditioning, if real—how many Americans actually think of their nation's border being in Korea?—is perverse, since the security of disparate countries in Asia is not as important as that of the West Coast. Somewhat similar is Hisahiko Okazaki's contention that "as long as America wants a world reputation, it can't afford to lose its bases in Japan."[208] If possessing the world's largest and most technologically advanced military and largest and most productive economy won't earn respect for the United States, then nothing will.

Finally, there are the "kitchen-sink" arguments, the intellectual dregs that invariably find their way into government reports. The Pentagon alleges that U.S. force deployments promote "democratic development in Asia, by providing a clear, readily observable example of the American military's apolitical role."[209] (If so, one wonders why it took decades for the ROK's military to get out of politics and stay in its barracks.) Moreover, contends the Department of Defense, through contact with foreign militaries, "we gain insight into, and personal ties with, their societies."[210] However, inserting tens of thousands of young males into foreign societies is not necessarily the best form of cultural contact—witness the tragic rape of a 12-year-old girl by three servicemen in Okinawa. Expanding business and tourist travel seems more likely to achieve the same end with fewer costly side effects.

One study group cited the dispatch of Marines based in Okinawa "during disaster relief operations in Bangladesh" as an example of the value of U.S. bases and forces for adding "to the credibility of America's commitment to regional stability."[211] An Army analyst advocates preserving existing force deployments to "counter terrorism," "counter (illegal) drug actions," "counter pollution," and "provide humanitarian assistance, disaster relief."[212] Those proposed goals demonstrate a fertile mind at work, but not much else. How U.S. soldiers would, say, "counter pollution" is unclear—would they seize Korean (or maybe Chinese) factories that violate environmental regulations and arrest, say, Japanese drivers of automobiles without catalytic converters? If so, we could bring the troops home to perform the same tasks. All of those proposed missions are curious justifications for risking war, spending $40 billion annually, and subsidizing economic competitors.

Conclusion

It is time for Washington to adjust its military deployments throughout East Asia. The hegemonic threat posed by the Soviet

Union appeared to link the security of America with that of such allies as Japan and South Korea. But today, observes Edward Olsen, "that linkage has completely dissipated. America's current alliances with other countries are intended totally to deter attacks *on them* or to fight *their* wars should deterrence fail."[213] During the Cold War, Washington's alliances were at least theoretically built on mutual interest. Today the benefits run almost solely in the direction of the allies. Thus, jettisoning treaties and deployments that commit Washington to fight for the security of allies rather than that of the United States would increase America's security by reducing the likelihood of its involvement in war.

Given the economic growth and political development of states throughout the region, disengagement would not leave Washington's friends militarily naked and helpless. Indeed, America's original deployments were not intended to be permanent. To the contrary, by its own terms, the Mutual Defense Treaty between the United States and the Republic of Korea envisioned replacement of the bilateral alliance with "a more comprehensive and effective system of regional security in the Pacific Area."[214] The United States should work to make such a security regime a reality.

Washington should start by withdrawing from Korea forces that are unnecessary even if America wishes to maintain its defense treaty with more important countries such as Japan. Next the United States should phase out its forces in Japan, while maintaining military cooperation—joint naval exercises, shared intelligence gathering, and base access rights in an emergency. Washington should reject proposals to revive facilities in the Philippines, which had become expensive anachronisms. Washington should also kill off ANZUS, putting the pained compact out of its misery, though again, it should continue cooperative activities, such as intelligence work, that benefit members. The United States should center its reduced force structure around Wake Island, Guam, and Hawaii. That would maintain forces in the Central Pacific and the ability to move farther west if absolutely necessary.[215] At the same time, America should encourage greater regional cooperation where U.S. security interests may be affected, particularly in maintaining open sea lanes, and continue to play an active role in nonconfrontational areas—cultural, economic, diplomatic, and political.[216] However, while the United States should mediate, encourage, facilitate, and observe, it should not see itself as the residual problem solver and enforcer for East Asia.

An American withdrawal would unsettle countries in East Asia, but not as much as it would have 10, 20, or more years ago. Not only has the threat environment changed dramatically, but those states are more able to care for themselves. There is "a growing confidence among the nations of Asia," observes William Clark.[217] Indeed, they have had to begin contemplating life without American troops: it may have taken a volcano to force the issue, but Washington finally relinquished its bases in the Philippines. And everyone concerned—America, the Philippines, and East Asia as a whole—survived the experience unscathed.[218] Concern was probably greater 20 years ago when President Carter proposed withdrawing U.S. ground forces from South Korea, but even then, in a palpably more dangerous time, other East Asian states ultimately accepted the decision with some equanimity.[219]

Were unforeseen circumstances to arise, Washington should act as what Olsen calls "a distant balancer model," intervening with friendly states if necessary to protect vital interests that would otherwise go undefended.[220] But the daisy chain necessary to connect most local and regional complications to vital U.S. interests is long. And we've been down that road before. As Carpenter warns, the Vietnam War proved to be "a classic example" of daisy-chain reasoning "leading to the absurd conclusion that the preservation of a friendly regime in a small Southeast Asian nation (actually, one-half of that nation) was imperative to the United States."[221] At least the daisy chain then led back to a ruthless global hegemonic threat. China, Japan, and Russia aren't adequate substitutes today. There simply is no there there.

Surely, having won World War II does not commit the United States to forever patrol East Asia, guarding nations that prefer to devote their resources to economic development rather than military protection and to avoid dealing with emotions still raw from past Japanese aggression. The military is America's "strong suit," argues James Kelly.[222] Maybe so, but the Cold War left the United States little choice. Washington has fulfilled its duty to contain communism. Americans shouldn't be expected to surrender more dollars and risk more lives to police East Asia for as long as Washington's allies find that convenient.

8. A New Foreign Policy for a Changed World

In the aftermath of World War II, America's interventionist foreign policy appeared to have a purpose: containment of the hegemonic threat posed by the Soviet Union and its satellite allies. Thus, military involvement in distant conflicts, financial aid to assorted brutal dictators, maintenance of an international presence worthy of imperial Rome, and creation of a domestic national security state all seemed to be necessary but temporary departures from America's traditions of individual liberty at home and nonintervention abroad.

Today, however, there is nothing left to contain. The USSR no longer exists; the communist governments that once dominated Central and Eastern Europe have ended up in history's garbage can. In practice, China and Vietnam today pay more attention to Adam Smith than to Karl Marx. Collectivist rhetoric has largely disappeared from the Third World's discourse. The United States now reigns supreme: it possesses the world's largest and most productive economy; most effective and sophisticated military; and a pervasive, even overpowering, culture. Most major countries have embraced democratic capitalism and are on friendly terms with the United States. America's enemies, such as they are, are a handful of dismal, impoverished dictatorships. There is, as it were, a threat vacuum.

In such a world, especially after the expenditure of more than $13 trillion on defense during the Cold War, one would expect Washington to reconsider its security policy. Must the United States continue to spend a quarter of a trillion dollars annually on the military, roughly as much as the rest of the industrialized world combined? Must it continue to deploy hundreds of thousands of soldiers abroad? Must it continue to maintain hundreds of bases and other military installations overseas?

New Rationales for Old Commitments

Successive administrations and Congresses have, without seriously considering the questions, answered yes, yes, yes, forever yes. In the Pacific and East Asia, explains the Defense Department, America's "bilateral commitments remain inviolable, and the end of the Cold War has not diminished their importance."[1] The Pentagon's watchword in Europe also is "now more than ever." Observes the Department of Defense, "With the end of the Cold War, some thought that . . . an American presence would no longer be necessary. But after only a few years, it is clear that American involvement remains essential for European stability."[2] Of course.

And not just involvement—*expanded* involvement. The United States is building security contacts with Singapore and seeking new multilateral ties throughout East Asia, though not at the cost of its bilateral commitments, the Department of Defense hastily assures us. NATO is preparing to grow, with numerous eager candidates for membership: the Czech Republic, Hungary, Poland, Romania, and most of their neighbors. Although the Pentagon admits that the United States has no vital security interests in sub-Saharan Africa, that hasn't stopped it from planning to use "its capabilities and expertise to help create and nurture an 'enabling environment,' which is conducive to democratization, human rights, conflict resolution, and economic and social prosperity" in the region.[3] Some Americans suggest extending security guarantees to the Transcaucasus, and even North Korea, if recent comments by DPRK officials to Selig Harrison of the Carnegie Endowment are to be believed, would like American protection. Such is the lure of getting the globe's most trusted cop to walk yet another beat—at his own expense.

The lack of an enemy would seem to pose a problem for those committed to preserving and extending Cold War institutions. For instance, Colin Powell, when chairman of the Joint Chiefs of Staff, worried that he was left with only Fidel Castro and Kim Il Sung as demon adversaries. But, as public-choice economists would have predicted, the collapse of hegemonic communism, a genuine threat to America, has spurred what Ted Galen Carpenter of the Cato Institute calls a "search for enemies," and thus new justifications for old policies and programs.[4] Indeed, for some people Kim Il Sung—followed by his successor, Kim Jong Il—alone was enough to warrant a military build-up in East Asia. And there is no shortage of candidates for enemy in chief. Germany and Japan, only yesterday considered loyal allies, often have been posited as tomorrow's possible and even likely aggressors. *New York Times* columnist Anthony

Lewis has suggested that Bosnian Serb Gen. Ratko Mladic is an even greater threat than was Joseph Stalin.[5] More widely cited is the generic fear of instability, as if America's future depended on the latest power struggle in, say, Phnom Penh. And then there are the creative masterminds who foresee using military alliances and forces to combat drug smuggling, enhance environmental protection, and promote student exchanges. Indeed, why not turn tanks into book-mobiles? That would simultaneously increase literacy and advance American influence.

The Search for Enemies

The search for enemies is well under way in East Asia. In 1953 the ROK was a wreck—impoverished, war ravaged, and ruled by an unloved autocrat whose belligerence had helped plunge his country into a disastrous war. Without an American security guarantee, South Korea would not have long survived. But four-plus decades later the South is prosperous and democratic, while its adversary is ruled by an autocrat who lacks both charisma and international friends. North Korea talks of avoiding absorption by Seoul, not of conquest. Why, then, are U.S. forces still necessary? Some ROK officials still point north. Hyun Hong-Choo, the South's ambassador to the United States from 1991 to 1993, writes that "American troops remain in South Korea to help deter" the threat from "the last communist bastion of the Cold War."[6]

There is no special gravitational field on the Korean peninsula that prevents those living in the South from constructing a military superior to that possessed by the DPRK. For years South Korea has consciously chosen not to match the North; indeed, ROK defense outlays have been falling as a percentage of the government's budget and the country's gross domestic product. That is a curious way for a nation that is seemingly on the verge of war to act. Yet ROK president Kim Young Sam warned in late 1995, "The last embers of the Cold War still flicker and could burst into the flames of war at any time."[7] His superheated rhetoric notwithstanding, even many South Koreans recognize that the argument that the South needs Washington's help is starting to sound ridiculous—rather like the United States' begging the Europeans for help in defending against Mexico.

That has led to a busy search for new regional threats requiring American attention. It hasn't taken long for Americans and South Koreans alike to find some: China and Japan, obviously, along with the ubiquitous demon of instability. Indeed, it has taken a century, but Seoul seems about to achieve its original objective in opening relations with the United States—finding a distant ally to guarantee its security against its three great-power neighbors.

The United States as Big Brother

South Korea's desire for a friendly big brother is understandable. After all, at different points in its history the peninsula has been dominated or occupied by Japan, China, and Russia.[8] Under pressure from Japan earlier this century, the Korean kingdom turned to America, which it viewed "as a nation having no territorial or political ambitions in Korea and one which could be relied on to check those states who did have."[9] When Japan asserted control over Korea, however, the United States did nothing. Observed President Theodore Roosevelt, "I do not see that any practical action . . . is open to us."[10]

With the passing of the North Korean threat, a worried Seoul is again looking at its geographical position and for that distant ally. As the Ministry of National Defense stated in 1990, "The Korean peninsula is located in a strategically sensitive area where the interests of the four major regional powers—the United States, the Soviet Union, China and Japan—converge."[11] Actually, America is not now and never was a regional power in East Asia on the basis of geography, but that is what the ROK wants Washington to think. In 1994 the ministry opined that U.S. forces "served as a balancing element in the Northeast Asian region."[12] Similarly, President Kim Young Sam told Congress during his trip to America in July 1995 that "to maintain peace in the Korean peninsula and to maintain stability in the Asia-Pacific region, the U.S. force in the Republic of Korea is necessary."[13]

The ROK's desire for continued protection is certainly understandable, even though Seoul can build a military sufficient to make the cost of aggression extremely high for any of its neighbors. But that desire is not a valid basis for U.S. policy. Nicholas Eberstadt of the American Enterprise Institute worries that "Korea will remain in harm's way throughout the foreseeable future." Thus, he contends that "surveying the possibilities for the future, in sum, the case for a continuing American security partnership with Korea would seem to be strong—even if the North Korean threat is removed and a free and peaceful reunification is consummated."[14] What remains strong, however, is the case for the South's desire, not the case for America's satisfying that desire. Without a connection to the threat of hegemonic Soviet communism, South Korea loses its connection to U.S. security, along with the rationale for Washington's maintaining a costly and dangerous military tripwire far from home.

After all, it would be desirable, from America's standpoint, for South Korea to garrison South Florida. Japan could help patrol the Atlantic. German and French forces (perhaps the joint brigade) could guard Alaska. Britain could provide radar and air defense for the continental states. All of those steps would be beneficial, since they would allow Americans to devote more of their resources to economic development. The allies, however, would probably not find the United States' desire for such assistance a persuasive reason for subsidizing America's defense.

Benefits to America

The United States should use the same calculus. At base, policymakers need to ask, does an interventionist foreign policy benefit Americans, the people who will be paying for and dying in any war? As Carpenter argues, "The lives, freedoms, and financial resources of the American people are not—or at least should not be—available for whatever foreign policy objectives suit the whims of the national political leaders."[15] That political elites in this nation enjoy greater influence (and travel opportunities) because of U.S. alliances and troop deployments is not enough. Common people, too, should benefit, and benefit enough to warrant the expense.[16]

That expense, in the case of Korea, and more broadly East Asia, is not negligible. It includes the risk of war in conflicts that no longer endanger America's security. Maintaining the forces necessary to defend the region runs upward of $40 billion annually. As a result, America's defense guarantees put the United States at a severe economic disadvantage when competing against tough trading partners. Moreover, the Mutual Defense Treaty with South Korea is one of many commitments that have forced America to adopt an imperial

185

rather than a republican policy. That imperial policy pervades America's national life, from an outsized military to a secretive national security establishment.

What are we getting in return, if no longer genuine "defense"? One answer is allies. In fact, if the United States wanted, it could have as an ally virtually every nation on earth. Washington could invite Bulgaria, Georgia, Latvia, and Ukraine to join NATO; propose greater military cooperation with Morocco and Macedonia; offer bilateral security guarantees to Vietnam; maybe even indicate a willingness to ensure North Korea's survival. We would have lots more allies.

But what good are allies? Seth Cropsey of the Heritage Foundation states simply, "America still needs allies and could not count on any if it fails to stand by" the ROK.[17] But why does the United States need allies? Alliances are supposed to serve a purpose, and they may have done so when the United States faced the Soviet Union and its satellites. However, America faces no comparable threat today. Certainly cooperation with friendly states remains a useful means of responding to common problems. Maintaining rigid alliances, security guarantees, and troop deployments for the sake of retaining allies is not just costly but dangerous, since the way we prove that we are a loyal ally is by, as Cropsey advocates, intervening in conflicts, even those with no direct impact on U.S. security.

Shed Allies

The United States needs to discard, not add, allies. Explains Edward Olsen of the Naval Postgraduate School,

> Were the United States to shed its unnecessary allies, what is likely to happen? Clearly we would be in no greater danger of an attack than we are today. In fact, the United States would face a greatly reduced risk of war. Virtually all the contemporary warfare contingencies contemplated by the American military establishment are predicated on the United States meeting a commitment to an ally or a regional security pact. Furthermore, without allies the United States would be rid of peacetime pressures to maintain our strategic credibility in their eyes, which permits allies to manipulate American public opinion and policy. In post–Cold War circumstances, there is no reason to endanger American credibility in defense of other countries' interests.[18]

Another reason to preserve America's Cold War military posture, explains the Clinton White House, is to contribute "to regional stability by deterring aggression and adventurism."[19] But it would be dangerous to choose stability as the lodestar for U.S. policy. It may conflict with other important goals, such as democracy (consider Washington's support of the dictatorship in Algeria). It may be irrelevant to American security (who governs Burma just isn't important). It may be impossible to impose from outside, as many nations have found—most recently the Soviet Union in Afghanistan. And it may be better achieved by other states in the affected region, as on the Korean peninsula, in the post–Cold War international environment with multiple centers of power. In the end, the chimera of stability is likely to lead Washington to risk thousands of lives day in and day out, and to spend tens of billions of dollars year after year, in hopes of preventing events that are not only purely speculative but also tangential to U.S. security.

Finally, America's military presence and treaties are supposed to yield a host of other benefits—national credibility, open trading systems, cultural exchange, greater democratization, and the like. Even if those benefits in fact result from U.S. military deployments, and some are quite doubtful, they are at best fringe benefits. They do not justify commitments that are both expensive and dangerous.

Of course, some say that disengagement may be the right policy, but not just yet. One argument is that U.S. cuts in Korea should be used as a "bargaining chip" to gain DPRK arms reductions.[20] Other pundits propose waiting until the nuclear issue is definitively resolved, or the North's communist regime has fallen, or South Korea has matched Pyongyang's military, or rapprochement has occurred between the two Koreas. However, then there will be another plausible reason to hold off another few years. In practice, "not yet" really means "never." The reason for creating the U.S.-Korean alliance has disappeared; the conditions that once warranted its continuation have disappeared. Now the bilateral treaty and troop deployments should also disappear.

And disappear completely. Disengagement must be total—all forces, all guarantees. To do otherwise, following the Carter plan of withdrawal-lite, offers little if any advantage to America. As Georgetown University professor Earl Ravenal explains, such a strategy "promises perpetual involvement but invites recriminations by allies. It is the typical middle position, with all the obvious contradictions of that position and with few earmarks of definitive choice."[21] The end of the Cold War and South Korea's dramatic growth call out for definitive choice.

Such a step would undoubtedly worry many South Koreans. Even Kim Dae Jung, long thought of as the grand radical of Korean politics, states that "Koreans remember all too well what happened in 1950 after the United States unilaterally pulled out its troops without securing peace."[22] Therefore, he urges Washington to remain. But today Seoul is capable of securing its own peace and security.

Doing so probably will entail eventual reunification.[23] There's no doubt that many South Koreans hope for and, indeed, expect a North Korean collapse, but to plan on one would be foolish.[24] Still, the ROK should be prepared for such a contingency, since Romania proved that even the most brutal totalitarian system may actually be so fragile as to be shattered by one good demonstration. Nevertheless, under no circumstances is reunification likely to be easy. The Korean War may have ended more than 40 years ago, but, writes Chongwook Chung, "the wounds inflicted by the war are still fresh and deep and cannot be healed merely by the passage of time."[25] Moreover, 40 years of development under different "social systems," as North Korean officials typically put it, has created another gap that will be difficult to bridge. In that endeavor the two Koreas are essentially on their own. Outside powers may have been able to divide the peninsula, but they can't put it back together again.

There are, of course, risks inherent in American disengagement from Korea and ultimately East Asia. As historian William Stueck observes, the original Korean War was "laden with miscalculation on all sides."[26] But that record is all the more reason to disengage. Mistakes were made between 1945 and 1950, and once they were made the United States had no choice but to fight another war less than five years after the end of World War II. With the end of the Cold War, however, Washington need no longer take on the burden of other nations' mistakes.

South Korea, in turn, would no longer have to help pay for America's mistakes. The ROK should ponder well the price of its continuing security dependence on the United States. Having such an "elder brother"—long Korea's goal—obviously has important advantages. But there are costs as well. First is the frequent negative social impact.

The 1995 subway brawl may have been sensationalized, but it nevertheless illustrated an important cost of dependence. Washington is used to having other nations treat its troops with deference, as occupying heroes; but tens of thousands of young American soldiers are not always going to act like gentlemen respectful of a foreign culture.

Second is the question of the respect accorded the ROK as a nation. "Most people in South Korea are beginning to feel more prestigious and self-confident," says newspaper columnist Kil Jeong Woo. "These kinds of things should be respected by our American friends, not ignored."[27] But they will be ignored so long as the South relies on what amounts to U.S. military charity to guarantee its defense. The United States has never established a security partnership with an equal; Washington believes in being either a big brother or a passing acquaintance. Washington will not treat South Koreans with respect as long as the United States remains the senior partner in a profoundly unequal security relationship. The latest evidence of America's attitude is its reluctance to renegotiate its Status-of-Forces Agreement with the ROK, as it has with Japan, since the ROK pays less base support.

That phenomenon may have consequences beyond simply wounding the ROK's national ego. While Washington is generally benevolent, there is no reason to expect it to put the South's policy objectives before its own. U.S. decisions—to, for instance, impose trade sanctions or launch military strikes against the North because of its nuclear program—could be very costly to Seoul. Moreover, U.S. commitments elsewhere, in the Persion Gulf region, for instance, may reduce the forces available for deployment to the ROK in a crisis.[28] As Ted Galen Carpenter says, "It is not in the best interest of the South Korean people for the ROK to have its national survival in the hands of decisionmakers in Washington."[29]

South Korea's Ministry of National Defense has already acknowledged the importance of developing "a future-oriented defense policy in preparation for the twenty-first century and the post-unification era."[30] As South Korea emerges as a significant international player in economic and political terms, it needs to begin planning to play an equally influential, and independent, military role as well.

In the end, however, only Washington can decide to terminate the Mutual Defense Treaty and return to America's noninterventionist roots, and to do so on the basis of U.S. interests. Seoul, Manila, Singapore, Tokyo, and others in East Asia will probably still want the United States to be prepared to fight to the last American for them. But their wishes should not matter. Washington should risk the lives and wealth of its citizens only when something fundamental is at stake for their own political community. U.S. soldiers' lives are not gambit pawns to be sacrificed in some global chess game.

This argument shouldn't be hard to grasp, but American policy-makers sometimes seem to have trouble seeing fundamental issues clearly. An outsider with nothing at stake can often do better. In this case that someone is Professor Makoto Momoi of Japan's National Defense College, who observed at the time of the controversy over the Carter withdrawal plan, "If I were an American, I would insist on removing the U.S. troops from South Korea. It is unnatural to keep troops in another country forever."[31] He's right—it is unnatural. It is time to bring our troops home.

Notes

Preface

1. Young Namkoong, "Assessment of the North Korean Economy: Status and Prospects," in *US-Korean Relations at a Time of Change* (Seoul: Research Institute for National Unification, 1994), p. 26.

2. Melvyn Krauss, *How NATO Weakens the West* (New York: Simon and Schuster, 1986), pp. 199–200.

3. In fact, my colleague Ted Galen Carpenter has written about both of them in recent years. See Carpenter, *Beyond NATO: Staying Out of Europe's Wars* (Washington: Cato Institute, 1994); and Carpenter, "Paternalism and Dependence: The U.S.-Japanese Security Relationship," Cato Institute Policy Analysis no. 244, November 1, 1995.

Chapter 1

1. Naturally, Pyongyang claims that the ROK started the war. Even some Western revisionist historians have argued that ROK president Syngman Rhee, who had threatened to attack north in order to recover the "lost territories," intentionally provoked the North Korean assault or that some U.S. officials knew of the impending attack and hoped to use it to support their desires for a major military build-up, or both. See, for example, Jon Halliday and Bruce Cumings, *Korea: The Unknown War* (London: Penguin Books, 1990), p. 74; Bruce Cumings, *The Origins of the Korean War: The Roaring of the Cataract* (Princeton, N.J.: Princeton University Press, 1990), pp. 568–621; and I. F. Stone, *The Hidden History of the Korean War: 1950–1951* (1952; Boston: Little, Brown, 1988), pp. 1–13.

2. Rhee, whose name is more accurately rendered as Yi Sing Man, earned a doctorate at Princeton University and was elected president of the Korean Provisional Government by a conference of Korean exiles in Philadelphia in 1919. I will use the Americanized form of his name by which he is widely known.

3. Quoted in Clay Blair, *The Forgotten War: America in Korea, 1950–1953* (New York: Times Books, 1987), p. 465.

4. Steven Rearden, *The Formative Years: 1947–1950* (Washington: Office of the Secretary of Defense, 1984), p. 361.

5. Rosemary Foot, *The Wrong War: American Policy and the Dimensions of the Korean Conflict, 1950–1953* (Ithaca, N.Y.: Cornell University Press, 1985), pp. 40–41.

6. David Callahan, *Dangerous Capabilities: Paul Nitze and the Cold War* (New York: HarperCollins, 1990), p. 100.

7. Rearden, p. 531.

8. See, for example, David McCullough, *Truman* (New York: Simon and Schuster, 1992), p. 773; and Rearden, p. 536.

9. William Stueck, *The Korean War: An International History* (Princeton, N.J.: Princeton University Press, 1995), p. 43. Similar is the assessment of John Lewis Gaddis, "Korea in U.S. Politics, Strategy, and Diplomacy, 1945–50," in *The Origins of the Cold War in Asia*, ed. Yonosuke Nagai and Akira Iriye (New York: Columbia University Press, 1977), p. 290.

191

10. Stueck, p. 43.

11. P. Edward Haley, "The Korean War and United States Strategy," in *The Korean War: 40-Year Perspectives*, ed. Chae-Jin Lee (Claremont, Calif.: Keck Center for International and Strategic Studies, 1991), pp. 36–37.

12. Quoted in Harry Summers, "Pursuit of Peace in the Pacific," *Washington Times*, August 31, 1995, p. A15.

13. For instance, Daryl Plunk, a visiting fellow at the Heritage Foundation, supported a permanent presence of U.S. forces during the question-and-answer period at a Cato Institute conference, "The U.S.–South Korean Alliance: Time for a Change," June 21, 1990.

14. U.S. Department of Defense, *United States Security Strategy for the East Asia–Pacific Region* (Washington: U.S. Department of Defense, February 1995), p. 10.

15. For example, in conversations as early as 1993 Park Hong-Kyoo of the Institute of Foreign Affairs and National Security was dismissing the importance of the threat from North Korea and promoting the role of U.S. forces in deterring Japan.

16. Jeane Kirkpatrick, "A Normal Country in a Normal Time," in *America's Purpose: New Visions of U.S. Foreign Policy*, ed. Owen Harries (San Francisco: ICS Press, 1991), p. 163.

17. See Patrick Tyler, "Pentagon Imagines New Enemies to Fight in Post-Cold-War Era," *New York Times*, February 17, 1992, p. A1.

18. One analyst worries that a succession struggle in the North "could very well spill over into a north-south fight." Thomas W. Robinson, "Post–Cold War Security in the Asia-Pacific Region," in *The Chinese and Their Future: Beijing, Taipei, and Hong Kong*, ed. Zhiling Lin and Thomas W. Robinson (Washington: American Enterprise Institute, 1994), p. 402. Others worry that a combination of famine in the North and political infighting in the South could encourage an attack. John Burton, "Seoul Warns of Military Threat from North Korea," *Financial Times*, November 29, 1995, p. 8; Shim Jae Hoon and Andrew Sherry, "Cutting the Knot," *Far Eastern Economic Review*, November 30, 1995, p. 68; Willis Witter, "War Fears Bubble Up amid Double Trouble," *Washington Times*, December 21, 1995, pp. A1, A17; and Kevin Sullivan, "Food Shortages Fuel Alarm over N. Korea," *Washington Post*, December 23, 1995, p. A11. However, DPRK officials today seem quite realistic about the likely outcome of any war; pervasive hunger and even starvation would make it harder to mount and sustain a successful military operation. Thus, it would be in no faction's interest to initiate a conflict since doing so would almost certainly end in the regime's destruction. Obviously, mistakes and miscalculations could still occur, but the peace should remain secure as long as Seoul avoids the temptation to intervene in any Northern power struggle.

19. International Institute for Strategic Studies, *The Military Balance: 1995–1996* (Oxford: Oxford University Press, 1995), pp. 183–85.

20. Stephen Goose, "The Comparative Military Capabilities of North Korean and South Korean Forces," in *The U.S.–South Korean Alliance: Time for a Change*, ed. Doug Bandow and Ted Galen Carpenter (New Brunswick, N.J.: Transaction, 1992), p. 41.

21. Some still do. In September 1995 radical students demonstrated before the American Center in Kwangju demanding that the U.S. government reveal what it knew of the 1980 crackdown and punish any wrongdoers.

22. See Doug Bandow, "Korea: The Case for Disengagement," Cato Institute Policy Analysis no. 96, December 8, 1987, pp. 6–9, 12–13.

23. For a recent discussion of human rights, or the lack thereof, in the DPRK, see Tae Hwan Ok, "Human Rights Violation in North Korea," *Korean Journal of National Unification* 4 (1995): 187–203.

24. Ted Galen Carpenter, "South Korea: A Vital or Peripheral U.S. Security Interest?" in *The U.S.–South Korean Alliance*, pp. 4, 13.

25. Callum MacDonald, *Korea: The War before Vietnam* (New York: Free Press, 1986), p. 13.

26. Ibid., p. 35; Michael Schaller, *Douglas MacArthur: The Far Eastern General* (New York: Oxford University Press, 1989), p. 163.

27. Joseph Goulden, *Korea: The Untold Story of the War* (New York: McGraw-Hill, 1982), p. 28. One Korean observes that "all these examples indicate that, during the immediate postwar years, the United States did not give strategically high priority to Korea, an attitude reminiscent of the late Yi dynasty period." Soong-Hoom Kil, "Japan in American-Korean Relations," in *Korea and the United States: A Century of Cooperation*, ed. Youngnok Koo and Dae-Sook Suh (Honolulu: University of Hawaii Press, 1984), p. 156.

28. Harry S. Truman, *Years of Trial and Hope: 1946–1952* (New York: Doubleday, 1956), p. 325.

29. Ibid., p. 337.

30. Ibid., pp. 339–40. Dean Acheson took a similar stance, admitting that "this attack did not amount to a *casus belli* against the Soviet Union" but that it was nevertheless "an open, undisguised challenge to our internationally accepted position as the protector of South Korea." Acheson, *Present at the Creation: My Years in the State Department* (New York: Norton, 1969), p. 405. A detailed discussion of the Truman administration's decision to go to war is provided in Glenn Paige, *The Korean Decision: June 24–30, 1950* (New York: Free Press, 1968).

31. MacDonald, pp. 28, 34.

32. See, for example, U.S. Department of Defense, *United States Security Strategy for the East Asia–Pacific Region*, p. 5.

33. Ministry of National Defense, *Defense White Paper: 1989* (Seoul: Republic of Korea, 1990), p. 27.

34. See, for example, Ronald McLaurin, "Security Relations: Burden-Sharing in a Changing Strategic Environment," in *Alliance under Tension: The Evolution of South Korean–U.S. Relations*, ed. Manwoo Lee, Ronald McLaurin, and Chung-in Moon (Boulder, Colo.: Westview, 1988), pp. 171–72; and Sang-Woo Rhee, "The Roots of South Korean Anxiety about National Security," in *Threats to Security in East Asia–Pacific: National and Regional Perspectives*, ed. Charles E. Morrison (Lexington, Mass.: Lexington Books, 1983), p. 76.

Chapter 2

1. For a discussion of America's earliest contacts with Asia and the Open Door policy, see A. Whitney Griswold, *The Far Eastern Policy of the United States* (New York: Harcourt, Brace, 1938); and Ernest May and James Thomson, eds., *American–East Asian Relations: A Survey* (Cambridge, Mass.: Harvard University Press, 1972).

2. Richard O'Connor, *Pacific Destiny: An Informal History of the U.S. in the Far East* (Boston: Little, Brown, 1969), p. 150. Two years later a former interpreter at the U.S. consulate in Shanghai joined a similar expedition. Pyong-Choon Hahm, "The Korean

Perception of the United States," in *Korea and the United States: A Century of Cooperation*, ed. Youngnok Koo and Dae-Sook Suh (Honolulu: University of Hawaii Press, 1984), p. 25.

3. Ibid., p. 26.

4. Ibid., p. 39.

5. Ibid., pp. 32–34; and John Chay, "The American Image of Korea to 1945," in *Korea and the United States*, pp. 64–70.

6. Dae-Sook Suh, "The Centennial: A Brief History," in *Korea and the United States*, p. 7.

7. James Matray, "Korea's Quest for Disarmament and Reunification," in *Korea and the Cold War: Division, Destruction, and Disarmament*, ed. Kim Chull Baum and James Matray (Claremont, Calif.: Regina Books, 1993), p. 234.

8. The entire long, sad tale is detailed in Hilary Conroy, *The Japanese Seizure of Korea, 1868–1910: A Study of Realism and Idealism in International Relations* (Philadelphia: University of Pennsylvania Press, 1960).

9. Dae-Sook Suh, p. 8. See also David Kwang-Sun Suh, "American Missionaries and a Hundred Years of Korean Protestantism," in *Korea and the United States*, pp. 319–49.

10. See James Matray, *The Reluctant Crusade: American Foreign Policy in Korea, 1941–1950* (Honolulu: University of Hawaii Press, 1985), pp. 7–19.

11. Robert Slusser, "Soviet Far Eastern Policy, 1945–50: Stalin's Goals in Korea," in *The Origins of the Cold War in Asia*, ed. Yonosuke Nagai and Akira Iriye (New York: Columbia University Press, 1977), pp. 133–36.

12. As Army historian James Schnabel notes, "The 38th Parallel cut more than 75 streams and 12 rivers, intersected many high ridges at variant angles, severed 181 small cart roads, 104 country roads, 15 provincial all-weather roads, 8 better-class highways, and 6 north-south rail lines." Schnabel, *Policy and Direction: The First Year* (Washington: U.S. Army, 1972), p. 11.

13. Dae-Sook Suh, p. 10.

14. The saga of the stillborn trusteeship is described in Matray, *The Reluctant Crusade*, pp. 52–124.

15. There is some controversy over how quickly the United States embraced Rhee. For instance, Matray argues that "administration officials, at least in Washington, honestly attempted to prevent a political triumph for Rhee during the first two years of the occupation." Matray, *The Reluctant Crusade*, p. 161. Compare the views of former State Department official Edward Olsen. Olsen, "South Korea under Military Rule: Friendly Tyrant?" in *Friendly Tyrants: An American Dilemma*, ed. Daniel Pipes and Adam Garfinkle (New York: St. Martin's, 1991), pp. 333–34. In any case, there is no doubt that Washington did eventually abandon its professed commitment to democracy.

Rhee deserves credit for his tireless fight for Korean independence. However, his reputation is stained by his suppression of democratic opponents and murder of political prisoners. Indeed, his regime slaughtered tens of thousands of people before the arrival of the advancing DPRK forces. See, for example, Callum MacDonald, *Korea: The War before Vietnam* (New York: Free Press, 1986), pp. 41–42.

16. Olsen, "South Korea under Military Rule," p. 332.

17. This may seem harsh, since U.S. policymakers undoubtedly did want the ROK to be free and democratic. But they had trouble conceiving of such a nation with a left-wing political orientation, and America's occupation policy left much to be

desired. See, for example, MacDonald, pp. 11–13; William Stueck, *The Korean War: An International History* (Princeton, N.J.: Princeton University Press, 1995), pp. 20–27; and Matray, *The Reluctant Crusade*, pp. 75–98.

18. Edward Olsen, *U.S. Policy and the Two Koreas* (Boulder, Colo.: Westview, 1988), p. 2. See also Selig Harrison, *The Widening Gulf: Asian Nationalism and American Policy* (New York: Free Press, 1978), pp. 237–44.

19. Hahm, p. 42.

20. For more information on the development of both Koreas, see Ralph Clough, *Embattled Korea: The Rivalry for International Support* (Boulder, Colo.: Westview, 1987); and Young Whan Kihl, *Politics and Policies in Divided Korea: Regimes in Contrast* (Boulder, Colo.: Westview, 1984).

21. MacDonald, p. 15. See also Okonogi Masao, "The Domestic Roots of the Korean War," in *The Origins of the Cold War in Asia*, pp. 299–320.

22. For a discussion of America's departure, see Kim Chull Baum, "U.S. Policy on the Eve of the Korean War: Abandonment or Safeguard?" in *Korea and the Cold War*, pp. 63–94.

23. Joint Chiefs of Staff, Memorandum, June 23, 1949, JCS 1483/74, RG 218, Box 25, Modern Military Records, National Archives, Washington.

24. For recent exculpations of Acheson, see John Merrill, "The Origins of the Korean War: Unanswered Questions," in *Korea and the Cold War*, pp. 106–7; and Philip Geyelin, "Don't Blame Acheson," *Washington Post*, August 8, 1995, p. A19.

25. Symptomatic of such overconfidence was a book, published in 1950 and written before the North's invasion in June of that year, that declared that "in a military sense the North Korea regime was undoubtedly the stronger at the outset, but it was rapidly being overtaken by the South Korean government." George McCune and Arthur Grey, *Korea Today* (Cambridge, Mass.: Harvard University Press, 1950), p. 266.

26. Matray, *The Reluctant Crusade*, p. 233.

27. Stueck, *The Korean War*, p. 11.

28. Although the Rhee regime was not without some blame for raising tensions on the peninsula before the war, there is no serious doubt that Kim Il Sung was the aggressor. See, for example, Merrill, "The Origins of the Korean War," pp. 95–100, 107–8. Why Kim chose June 25 to strike is still not clear. Speculations include the failure of DPRK guerrillas to topple Rhee, domestic political pressure on Kim, and an impending visit to South Korea by John Foster Dulles. MacDonald, pp. 27–28; and A. James Gregor and Maria Hsia Chang, *The Iron Triangle: A U.S. Security Policy for Northeast Asia* (Stanford, Calif.: Hoover Institution, 1984), p. 69. One of the most detailed looks at the start of the conflict is provided by John Merrill, *Korea: The Peninsular Origins of the War* (Newark: University of Delaware Press, 1989).

29. Glenn Paige, *The Korean Decision: June 24–30, 1950* (New York: Free Press, 1968), p. 132. See also Matray, *The Reluctant Crusade*, pp. 236–37; and Rosemary Foot, *The Wrong War: American Policy and the Dimensions of the Korean Conflict, 1950–1953* (Ithaca, N.Y.: Cornell University Press, 1985), pp. 58–62.

30. The roles of China and Russia have been much debated; archival material unearthed since the end of the Cold War has proved to be particularly illuminating. See, for example, Stueck, *The Korean War*, pp. 31–41; Merrill, "The Origins of the Korean War," pp. 95–109; and William Stueck, "The Soviet Union and the Origins of the Korean War," in *Korea and the Cold War*, pp. 111–24; Kathryn Weathersby, "Korea, 1949–50," Woodrow Wilson International Center for Scholars *Bulletin*, issue 5 (Spring 1995): 1, 2–9; Kim Hakjoon, "Russian Foreign Ministry Documents on the

Origins of the Korean War," Paper presented to Korea Society conference, "The Korean War: An Assessment of the Historical Record," Washington, July 24–25, 1995; Kim Chull-Baum, "A Triangle of Kim, Stalin, and Mao in the Korean War," Paper presented at "The Korean War: An Assessment of the Historical Record"; and Evgueni Bajanov, "Assessing the Politics of the Korean War," Paper presented at "The Korean War: An Assessment of the Historical Record."

31. See Natalia Bajanova, "Assessing the Conclusion and Outcome of the Korean War," Paper presented at "The Korean War: An Assessment of the Historical Record."

32. People who are interested in the details of the conflict have never quite "forgotten" the war, despite its nickname. For instance, see Stueck *The Korean War;* John Toland, *In Mortal Combat: Korea, 1950–1953* (New York: Morrow, 1991); Doris Condit, *The Test of War: 1950–1953* (Washington: U.S. Department of Defense, 1988); Clay Blair, *The Forgotten War: America in Korea, 1950–1953* (New York: Times Books, 1987); Max Hastings, *The Korean War* (New York: Simon and Schuster, 1987); MacDonald; and T. R. Fehrenbach, *This Kind of War: A Study in Unpreparedness* (New York: Macmillan, 1963). A shorter, more policy-oriented discussion is provided by Foot.

33. Blair, p. 336.

34. See, for example, Toland, pp. 233–54; Blair, pp. 336–72; MacDonald, pp. 51–67; and Stueck, *The Korean War*, pp. 93–126.

35. Exactly why China intervened is important and interesting but not terribly relevant to policy today. For more information on that issue, see, for example, Stueck, *The Korean War*, pp. 85–126; Chen Jian, *China's Road to the Korean War: The Making of the Sino-American Confrontation* (New York: Columbia University Press, 1994); Edwin Hoyt, *The Day the Chinese Attacked: Korea, 1950* (New York: McGraw-Hill, 1990); Russell Spurr, *Enter the Dragon: China's Undeclared War against the U.S. in Korea, 1950–51* (New York: Newmarket, 1988); Allen S. Whiting, *China Crosses the Yalu: The Decision to Enter the Korean War* (Stanford, Calif.: Stanford University Press, 1968); Zhai Zhihai, "China's Decision to Enter the Korean War: History Revisited," in *Korea and the Cold War*, pp. 141–66; and Zhang Xi, "Peng Dehuai and China's Entry into the Korean War," *Chinese Historians* 6, no. 1 (Spring 1993): 1–29. Newly released documents continue to illuminate the Chinese decisionmaking process. See, for example, Walter Pincus, "Papers Show Mao Wary of Korean War," *Washington Post,* December 20, 1995, pp. D28, D29.

36. L'affaire MacArthur has generated an enormous amount of ink. A concise and persuasive critique of the general and his role is provided by Michael Schaller, "Douglas MacArthur: The China Issue, Policy Conflict, and the Korean War," in *Korea and the Cold War*, pp. 167–91.

37. Blair, p. 973.

38. The conflict between the ROK and the United States is explored in Ohn Chang-il, "South Korea, the United States, and the Korean Armistice Negotiations," in *Korea and the Cold War*, pp. 209–29; and Stueck, *The Korean War*, pp. 210–15, 320–25, 330–39.

39. Barton Bernstein, "Dubious Venture," *Inquiry,* June 1982, p. 44; and Council of Economic Advisers, *Economic Report to the President* (Washington: Government Printing Office, 1987), p. 244.

40. See, for example, J. Y. Ra, "The Politics of Conference: The Political Conference at Geneva, April 26–June 15, 1954," Paper presented at "The Korean War: An Assessment of the Historical Record."

41. For more details on the armistice system, see Ministry of National Defense, *Defense White Paper: 1989* (Seoul: Republic of Korea, 1990), pp. 86–94.

42. Youngnok Koo, "The First Hundred Years and Beyond," in *Korea and the United States*, p. 359.

43. Ibid., p. 360. The difficult negotiations are covered by Ohn Chang-il, "South Korea, the United States, and the Korean Armistice Negotiations," in *Korea and the Cold War*, pp. 223–29.

44. Dae-Sook Suh, p. 12.

45. For a detailed look at the collapse of the Rhee regime, see Quee-Young Kim, *The Fall of Syngman Rhee* (Berkeley, Calif.: Institute of East Asian Studies, 1983). A broader look at opposition to Rhee can be found in Chi-Young Pak, *Political Opposition in Korea, 1945–1960* (Seoul: Seoul National University Press, 1980).

46. America's ambivalence is discussed in Olsen, "South Korea under Military Rule," pp. 336–37.

47. John Spanier, *American Foreign Policy since World War II*, 7th ed. (New York: Praeger, 1977), p. 212.

48. Young-Sun Ha, "American-Korean Military Relations: Continuity and Change," in *Korea and the United States*, p. 119.

49. Quoted in Koo, p. 361.

50. Astri Suhrke and Charles Morrison, "Carter and Korea: The Difficulties of Disengagement," *World Today*, October 1977, p. 371.

51. Manwoo Lee, "Double Patronage toward South Korea: Security vs. Democracy and Human Rights," in *Alliance under Tension: The Evolution of South Korean–U.S. Relations*, ed. Manwoo Lee, Ronald McLaurin, and Chung-in Moon (Boulder, Colo.: Westview, 1988), pp. 35–36.

52. Quoted in Ralph Clough, *Deterrence and Defense in Korea: The Role of U.S. Forces* (Washington: Brookings Institution, 1976), p. 3.

53. Dae-Sook Suh, pp. 15–16.

54. Quoted in "Should U.S. Withdraw Troops from Korea?" *U.S. News & World Report*, June 20, 1977, p. 27.

55. Olsen, *U.S. Policy and the Two Koreas*, p. 12.

56. Lee, p. 29. See also Olsen, "South Korea under Military Rule," pp. 339–40.

57. "Weinberger Assures South Koreans 40,000 U.S. Troops Will Not Pull Out," *Washington Times*, April 3, 1986, p. A6.

58. See, for example, A. James Gregor and Maria Hsia Chang, *The Iron Triangle: A U.S. Security Policy for Northeast Asia* (Stanford, Calif.: Hoover Institution Press, 1984), pp. 69–70.

59. Those and other instances are discussed in Manwoo Lee, "Anti-Americanism and South Korea's Changing Perception of America," in *Alliance under Tension*, pp. 7–27, 221–23; and Kim Kyong-Dong, "Korean Perceptions of America," in *Korea Briefing, 1993: Festival of Korea*, ed. Donald Clark (Boulder, Colo.: Westview, 1993), pp. 172–74.

60. Lee, "Double Patronage toward South Korea," pp. 43–44.

61. See, for instance, Nicholas Kristof, "Subway Brawl Inflames Issue of G.I.'s in Korea," *New York Times*, August 24, 1995, p. A3.

62. Steve Glain, "For South Korea Firms, Speaking Too Freely May Carry Steep Price," *Wall Street Journal*, August 18, 1995, pp. A1, A6.

63. Nicholas Eberstadt, *Korea Approaches Reunification* (Armonk, N.Y.: M. E. Sharpe, 1995), pp. 158–61.

64. Quoted in Chae-Jin Lee, "U.S. Policy toward South Korea," in *Korea Briefing, 1993*, p. 59.

65. U.S. Department of Defense, *United States Security Strategy for the East Asia–Pacific Region* (Washington: U.S. Department of Defense, February 1995), p. 10.

66. Eui-Young Yu, "Korean Communities in the United States," in *Korea and the United States*, p. 288. A detailed look at this community is provided by Eui-Young Yu, "The Korean American Community," in *Korea Briefing, 1993*, pp. 139–62.

67. For a discussion of the role of American-educated Koreans, see Dong Suh Bark, "The American-Educated Elite in Korean Society," in *Korea and the United States*, pp. 263–80.

68. Gus Constantine, "Only South Koreans over 40 Favor U.S. Troops," *Washington Times*, November 22, 1995, p. A11.

Chapter 3

1. U.S. Department of Defense, *United States Security Strategy for the East Asia–Pacific Region* (Washington: U.S. Department of Defense, February 1995), p. 10. Cited hereinafter as *United States Security Strategy*.

2. Ibid.

3. U.S. Department of State, *U.S. Treaties and Other International Agreements*, vol. 5, part 3 (Washington: Government Printing Office, 1956), pp. 2372–73.

4. *United States Security Strategy*, p. 26. A detailed breakdown of the units is provided by the International Institute for Strategic Studies, *The Military Balance: 1995–1996* (Oxford: Oxford University Press, 1995), pp. 30–31.

5. Earl Ravenal, *Designing Defense for a New World Order: The Military Budget in 1992 and Beyond* (Washington: Cato Institute, 1991), p. 2. Although the post–Cold War drawdown has reduced U.S. forces in Europe by about two-thirds, it has left East Asia's deployments relatively untouched. For instance, total personnel in Korea edged down only from 41,800 in 1991 to 36,250 in 1994. Over the same period, total forces in Japan remained essentially static, going from 45,100 to 44,800. International Institute for Strategic Studies, *The Military Balance 1991–1992* (London: Brassey's, 1991), p. 27; and International Institute for Strategic Studies, *The Military Balance 1994–1995*, p. 32.

6. Quoted in Stephen Goose, "The Military Situation on the Korean Peninsula," in *Two Koreas—One Future?* ed. John Sullian and Roberta Foss (Lanham, Md.: University Press of America, 1987), p. 82.

7. As noted in chapter 2, the price paid by Koreans, both South and North, was much greater.

8. See, for example, Robert Hall and Ian Kemp, eds., "North Korea: The Final Act," *Jane's Intelligence Review*, Special Report no. 2 (1994), pp. 21–24; Bruce Bennett, "The Prospects for Conventional Conflict on the Korean Peninsula," *Korean Journal of Defense Analysis* 7, no. 1 (Summer 1995): 95–127; "Seoul Is Confident: North Couldn't Win," *International Herald Tribune*, March 29, 1994, p. 4; William Taylor, "Heading Off a Korea Showdown," *Washington Post*, November 21, 1993, p. A29; and Eugene Carroll, "Overstating the Danger of North Korea," *Washington Post*, April 22, 1994, p. A25.

For a contrary view, see Robert Gaskin, "Faulty Assessment of the Dangers," *Washington Times*, November 30, 1993, p. A15.

9. Melvyn Krauss, *How NATO Weakens the West* (New York: Simon and Schuster, 1986), p. 189. For similar sentiments, see Franklin Weinstein, "The U.S. Role in East and Southeast Asia," in *A U.S. Foreign Policy for Asia: The 1980s and Beyond,* ed. Ramon Myers (Stanford, Calif.: Hoover Institution Press, 1982); and the comments of Selig Harrison of the Carnegie Endowment in Franklin Weinstein and Fuji Kamiya, eds., *The Security of Korea: U.S. and Japanese Perspectives on the 1980s* (Boulder, Colo.: Westview, 1980), p. 72.

10. Ibid.

11. Quoted in Doug Bandow, "Seoul Long," *American Spectator,* November 1990, p. 35.

12. Even a decade ago an overwhelming majority of Koreans were demanding a more equal security partnership. Youngnok Koo, "The First Hundred Years and Beyond," in *Korea and the United States: A Century of Cooperation,* ed. Youngnok Koo and Dae-Sook Suh (Honolulu: University of Hawaii Press, 1984), p. 368. Later polls found that large numbers of Koreans believed America had taken advantage of its dominant role in the alliance. Kim Kyong-Dong, "Korean Perceptions of America," in *Korea Briefing, 1993: Festival of Korea,* ed. Donald Clark (Boulder, Colo.: Westview, 1993), p. 181.

13. Quoted in Weinstein and Kamiya, p. 84.

14. See Ted Galen Carpenter, *A Search for Enemies: America's Alliances after the Cold War* (Lexington, Mass.: Lexington Books, 1992), p. 86.

15. Krauss, p. 188.

16. Stephen Goose, "U.S. Forces in Korea: Assessing a Reduction," in *Collective Defense or Strategic Independence? Alternative Strategies for the Future,* ed. Ted Galen Carpenter (Washington: Cato Institute, 1989), p. 88.

Up through 1986 the United States also provided Seoul with hundreds of millions of dollars in grants and loans annually for its defense, with a cumulative total of over $15 billion. Ministry of National Defense, *Defense of Korea: 1991–1992* (Seoul: Republic of Korea, 1992), p. 50; and International Institute for Strategic Studies, *The Military Balance: 1988–1989* (London: International Institute for Strategic Studies, 1988), p. 223. The role of American military aid is discussed in Young-Sun Ha, "American-Korean Military Relations: Continuity and Change," in *Korea and the United States,* pp. 117–20.

17. Quoted in Goose, p. 89.

18. *United States Security Strategy,* p. 28. See also the cost breakdown in Ministry of National Defense, *Defense White Paper: 1990* (Seoul: Republic of Korea, 1991), p. 144.

19. Ministry of National Defense, *Defense White Paper: 1989* (Seoul: Republic of Korea, 1990), p. 130.

20. Compare Ted Galen Carpenter and Rosemary Fiscarelli, "Defending America in the 1990s: A Budget for Strategic Independence," in *America's Peace Dividend: Income Tax Reductions from the New Strategic Realities* (Washington: Cato Institute, 1990), pp. 46–48, with Earl Ravenal, *Defining Defense: The 1985 Military Budget* (Washington: Cato Institute, 1984), p. 16. I have adjusted both sets of numbers to 1996 dollars. Obviously, these sorts of computations are not precise, but the figures demonstrate the magnitude of the cost.

21. Earl Ravenal, "The Way Out of Korea," *Inquiry,* December 5, 1977. p. 16. The Defense Department has denied that there are any units outside the ROK "whose primary mission is reinforcement in Korea," but that department simultaneously conceded that there are "several units, all of which are assigned responsibilities in

other areas of the world, which have a potential secondary mission of reinforcement in Korea." U.S. Department of Defense, "Report to Congress on the Military Situation on the Korean Peninsula," February 1987, p. 8.

22. Earl Ravenal, *Designing Defense for a New World Order*, p. 51. That estimate is comparable to later ones by Ted Galen Carpenter of Cato and by the Center for Defense Information. See, for example, Carpenter, "The Case for U.S. Strategic Independence," Cato Institute Foreign Policy Briefing no. 16, January 16, 1992, p. 1; and Center for Defense Information, "The U.S. as the World's Policeman? Ten Reasons to Find a Different Role," *Defense Monitor* 20, no. 1 (1991): 3. Back in 1984, Ravenal's estimate was higher. He figured that of the $305 billion defense authorization requested in fiscal year 1985, $47 billion was designated for eastern Asia. Ravenal, *Defining Defense*, p. 16.

23. Ravenal, "The Way Out of Korea," p. 16.

24. Callum MacDonald, *Korea: The War before Vietnam* (New York: Free Press, 1986), pp. 13–14.

25. Ibid., pp. 41, 60.

26. "Banner Battle Rouses Crowd at Seoul Rally," *Washington Post*, July 19, 1987, p. A18.

27. Quoted in Selig Harrison, "Dateline South Korea: A Divided Seoul," *Foreign Policy*, no. 67 (Summer 1987): 157. Also quoted in Jinwung Kim, "Recent Anti-Americanism in South Korea: The Causes," *Asian Survey* 29, no. 8 (August 1989): 755.

28. Linda Lewis, "The 'Kwangju Incident' Observed: An Anthropological Perspective on Civil Uprisings," in *The Kwangju Uprising: Shadows over the Regime in South Korea*, ed. Donald Clark (Boulder, Colo.: Westview, 1988), p. 23.

29. Sanford Ungar, "South Korea: Old Ally, New Competitor," *Atlantic Monthly*, December 1983, p. 23. The issue still rankles many South Koreans. See Chungmoo Choi and Eun Meekim, "U.S. Must Face Role in South Korean Scandal," letter to the editor, *New York Times*, January 14, 1996, p. 12E.

30. Washington's encouragement was due primarily to the efforts of Gaston Sigur, then assistant secretary of state for East Asia. See Sigur, "A Historical Perspective on U.S.-Korean Relations and the Development of Korean Democracy: 1987–1992," in *Democracy in Korea: The Roh Tae Woo Years*, ed. Christopher Sigur (New York: Carnegie Council on Ethics and International Affairs, 1992), pp. 8–17.

31. Edward Olsen, "South Korea under Military Rule: Friendly Fascism?" in *Friendly Tyrants: An American Dilemma*, ed. Daniel Pipes and Adam Garfinkle (New York: St. Martin's, 1991), p. 340. Stephen Gilbert of Georgetown University contends that it is "likely that in the absence of American troops President Chun's government would not have agreed to the election of his successor in the fall of 1987 nor would he have relinquished his post to Roh Tae-Woo in February 1988." Gilbert, "Approaching the Pacific Century," in *Security in Northeast Asia: Approaching the Pacific Century*, ed. Stephen Gilbert (Boulder, Colo.: Westview,, 1988), p. 182. Yet it was South Korean protests that made the continuation of military rule untenable. Unless it threatened to withdraw its forces—and it had at least tolerated every previous dictator—Washington had precious little leverage.

32. James Matray, "Korea's Quest for Disarmament and Reunification," in *Korea and the Cold War: Division, Destruction, and Disarmament*, ed. Kim Chull Baum and James Matray (Claremont, Calif.: Regina Books, 1993), p. 237. More generally, see Jinwung Kim, pp. 749–63; and Donald Clark, "Bitter Friendship: Understanding Anti-Americanism in South Korea," in *Korea Briefing, 1991*, ed. Donald Clark (Boulder, Colo.: Westview, 1991), pp. 147–67.

33. That was not the first time that crimes committed by American servicemen created pressure for revising the SOFA. Jinwung Kim, pp. 756–58.

34. On the media, see, for example, Jim Lea, "High DOD Aide Assails ROK Press," *Pacific Stars & Stripes*, September 8, 1995, p. 1.

35. Quoted in Nicholas Kristof, "Subway Brawl Inflames Issue of G.I.'s in Korea," *New York Times*, August 24, 1995, p. A3. See also Kevin Sullivan and Mary Jordan, "S. Korea Wants to Be Grown-Up Ally," *Washington Post*, October 19, 1995, pp. A31, A33.

36. Jack Anderson and Michael Binstein, "Korean Press Distorts 'Crime' by GIs," *Washington Post*, August 31, 1995, p. B23.

37. Quoted in Kristof.

38. See, for example, accounts of anti-American student demonstrations in Seoul, Kwangju, and elsewhere in Foreign Broadcast Information Service, *Daily Report: East Asia*, September 27, 1995, pp. 54–55.

39. Manwoo Lee, "Anti-Americanism and South Korea's Changing Perception of America," in *Alliance under Tension: The Evolution of South Korean–U.S. Relations*, ed. Manwoo Lee, Ronald McLaurin, and Chung-in Moon (Boulder, Colo.: Westview, 1988), p. 26.

40. Kim Kyong-Dong, p. 177.

41. See, for example, Jack Anderson and Dale Van Atta, "Arab Americans: Suspects without Probable Cause," *Washington Post*, January 27, 1991, p. C7.

42. See, for example, Morton Halperin and Jeanne Woods, "Ending the Cold War at Home," *Foreign Policy* (Winter 1990–91): 128–43.

43. Burton Yale Pines, "Ten Principles of a Conservative Foreign Policy," Heritage Talking Points, Heritage Foundation, 1991, p. 3.

44. Arthur Burns, "The Defense Sector: An Evaluation of Its Economic and Social Impact," in *The War Economy of the United States: Readings in Military Industry and Economy*, ed. Seymour Melman (New York: St. Martin's, 1971), pp. 115–21.

45. Robert Higgs, *Crisis and Leviathan: Critical Episodes in the Growth of American Government* (New York: Oxford University Press, 1987), pp. 235–36.

46. See Doug Bandow, "The Persian Gulf: Restoring the Congressional War Power," in *America Entangled: The Persian Gulf Crisis and Its Consequences*, ed. Ted Galen Carpenter (Washington: Cato Institute, 1991), pp. 97–103.

47. See, for example, Doug Bandow, ". . . But Congressional Voodoo Turns Doves into Hawks," *Wall Street Journal*, September 15, 1995, p. A14; Doug Bandow, "Who Has the Power to Take Us to War?" *Washington Times*, September 13, 1995, p. A17; and Doug Bandow, "Another Crisis of Presidential War-Making," *Los Angeles Times*, July 7, 1994, p. A11.

48. See, for example, Peter Lewis, "Technology," *New York Times*, September 11, 1995, p. D7; Robert Holleyman, president, Business Software Alliance, "The Export of Software with Encryption Capabilities," September 6, 1995; Sheldon Richman, "In the Cybersnoop Age," *Washington Times*, April 18, 1995, p. A17; Rebecca Gould, director of policy, Business Software Alliance, Testimony before the Committee to Study National Cryptography Policy, National Research Council, April 12, 1995; and Frost & Sullivan Market Intelligence, "The Demand for Information Security and Encryption in Fortune 500 Companies in the United States," October 1, 1993.

49. Quoted in "The U.S. as the World's Policeman? Ten Reasons to Find a Different Role," *Defense Monitor* 20, no. 1 (1991): p. 2.

50. Quoted in George Will, "Worthy of Contempt," *Washington Post*, August 3, 1995, p. A31.

51. Ted Galen Carpenter, "The Military Budget," in *The Cato Handbook for Congress: 104th Congress* (Washington: Cato Institute, 1995), pp. 99–105. See also Carpenter and Fiscarelli, pp. 7–54. Obviously, there is no consensus on exactly what would be necessary for a defense budget genuinely limited to America's defense; the Center for Defense Information proposes steady-state military outlays of $175 billion starting in 1999, about $10 billion more than suggested by Carpenter. Center for Defense Information, "A Post–Cold War Military Force," *Defense Monitor* 24, no. 3 (1995). For an earlier proposal, see Center for Defense Information, "Defending America: A Force Structure for 1995," February 28, 1992. For other alternatives, see Philip Morrison et al., "The Future of American Defense," *Scientific American*, February 1994, pp. 38–45; Jeffrey Gerlach, "Pentagon Myths and Global Realities: The 1993 Military Budget," Cato Institute Policy Analysis no. 171, May 24, 1992, p. 18; and Center for Defense Information, "Defending America: CDI Options for Military Spending," *Defense Monitor* 21, no. 4 (1992). All of those proposals, despite their differences, offer a dramatic alternative to the Pentagon's proto–Cold War plans.

52. See, for example, Baker Spring, "Clinton's Bankrupt National Security Strategy," Heritage Foundation Backgrounder no. 1000, September 27, 1994, along with the slightly hysterical Baker Spring, "Budget Cuts Could Spell End of American Global Power," Heritage Foundation Backgrounder Update no. 258, August 1, 1995.

53. See Center for Defense Information, "A Post–Cold War Military Force"; Center for Defense Information, "Far Flung Frontiers of Security," *Defense Monitor* 24, no. 1 (1995); and David Isenberg, "The Pentagon's Fraudulent Bottom-Up Review," Cato Institute Policy Analysis no. 206, April 21, 1994.

54. Paul Kennedy, *The Rise and Fall of the Great Powers: Economic Change and Military Conflict from 1500 to 2000* (New York: Random House, 1987), p. 517.

55. Quoted in "Overheard," *Newsweek*, April 22, 1991, p. 19.

56. Robert Higgs, "The Cold War Economy: Opportunity Costs, Ideology, and the Politics of Crisis," *Exploration in Economic History* 31 (1994): 283–312. See also Robert Higgs, "U.S. Military Spending in the Cold War Era: Opportunity Costs, Foreign Crises, and Domestic Constraints," Cato Institute Policy Analysis no. 114, November 30, 1988.

57. Lloyd Jeffry Dumas, *The Overburdened Economy: Uncovering the Causes of Chronic Unemployment, Inflation, and National Decline* (Berkeley: University of California Press, 1986), p. 208.

58. David Mowery and Nathan Rosenberg, *Technology and the Pursuit of Economic Growth* (New York: Cambridge University Press, 1989), p. 123.

59. Oddly, the most recent boosters of military spending as a means of creating jobs have been conservatives, who otherwise deplore Keynsian economics and the idea that government outlays do anything except rearrange output and employment. For comments by Defense Secretary Caspar Weinberger and others, see Robert DeGrasse, *Military Expansion, Economic Decline: The Impact of Military Spending on U.S. Economic Performance* (Armonk, N.Y.: M. E. Sharpe, 1983), pp. 1–3. However, the myth also has long had some support on the left. See, for example, Sidney Lens, *Poverty: America's Enduring Paradox* (New York: Crowell, 1969), pp. 296–97.

60. Robert Higgs, "Wartime Prosperity? A Reassessment of the U.S. Economy in the 1940s," *Journal of Economic History* 52, no. 1 (March 1992): 56.

61. Center for Defense Information, "Reduce Military Spending: Create More Jobs," *Defense Monitor* 23, no. 6 (1994): 6.

62. For a detailed look at the impact on particular states and localities, see Congressional Budget Office, *The Economic Effects of Reduced Defense Spending* (Washington: Congressional Budget Office, February 1992), pp. 21–42. Transition assistance is covered in Murray Weidenbaum, *Small Wars, Big Defense: Paying for the Military after the Cold War* (New York: Oxford University Press, 1992), pp. 75–88.

63. Robert DeGrasse et al., *The Costs and Consequences of Reagan's Military Build-Up* (New York: Council on Economic Priorities, 1982), p. 24.

64. Congressional Budget Office, p. ix.

65. William A. Niskanen, "Fiscal Effects on U.S. Economic Growth," Paper presented at the Milken Institute's conference, "Economic Policy, Financial Markets, and Economic Growth," Santa Monica, California, October 22–23, 1992, p. 19.

66. See, for example, Jules Backman, *The Economics of Armament Inflation* (New York: Rinehart, 1951); Terence McCarthy, "What the Vietnam War Has Cost," in *The War Economy of the United States*, pp. 160–69; and Seymour Melman, *The Permanent War Economy: American Capitalism in Decline* (New York: Touchstone, 1985), pp. 69–70.

67. William Leonard Crum et al., *Fiscal Planning for Total War* (New York: National Bureau of Economic Research, 1942), p. 127.

68. DeGrasse, pp. 12–15.

69. Dumas, p. 208. Similar language is used by Melman, *The Permanent War Economy*, pp. 62–64.

70. Dumas, p. 221.

71. Bruce Russett, "The Price of War," in *The War Economy of the United States*, p. 156. One estimate of total lost production between 1946 and 1973 alone is $1.9 trillion. Melman, *The Permanent War Economy*, p. 67. See also Glenn Pascall and Robert Lamson, *Beyond Guns and Butter: Recapturing America; Economic Momentum after a Military Decade* (Washington: Brassey's, 1991), pp. 33–40.

72. DeGrasse et al., p. 16.

73. Mowery and Rosenberg, p. 209. See also Pascall and Lamson, pp. 42–46.

74. Amitai Etzioni, "Federal Science, an Economic Drag, Not Propellent," in *The War Economy of the United States*, p. 133. See also DeGrasse et al., p. 21; and Dumas, p. 214.

75. DeGrasse, pp. 80–83; and Dumas, pp. 215–16.

76. Weidenbaum, p. 90. For an even more detailed look at Washington's failed semiconductor research record, see Mowery and Rosenberg, pp. 144–46; and DeGrasse, pp. 84–94.

77. Mowery and Rosenberg, p. 129. See also Pascall and Lamson, pp. 62–68.

78. Albert Teich et al., *Interim Report on Congressional Appropriations for R&D in FY 1996* (Washington: American Association for the Advancement of Science, 1995), p. v.

79. Projects such as the supercollider, canceled in 1994, have generated support as much for reasons of pork as of science. And whatever their abstract scientific interest, they are hardly essential to the nation's economic or scientific health. Other federal projects, such as the Department of Energy's venture into synthetic fuels, have turned out be complete wastes as well as pork. Weidenbaum, p. 98. A broader look at the dangers of government-subsidized research is provided by Daniel Greenberg, *The Politics of Pure Science* (New York: New American Library, 1967). Moreover, the GOP's largest proposed cuts were for the National Aeronautics and Space Administration, which generates more rhapsodic poetry than economically essential work.

There is no reason to assume that worthwhile work will not be done without federal subsidies. Private R&D has been growing as a share of total R&D expenditures since 1964 and now makes up more than half of all such outlays. Private firms' responsibility for industrial R&D has grown particularly quickly, even as federal funding has stagnated. Mowery and Rosenberg, pp. 126, 141. Generous private contributions also promote medical research. Sandra Blakeslee, "With Huge Gift, Utah Researchers to Study Cancers' Earliest Stages," *New York Times*, October 17, 1995, p. C3.

Indeed, Congress has made its most significant trims of research with commercial applications, precisely the sort that private business is most likely to undertake. Further, more money left in private hands will create a larger pool for nonprofit institutions to use to conduct worthwhile work.

Romer is quoted in Troy Goodman et al., "Should the Labs Get Hit?" *U.S. News & World Report*, November 6, 1995, p. 84. Twenty-five billion dollars a year is hardly pocket change; as Rep. Robert Walker, chairman of the House Science Committee, argued, the proposed budget would keep "a robust science policy while providing for the fundamental science we need to move forward." Quoted in William Broad, "G.O.P. Budget Cuts Would Fall Hard on Civilian Science," *New York Times*, May 22, 1995, p. A1. See also Daniel Greenberg, ". . . And Doomsters in Science," *Washington Post*, September 14, 1995, p. A23.

80. Etzioni, p. 133; and Dumas, p. 208. See also DeGrasse et al., p. 26; Melman, *The Permanent War Economy*, pp. 20, 80–81; and DeGrasse, pp. 14–15, 79–80.

81. Burns, p. 115. See also Dumas, p. 213; and Pascall and Lamson, pp. 40–41, 68–71.

82. Otto Eckstein, "Symposium on the Impact of Higher Defense Expenditures on the United States Economy in the 1980s," in U.S. Department of Defense, Transcript of 15th Annual OSD Cost Analysis Symposium, October 26–29, 1980, p. 126.

83. DeGrasse, pp. 47–48.

84. Those figures are for 1993. See U.S. Arms Control and Disarmament Agency, *World Military Expenditures and Arms Transfers: 1993–1994* (Washington: Government Printing Office, 1995); and International Institute for Strategic Studies, *The Military Balance: 1994–1995*, pp. 22, 180. Only the International Institute for Strategic Studies had released its 1994 figures, 3.5 percent to 4.1 percent, when this book went to press. International Institute for Strategic Studies, *The Military Balance: 1995–1996* (Oxford: Oxford University Press, 1995), pp. 23, 185.

85. U.S. Arms Control and Disarmament Agency, *World Military Expenditures and Arms Transfers: 1993–1994*, p. 70; and U.S. Arms Control and Disarmament Agency, *World Military Expenditures and Arms Transfers: 1987* (Washington: Government Printing Office, 1988), p. 64. All numbers are approximate. The estimates not only vary between organizations, such as the International Institute for Strategic Studies and the Stockholm International Peace Research Institute, but have also been adjusted over time by those organizations. Nevertheless, the figures are generally consistent. For instance, the Stockholm International Peace Research Institute figures the ROK's effort to have peaked at 6 percent of GDP (rather than the similar GNP) in 1980 and 1981. Stockholm International Peace Research Institute, *SIPRI Yearbook 1988: World Armaments and Disarmament* (New York: Oxford University Press, 1988), p. 170.

86. A short review of Korean economic policies is provided by Silvio de Franco et al., *Korea's Experience with Development of Trade and Industry* (Washington: World Bank, 1988). The ROK has a complex mixture of industrial policy and economic liberalization. For more detail, see Chung-Yum Kim, *Policymaking on the Front Lines: Memoirs of a Korean Practitioner, 1945–79* (Washington: World Bank, 1994); Vittorio

Corbo and Sang-Mok Suh, eds., *Structural Adjustment in a Newly Industrialized Country: The Korean Experience* (Washington: World Bank, 1992); Lee-Jay Cho and Yoon Hyung Kim, eds., *Economic Development in the Republic of Korea: A Policy Perspective* (Honolulu: East-West Center, 1991); and Jene Kwon, ed., *Korean Economic Development* (Westport, Conn.: Greenwood, 1990).

87. Dan Biers, "Asian Countries Aim to Boost Research," *Wall Street Journal*, October 24, 1995, p. A18.

88. T. W. Kang, *Is Korea the Next Japan?: Understanding the Structure, Strategy, and Tactics of America's Next Competitor* (New York: Free Press, 1989), p. 23.

89. Ernest Oppenheimer, "The War against Ourselves: Unequal Defense Costs Are the Villain in U.S.-Japan Trade Saga," *Barron's*, May 29, 1995, p. 43. Oppenheimer exaggerates, since other countries, such as the ROK, also bear responsibility for the differential, but his basic point remains valid.

90. Akio Torii and Richard Caves, "Technical Efficiency in Japanese and U.S. Manufacturing Industries," in *Industrial Efficiency in Six Nations*, ed. Richard Caves (Cambridge, Mass.: MIT Press, 1992), p. 455. A more anecdotal account is provided by Melman, *The Permanent War Economy*, pp. 84–104. For a specific review of Japanese R&D policy, see Mowery and Rosenberg, pp. 219–37; for a more general look at the Japanese economy, see Takatoshi Ito, *The Japanese Economy* (Cambridge, Mass.: MIT Press, 1992).

91. Seymour Melman, "Profits without Productivity," in *The War Economy of the United States*, p. 125; Melman, *The Permanent War Economy*, pp. 82–84; and Dumas, pp. 223–24.

92. Daniel Burstein, *Yen! Japan's New Financial Empire and Its Threat to America* (New York: Simon and Schuster, 1988), p. 49.

93. Especially during Japan's boom years, some analyses of Tokyo's incredible economic performance verged on the hysterical. See, for example, William Holstein, *The Japanese Power Game: What It Means for America* (New York: Scribner's, 1990); Clyde Prestowitz, *Trading Places: How We Allowed Japan to Take the Lead* (New York: Basic Books, 1988); and Burstein. The most extreme versions of that argument, which has been vented on both sides of the Pacific, are probably George Friedman and Meredith Lebard, *The Coming War with Japan* (New York: St. Martin's, 1991); and Shintaro Ishihara, *The Japan That Can Say No: Why Japan Will Be First among Equals* (New York: Simon and Schuster, 1991).

94. See, for example, J.-J. Servan-Schreiber, *The American Challenge* (New York: Atheneum, 1968).

95. What Japan's economy actually requires is sustained deregulation. See Emily Thornton, "Deregulation Dawdle," *Far Eastern Economic Review*, September 29, 1995, pp. 58, 60; David Hamilton et al., "Japan's Big Problem: Freeing Its Economy from Over-Regulation," *Wall Street Journal*, April 25, 1995, pp. A1, A13; and "Japan's Economy Needs a Heavy Dose of Deregulation," editorial, *Wall Street Journal*, September 25, 1995, p. B5. Even so, serious economic problems would probably persist. A. Gary Shilling, "Japan's Virulent Deflation," *Forbes*, August 14, 1995, p. 188.

96. For many years the problem was not only that allied states were not spending as much on defense as they otherwise would have had to; the United States was also directly subsidizing their efforts. In the mid-1980s, when South Korea had sprinted past the North and was enjoying one of the top economic growth rates in the world, Washington was still providing hundreds of millions of dollars in loans for weapons purchases. During the first half of the 1980s the United States spent some $1 billion

on military construction projects in the ROK. Congress finally killed those programs, over the objection of the Reagan administration and conservative organizations such as the Heritage Foundation. See Doug Bandow, "Korea: The Case for Disengagement," Cato Institute Policy Analysis no. 96, December 8, 1987, pp. 20–21.

Chapter 4

1. A detailed review of U.S.-ROK trade squabbles is provided in Chung-in Moon, "Irony of Interdependence: Emerging Trade Frictions between South Korea and the U.S.," in *Alliance under Tension: The Evolution of South Korean–U.S. Relations*, ed. Man-woo Lee, Ronald McLaurin, and Chung-in Moon (Boulder, Colo.: Westview, 1988), pp. 47–77.

2. Quoted in Steve Glain, "Reporter's Notebook: In North Korea Foundation Shifts but Juche Still Stands," *Wall Street Journal*, September 26, 1995, p. A15. U.S. firms in South Korea have bitterly attacked ROK restrictions on trade and investment. American Chamber of Commerce, *Pillars of Protectionism in Korea* (Seoul: American Chamber of Commerce in Korea, August 1990).

3. William Taylor Jr., *The Future of Conflict into the 21st Century* (Seoul: Korea Institute for Defense Analyses, 1987), p. 20.

4. Sung-Hoon Kim, "Discussion," in *Economic Relations between the United States and Korea: Conflict or Cooperation?* ed. Thomas Bayard and Soo-Gil Young (Washington: Institute for International Economics, 1988), p. 165. For a detailed look at trade frictions, see Moon, "Irony of Interdependence." The fall in the ROK's economically insignificant but symbolically important trade surplus with America has eased economic strains between the two nations. Tough issues are bound to recur, however. See, for example, Donna Smith, "Trade Fight with Seoul over Cars Expected," *Washington Times*, September 5, 1995, p. B7.

5. The DPRK may offer only limited market opportunities, but a number of U.S. firms have indicated their interest in venturing north. Michael Newman, "Mission Impossible?" *Far Eastern Economic Review*, September 29, 1994, pp. 56, 58. Although international trade with the North has been falling, one analysis suggests that the uninhibited entry of Pyongyang into the world economy would result in a fivefold increase in its international commerce, 7 percent of which would be America's "natural" share. Marcus Noland, "The North Korean Economy," *Korea Economic Update*, July 1995, p. 3.

6. In fact, South Korea's access to advanced weaponry from the United States and other Western nations provides it an important military advantage over the North, given the virtual end of arms shipments from Moscow to Pyongyang. See Stephen Goose, "The Comparative Military Capabilities of North Korean and South Korean Forces," in *The U.S.–South Korean Alliance: Time for a Change*, ed. Doug Bandow and Ted Galen Carpenter (New Brunswick, N.J.: Transaction, 1992), pp. 43–46.

7. Ministry of National Defense, *Defense White Paper: 1994–1995* (Seoul: Republic of Korea, 1995), p. 235. Cited hereafter as *Defense White Paper: 1994–1995*.

8. Changsu Kim, "Competing Security Needs of the Republic of Korea in the 1990s: In Search of a Peaceful Reunification," in *The U.S.–South Korean Alliance*, p. 61.

9. U.S. Department of Defense, *Congressional Presentation for Security Assistance Programs, FY 1987* (Washington: U.S. Department of Defense, 1986), vol. 1, p. 74. Oddly enough, shortly thereafter the very same department stated that "the South's economy has currently reached the dynamic growth levels of the 1970s and can

support increased defense production should the government make that decision." U.S. Department of Defense, "Report to Congress on the Military Situation on the Korean Peninsula," February 1987, p. 1.

10. William Taylor and Michael Mazarr, Letter to the editor, *Foreign Policy*, no. 79 (Summer 1990): 188.

11. Richard Fisher and John Dori, *U.S. and Asia Statistical Handbook: 1995* (Washington: Heritage Foundation, 1995), p. 55.

12. Gerald Ford, *A Time to Heal* (New York: Berkley Books, 1980), p. 208.

13. Quoted in Eduardo Lachica, "Two Opposition Leaders Figure Heavily in U.S. Efforts to Quell Chaos in Korea," *Wall Street Journal*, June 24, 1987, p. 23.

14. Quoted in John Hughes, "Korea: The U.S. Role," *Christian Science Monitor*, June 12, 1987, p. 14.

15. Quoted in Nicholas Kristof, "Anti-Americanism Grows in South Korea," *New York Times*, July 12, 1987, p. E3.

16. Joseph Harsch, "South Korea: A Classic Imperial Problem," *Christian Science Monitor*, June 23, 1987, p. 16.

17. Quoted in Gregory Henderson, "Time to Change the US–South Korea Military Relationship," *Far Eastern Economic Review*, September 24, 1987, p. 36.

18. Quoted in "As South Korea Goes Its Own Way," *U.S. News & World Report*, September 8, 1980, p. 32.

19. William Berry, *North Korea's Nuclear Program: The Clinton Administration's Response* (Colorado Springs: Institute for National Security Studies, 1995), p. 22.

20. Quoted in Clay Blair, *The Forgotten War: America in Korea, 1950–1953* (New York: Times Books, 1987), p. 44. Rhee unsuccessfully attempted to wring a similar declaration out of the Truman administration. James Irving Matray, *The Reluctant Crusade: American Foreign Policy in Korea, 1941–1950* (Honolulu: University of Hawaii Press, 1985), p. 191.

21. John Lewis Gaddis, "Korea in American Politics, Strategy, and Diplomacy, 1945–50," in *The Origins of the Cold War in Asia*, ed. Yonosuke Nagai and Akira Iriye (New York: Columbia University Press, 1977), p. 281. In fact, that position was held by most military officials, including Gen. Douglas MacArthur, though some in the State Department, including America's ambassador to the ROK, John Muccio, felt otherwise. Callum MacDonald, *Korea: The War before Vietnam* (New York: Free Press, 1986), pp. 26–27, 35; and Matray, pp. 194–97.

22. Despite all the public attention received by the South's economic "miracle," the ROK "is clearly not in the big leagues," admits businessman T. W. Kang. Kang, *Is Korea the Next Japan? Understanding the Structure, Strategy, and Tactics of America's Next Competitor* (New York: Free Press, 1989), p. 43. For instance, South Korea's GDP remains a fraction of those of Britain and Italy, let alone those of France, Germany, and Japan.

23. Ted Galen Carpenter, "South Korea: A Vital or Peripheral U.S. Security Interest?" in *The U.S.–South Korean Alliance*, p. 3.

24. Richard D. Detrio, *Strategic Partners: South Korea and the United States* (Washington: Government Printing Office, 1989), pp. 84–85; and Norman Levin and Richard Sneider, *Korea in Postwar U.S. Security Policy* (Santa Monica, Calif.: Rand Corporation, 1982), p. 41.

25. Quoted in David Pitt, "Seoul, U.S. Forces and the North: The Balance Is as Delicate as Ever," *New York Times*, April 8, 1987, p. A10.

26. William Gleysteen and Alan Romberg, "Korea: Asian Paradox," *Foreign Affairs* 65 (Spring 1987): 1052.

27. Edwin Feulner Jr., "The U.S.–Republic of China Partnership in the Year 2000," Heritage Foundation Lecture no. 85, 1987, p. 5.

28. Quoted in Marcus Corbin et al., "Mission Accomplished in Korea: Bringing U.S. Troops Home," *Defense Monitor* 9, no. 2 (1990): 5.

29. U.S. Department of Defense, *United States Security Strategy for the East Asia–Pacific Region* (Washington: U.S. Department of Defense, February 1995), p. 10.

30. Quoted in Jim Lea, "N. Korea Threat Alive, Official Says," *Pacific Stars & Stripes*, September 9, 1995, p. 1.

31. MacDonald, p. 33.

32. Carpenter, p. 9.

33. MacDonald, pp. 13, 30, 35. See also Soong-Hoom Kil, "Japan in American-Korean Relations," in *Korea and the United States*, ed. Youngnok Koo and Dae-Sook Suh (Honolulu: University of Hawaii Press, 1984), pp. 155–56.

34. Carpenter, p. 6.

35. MacDonald, p. 26.

36. Joseph Goulden, *Korea: The Untold Story of the War* (New York: McGraw-Hill, 1982), p. 28.

37. Chin-Wee Chung, "American–North Korean Relations," in *Korea and the United States*, p. 185.

38. U.S. Department of Defense, *United States Security Strategy for the East Asia–Pacific Region*, p. 10.

39. Ministry of National Defense, *Defense White Paper: 1989* (Seoul: Republic of Korea, 1990), pp. 144–45. Cited hereafter as *Defense White Paper: 1989*.

40. International Institute for Strategic Studies, *The Military Balance: 1995–1996* (Oxford: Oxford University Press, 1995), pp. 183–86. Unclassified studies by the Korean and U.S. governments reflect similar numbers and conclusions. *Defense White Paper: 1994–1995*, p. 80; U.S. Department of Defense, "Report to Congress."

41. Ministry of National Defense, *Defense White Paper: 1990* (Seoul: Republic of Korea, 1991), p. 87. Cited hereafter as *Defense White Paper: 1990*.

42. Stephen Goose, "The Military Situation on the Korean Peninsula," in *Two Koreas—One Future?* ed. John Sullivan and Roberta Foss (Lanham, Md.: University Press of America, 1987), p. 57. The South Korean Ministry of National Defense has acknowledged being criticized for emphasizing quantity over quality in its publications. *Defense White Paper: 1990*, p. 5.

43. Goose, "The Military Situation," p. 57. For that reason he believed that even in the absence of U.S. Air Force units, "the battle for the skies would clearly be won by the South" (p. 67).

44. U.S. Department of Defense, "Report to Congress," p. 1.

45. Ministry of National Defense, *Defense White Paper: 1991–1992* (Seoul: Republic of Korea, 1992), p. 119. Cited hereafter as *Defense White Paper: 1991–1992*.

46. Robert Hall and Ian Kemp, eds, "North Korea: The Final Act," *Jane's Intelligence Review*, Special Report no. 2, 1994, p. 24.

47. See, for example, Goose, "The Comparative Military Capabilities," p. 50; and Donald Cotter and N. F. Wilkner, "Korea: Force Imbalances and Remedies," *Strategic Review* (Spring 1982): 67.

48. Congressional Budget Office, *U.S. Ground Forces: Design and Cost Alternatives for NATO and Non-NATO Contingencies* (Washington: Government Printing Office, 1980), p. 69.

49. Quoted in Edward Neilan, "South Korea Faces Constant Threat of Northern Invasion," *Washington Times*, May 6, 1987, p. B9.

50. Goose, "The Military Situation," pp. 73–76; and Goose, "The Comparative Military Capabilities," pp. 50–52.

51. International Institute for Strategic Studies, *The Military Balance: 1985–86* (London: International Institute for Strategic Studies, 1985), p. 118.

52. Compare *Defense White Paper: 1991–1992*, pp. 55, 59, with *Defense White Paper: 1994–1995*, pp. 132–33. Growing South Korean economic ties with China and Russia also militate against their support for the DPRK in any crisis. On the latter, see, for example, In-Kon Yeo, "Economic Cooperation between South Korea and Russia: Current Developments and Future Prospects," *Korean Journal of National Unification*, Special Edition (1993): 151–65. At the same time, commerce between Russia and the DPRK has dwindled dramatically. Nicholas Eberstadt et al., "The Collapse of Soviet and Russian Trade with the DPRK, 1989–1993: Impact and Implications," *Korean Journal of National Unification* 4 (1995): 87–104.

53. *Defense White Paper: 1990*, p. 55.

54. U.S. Department of Defense, "Report to Congress," p. 2.

55. Denny Roy, "North Korea and the 'Madman' Theory," *Security Dialogue* 25, no. 3 (September 1994): 311.

56. Bruce Bennett, "The Prospects for Conventional Conflict on the Korean Peninsula," *Korean Journal of Defense Analysis* 7, no. 1 (Summer 1995): 95.

57. Quoted in Kevin Sullivan, "S. Korean President Calls North's Leaders 'Weaker,' " *Washington Post*, July 29, 1995, p. A20.

58. As the ROK Ministry of Defense points out, the list of North Korean terrorist provocations is long. *Defense White Paper: 1991–1992*, pp. 357–66. For criticism, see, for example, Robert Gaskin, "Faulty Assessment of the Dangers?" *Washington Times*, November 30, 1993, p. A15. Even the ROK Ministry of National Defense acknowledges problems of morale and low retention rates for noncommissioned officers. *Defense White Paper: 1994–1995*, pp. 24–25. And, of course, U.S. observers heaped praise upon Syngman Rhee's doomed forces. See Matray, p. 231. Nevertheless, there is a world of difference between ROK forces in 1950 and nearly five decades later.

59. See the discussion of a potential attack in Hall and Kemp, pp. 22–24.

60. Quoted in Jim Lea, p. 2.

61. *Defense White Paper: 1990*, p. 105.

62. Quote from *Defense White Paper: 1994–1995*, p. 128. Similarly, Norman Levin and Richard Sneider of the Rand Corporation wrote, "The current modernization of the Korean armed forces is likely to permit some reduction in the U.S. military presence later in the 1980s, *provided that the North Korean build-up does not keep pace.*" Levin and Sneider, p. 41; emphasis added. Of course, it was South Korea's duty to ensure that the DPRK did not keep pace.

63. That seems to have long been the case with NATO. Writes former secretary of state Henry Kissinger, "The greater the pressures for troop withdrawal in the United States, the greater the disinclination of our allies to augment their military establishments lest they justify further American withdrawals." Kissinger, *White House Years* (Boston: Little, Brown, 1979), p. 394.

64. Claude Buss, *The United States and the Republic of Korea: Background for Policy* (Stanford, Calif.: Hoover Institution, 1982), p. 142.

65. Quoted in ibid., p. 144.

66. Quoted in Astri Suhrke and Charles Morrison, "Carter and Korea: The Difficulties of Disengagement," *World Today*, October 1977, p. 371.

67. Franklin Weinstein and Fuji Kamiya, eds., *The Security of Korea: U.S. and Japanese Perspectives on the 1980s* (Boulder, Colo.: Westview, 1980), p. 75.

68. Larry Niksch, "Korea: U.S. Troop Withdrawal and the Question of Northeast Asian Stability," Congressional Research Service, Issue Brief no. IB79053, April 16, 1980, p. 17.

69. House Appropriations Committee, "Foreign Assistance Appropriation, FY 1983," part 1, March 11, 1982, p. 152.

70. *A Handbook of Korea*, 4th ed. (Seoul: Ministry of Culture and Information, 1982), p. 454.

71. *DMS Intelligence Report*, September 19, 1983, p. 1.

72. Senate Armed Services Committee, "Department of Defense Appropriation for FY 1985," part 2, p. 1253.

73. Quoted in *Korea Herald*, July 7, 1985, and *Army*, October 1985, p. 134.

74. Quoted in Gus Constantine, "Imbalance in Arms Endangers South Korea," *Washington Times*, May 11, 1987, p. C8.

75. Quoted in Pitt.

76. Lee Suk Bok, *The Impact of US Forces in Korea* (Washington: National Defense University, 1987), p. 66.

77. Taylor, p. 19.

78. Amos Jordan and William Taylor, "Cut U.S. Troops in Korea Now," *New York Times*, December 2, 1988.

79. Quoted in Richard Halloran, "General Sees End to U.S. Troops in Korea in 90's," *New York Times*, August 13, 1989, p. 4.

80. U.S. Department of Defense, "A Strategic Framework for the Asian Pacific Rim: Looking toward the 21st Century," April 1990, pp. 3, 12.

81. *Defense White Paper: 1991–1992*, p. 116.

82. Goose, "The Comparative Military Capabilities," p. 40.

83. U.S. Department of Defense, "Report to Congress," p. 2.

84. Ministry of National Defense, *Defense White Paper: 1992–1993* (Seoul: Republic of Korea, 1993), p. 31. Cited hereafter as *Defense White Paper: 1992–1993*.

85. On the DPRK's military expansion, see, for example, *Defense White Paper: 1990*, p. 90.

86. That is hardly a state secret. See, for example, Yong-Sup Han, "Breaking Off the Cold War Chains on the Korean Peninsula: The Relevance of Arms Control Measures," *Journal of Korean Unification*, no. 4 (1995): 61.

87. *Defense White Paper: 1991–1992*, p. 31.

88. *Defense White Paper: 1989*, p. 118.

89. *Defense White Paper: 1994–1995*, p. 22.

90. Goose, "The Comparative Military Capabilities," p. 49.

91. See also the estimate of 18.5 to 1 in Fisher and Dori, pp. 52–55.

92. Buss, p. 139.

93. "Up until 1971," writes Lee,

the ROK Armed Forces had relied on the US forces and their military aid too heavily. There had been some military leaders who could not do anything without the assistance of the US forces. This tendency had been present from the beginning of the ROK forces' establishment and was accelerated by the

Korean War. Habitual assistance from the US military adviser, training by the US instructor, study at a US military school, and the basic field manual (which was translated directly from the US manual) seemed to result in a mental attitude in some Korean officers that can best be described as passive and dependent (p. 63).

94. The differences between GDP and GNP are small and technical; in the case of South Korea, GDP tends to exceed GNP. Most analysts today rely on GDP rather than GNP. Lee is quoted in Doug Bandow, "Leaving Korea," *Foreign Policy* 77 (Winter 1989–90): 90.

95. Private conversations with the author during a visit to Seoul in July 1995.

96. Ministry of National Defense, *Defense White Paper: 1993–1994* (Seoul: Republic of Korea, 1994), p. 188.

97. Quoted in Bandow, "Seoul Long," p. 35.

98. William Stueck, *The Korean War: An International History* (Princeton, N.J.: Princeton University Press, 1995), p. 11.

99. For various analyses of why the ROK succeeded, see Vittorio Corbo and Sang-Mok Suh, eds., *Structural Adjustment in a Newly Industrialized Country: The Korean Experience* (Baltimore: Johns Hopkins University Press, 1992); Jene Kwon, ed., *Korean Economic Development* (Westport, Conn.: Greenwood, 1990); Silvio de Franco et al., *Korea's Experience with the Development of Trade and Industry* (Washington: World Bank, 1988); and Norman Jacobs, *The Korean Road to Modernization and Development* (Urbana: University of Illinois Press, 1985). For a broad look at U.S.-ROK economic relations, see Dong Sung Cho, "From Unilateral Asymmetry to Bilateral Symmetry," in *Korea and the United States*, pp. 219–40; and Eul Young Park, "From Bilateralism to Multilateralism: Korea's Economic Relations with the United States, 1945–1980," in *Korea and the United States*, pp. 241–60.

100. World Bank, *World Tables: 1995* (Baltimore: Johns Hopkins University Press, 1995), p. 397. The figures from the International Institute for Strategic Studies are slightly lower but of the same magnitude. Such estimates are sensitive to exchange rate fluctuations, among other things.

101. Kyu-Ryoon Kim, "Economic Cooperation in Northeast Asia: The Role of Korea," *Korean Journal of National Unification*, Special Edition (1993): 167–77.

102. Ju-Yeon Kim, "Korean Emigrés Return for Economic, Cultural Reasons," *Washington Times*, October 27, 1995, p. A20; and Pam Belluck, "Healthy Korean Economy Draws Immigrants Home," *New York Times*, August 22, 1995, pp. A1, B4.

103. For estimates that the DPRK's economic contraction was in its sixth or seventh straight year by 1995, see Young Namkoong, "Assessment of the North Korean Economy: Status and Prospects," in *US-Korean Relations at a Time of Change* (Seoul: Research Institute for National Unification, 1994), pp. 9, 26; and Kevin Sullivan, "All Eyes—and Ears—on N. Korea," *Washington Post*, October 27, 1995, p. A27. By virtually every measure, ranging from agricultural production to foreign trade, the North's economic future looks bleak. Robert Delfs, ed., *Asia Yearbook: 1994* (Hong Kong: Far Eastern Economic Review, 1994), p. 149; and Aidan Foster-Carter, *North Korea after Kim Il-Sung* (London: The Economist Intelligence Unit, 1994), pp. 26–28.

104. Young-Ho Park, "Will North Korea Survive the Current Crisis? A Political Economy Perspective," *Korean Journal of National Reunification* 2 (1993): 105–25. For other looks at the DPRK economy, see Seung-Yul Oh, "Shortage in the North Korean Economy: Characteristics, Sources, and Prospects," *Korean Journal of National Unification* 4 (1995): 105–31; Namkoong, pp. 7–27; Richard Grant, "Juche's Last Gasp,"

Korean Journal of Defense Analysis 6, no. 2 (Winter 1994): 131–44; Robert Manning, "Economic Sanctions or Economic Incentives?" Paper presented to Carnegie Endowment for International Peace symposium, "The United States and North Korea: What Next?" Washington, November 16, 1993; Sang-In Jun, "A Maker of vs. a Victim of History: A Comparative-Historical Study of Economic Reforms and Developments in Vietnam and North Korea," *Korean Journal of National Unification*, Special Edition (1993): 59–96; and Marcus Noland, "The North Korean Economy," reprint, Korean Economic Institute of America, 1995.

105. "North Korea Asks U.N. for Aid," *Washington Times*, August 30, 1995, p. A11; and Stephen Linton, "The New Moses," *Far Eastern Economic Review*, July 20, 1995, p. 30.

106. Hwang Dong Joon, "South Korea's Defense Industry: An Asset for the U.S.," Heritage Foundation Backgrounder no. 38, December 10, 1985; and Goose, "The Comparative Military Capabilities," pp. 46–47. For a discussion of the development of the ROK's military-industrial complex, see Chung-in Moon, "U.S. Third Country Arms Sales Regulation and the South Korean Defense Industry," in *Alliance under Tension*, pp. 81–90.

107. For estimates, see U.S. Arms Control and Disarmament Agency, *World Military Expenditures and Arms Transfers: 1990* (Washington: Government Printing Office, 1991), p. 69; and U.S. Arms Control and Disarmament Agency, *World Military Expenditures and Arms Transfers: 1987* (Washington: Government Printing Office, 1988), p. 65. For a discussion of the agency's figures, see Goose, "The Comparative Military Capabilities," pp. 42–43. On ROK claims, see *Defense White Paper 1991–1992*, p. 116. See also Han, p. 66.

108. Sang-Woo Rhee, "The Roots of South Korean Anxiety about National Security," in *Threats to Security in East Asia–Pacific*, ed. Charles Morrison (Lexington, Mass.: Lexington Books, 1983), p. 67.

109. Han, p. 66.

110. Sang-Hun Choe, "S. Korea to Double Defense Outlays," *Washington Times*, December 24, 1995, p. A7.

111. See, for example, James Schnabel, *Policy and Direction: The First Year* (Washington: U.S. Army, 1972), p. 37.

112. Shipments will include anti-aircraft missiles, anti-tank missiles, tanks, and armored vehicles. "Moscow Pays Debt to Seoul with Arms," *Washington Times*, September 27, 1995, p. A10; and Anton Zhigulsky, "Russians Court S. Korea with Technology Transfer, Arms," *Defense News*, October 9–15, 1995, p. 12.

113. Vladimir Miasnikov, "Russian–South Korean Security Cooperation," *Korean Journal of Defense Analysis* 6, no. 2 (Winter 1994): 335. For more cautious views, see Stephen Blank, "Russian Policy and the Changing Korean Question," *Asian Survey* 35, no. 8 (August 1995): 711–25; and Alexander Zhebin, "Russia and North Korea: An Emerging, Uneasy Partnership," *Asian Survey* 35, no. 8 (August 1995): 726–39.

114. See, for example, Cameron Barr, "Democracy's Roots Deepen in S. Korea with Local Voting," *Christian Science Monitor*, June 16, 1995, p. 7.

115. Taylor and Mazarr, p. 188.

116. The ROK government has certainly spelled out the danger. See, for example, *Defense White Paper: 1989*, pp. 57–82.

117. Ralph Clough, *Embattled Korea: The Rivalry for International Support* (Boulder, Colo.: Westview, 1987), p. 99.

118. *Defense White Paper: 1991–1992*, p. 31.

119. Lee, p. 97.
120. These are International Institute for Strategic Studies figures. The U.S. Arms Control and Disarmament Agency shows a steady, but somewhat less dramatic, increase.
121. *Defense White Paper: 1994–1995*, pp. 221, 235. This has been a theme for a number of years. See, for example, *Defense White Paper: 1991–1992*, p. 169.
122. *Defense White Paper: 1994–1995*, p. 19.
123. Richard Solomon, "The Last Glacier: The Korean Peninsula and the Post–Cold War Era," *U.S. Department of State Dispatch*, February 11, 1991, p. 106.
124. *Defense White Paper: 1990*, p. 141.
125. Quoted in Nicholas Kristof, "Subway Brawl Inflames Issue of G.I.'s in Korea," *New York Times*, August 24, 1995, p. A3. The Ministry of National Defense also argues that America has an interest in basing troops in Korea "as an underpinning of strategic stability in this region." *Defense White Paper: 1990*, p. 141.
126. *Defense White Paper: 1994–1995*, pp. 11–12.
127. *Defense White Paper: 1989*, pp. 131, 149.
128. *Defense White Paper: 1994–1995*, pp. 223–24; and *Defense White Paper: 1990*, p. 154.
129. *Defense White Paper: 1992–1993*, p. 169.
130. *Defense White Paper: 1991–1992*, pp. 201, 255.
131. Clough, p. 98.
132. *Defense White Paper: 1992–1993*, p. 117. Interestingly, this section, which first appeared in the 1989 volume, disappeared from the 1994–95 volume.
133. *Defense White Paper: 1989*, p. 27.
134. Quoted in Georgie Anne Geyer, "South Korea Grateful for U.S. Help," *San Diego Union-Tribune*, July 23, 1995.

Chapter 5

1. Kim Kyong-Dong, "Korean Perceptions of America," in *Korea Briefing, 1993: Festival of Korea*, ed. Donald Gregg (Boulder, Colo.: Westview, 1993), p. 180.
2. Ministry of National Defense, *Defense White Paper: 1992–1993* (Seoul: Republic of Korea, 1993), p. 168. Cited hereafter as *Defense White Paper: 1992–1993*.
3. Quoted in Claude Buss, *The United States and the Republic of Korea: Background for Policy* (Stanford, Calif.: Hoover Institution Press, 1982), p. 143.
4. Ibid., p. 139.
5. The bureaucratic battle was extended and bitter. See, for example, James Irving Matray, *The Reluctant Crusade: American Foreign Policy in Korea, 1941–1950* (Honolulu: University of Hawaii Press, 1985), pp. 151–99; Kim Chull Baum, "U.S. Policy on the Eve of the Korean War: Abandonment or Safeguard?" in *Korea and the Cold War: Division, Destruction, and Disarmament*, ed. Kim Chull Baum and James Matray (Claremont, Calif.: Regina Books, 1993), pp. 63–94; and James Schnabel, *Policy and Direction: The First Year* (Washington: U.S. Army, 1972), pp. 28–30.
6. See Baum, pp. 72–73, 75–77.
7. Lee Suk Bok, *The Impact of US Forces in Korea* (Washington: National Defense University Press, 1987), pp. 24–29. Unfortunately, those initiatives achieved only moderate success. See, for example, Clay Blair, *The Forgotten War: America in Korea, 1950–1953* (New York: Times Books, 1987), pp. 51–52.
8. Quoted in Baum, p. 90.

9. Dean Acheson, "Crisis in Asia—An Examination of U.S. Policy," *Department of State Bulletin* 22 (January 23, 1950): 111–18.

10. Baum, pp. 82–83, 89. At least one Korean observer argues that the Pentagon belief that the peninsula was too rough for tanks was more important than Rhee's bellicosity. Lee, p. 28. However, Rhee's threats are widely cited by historians. William Stueck, *The Korean War: An International History* (Princeton, N.J.: Princeton University Press, 1995), p. 30; Blair, p. 44; Max Hastings, *The Korean War* (New York: Simon and Schuster, 1987), p. 43; Callum MacDonald, *Korea: The War before Vietnam* (New York: Free Press, 1986), pp. 15–16; and Matray, pp. 173, 183, 230, 233.

11. Lee, p. 60.

12. Ralph Clough, *Embattled Korea: The Rivalry for International Support* (Boulder, Colo.: Westview, 1987), p. 96; and Buss, pp. 89–91.

13. Richard Nixon, *U.S. Foreign Policy for the 1970s: Shaping a Durable Peace* (Washington: Government Printing Office, 1973), p. 110.

14. Clough, pp. 98–99. Buss speaks of the ROK's being "traumatized" (p. 141).

15. See, for example, Lee, p. 62.

16. Quoted in Buss, p. 145.

17. See, for example, ibid., p. 148.

18. Japan's position is discussed in Frank Baldwin, "Japan: Roadblock on the Way Out of Korea," *Inquiry*, April 3, 1978, pp. 19–22. Tokyo was concerned both about preserving peace on the Korean peninsula and about the credibility of America's security guarantee to Japan.

19. In a private conversation with the author, one of his former aides described President Carter's particular frustration at being undercut by his own appointees.

20. The entire Carter experience is covered in Buss, pp. 148–58.

21. Earl Ravenal, "The Way Out of Korea," *Inquiry*, December 5, 1977, p. 15.

22. Quoted in ibid.

23. Ibid.

24. Not surprisingly, the latter was of most concern to Japanese leaders. See, for example, Chong-Sik Lee, *Japan and Korea: The Political Dimension* (Stanford, Calif.: Hoover Institution Press, 1985), pp. 98–99.

25. Among those who noted the suspicious timing of the new assessments was New York University's Melvyn Krauss. Krauss, *How NATO Weakens the West* (New York: Simon and Schuster, 1987), p. 186.

26. So pitiful was the result that Carter does not even mention his efforts in his biography, *Keeping Faith: Memoirs of a President* (New York: Bantam Books, 1982). Nor did his national security adviser Zbigniew Brzezinski in *Power and Principle: Memoirs of the National Security Adviser, 1977–1981*, 2d ed. (New York: Farrar Straus Giroux, 1985).

27. Lee, p. 65.

28. Quoted in Krauss, p. 188.

29. Quoted in Lee, p. 65.

30. The plan is reviewed in Ministry of National Defense, *Defense White Paper: 1994–1995* (Seoul: Republic of Korea, 1995), pp. 122–23. Cited hereafter as *Defense White Paper: 1994–1995*. See also Ahn Byung-joon, "The United States, Korea, and Arms Control: A Strategic Review," in *Korea and the Cold War*, pp. 255–56.

31. *Defense White Paper: 1992–1993*, pp. 142–43. See also the discussion of a "shrinking" American role and "Koreanization of Korean defense." *Defense White Paper: 1994–1995*, p. 123.

32. Private meeting with the author in Seoul in August 1989.

33. See, for example, Doug Bandow, "Korea: The Case for Disengagement," Cato Institute Policy Analysis no. 96, December 8, 1987, p. 10; Amos Jordan and William Taylor, "Cut U.S. Troops in Korea Now," *New York Times*, December 2, 1988; William Taylor and Michael Mazarr, "Strategic Opportunities in Northeast Asia," *Korean Journal of Defense Analysis* 1, no. 2 (Winter 1989): 17; and Ralph Clough, *Deterrence and Defense in Korea: The Role of U.S. Forces* (Washington: Brookings Institution, 1976), pp. 59–61.

34. William Gleysteen Jr. and Alan Romberg, "Korea: Asian Paradox," *Foreign Affairs* 65, no. 3 (Spring 1987): 1048.

35. Franklin Weinstein and Fuji Kamiya, eds., *The Security of Korea: U.S. and Japanese Perspectives on the 1980s* (Boulder, Colo.: Westview, 1980), p. 70.

36. Trade concerns have complicated similar arrangements in the past, such as the FX, or Korean fighter, program. Robert Sutter, "U.S. Relations with South Korea in a Time of Transition," *Korean Journal of National Unification*, Special Edition (1993): 137.

37. Rhee's views in this regard appear to have differed little from those of Kim Il Sung, since Rhee asserted that the matter of reunification was purely a domestic concern. See, for example, Okonogi Masao, "The Domestic Roots of the Korean War," in *The Origins of the Cold War in Asia*, ed. Yonosuke Nagai and Akira Iriye (New York: Columbia University Press, 1977), p. 313.

38. Weinstein and Kamiya, p. 73.

39. Sens. Gordon Humphrey (R-N.H.) and John Glenn (D-Ohio) cited that as one reason for opposing the Carter withdrawal program. Pat Towell, "Carter's Korea Troop Withdrawal Faulted," *Congressional Quarterly*, February 25, 1978, p. 544. However valid their concern may have been then, today's democracy is far less likely to initiate an attack than was yesterday's dictatorship. Nevertheless, Selig Harrison of the Carnegie Endowment for International Peace worries that American arms sales might "encourage the South to think it could conquer the North." Conversation with the author, November 1995. But Seoul would need to undertake a massive build-up—for which the United States could refuse to supply weapons—before it could have any confidence of being able to win an offensive war. In any case, the dominant sentiment in the South appears to be that the DPRK will eventually collapse, so there is no reason for military adventurism.

40. For instance, former Army chief of staff Gen. E. C. Meyer has called Germany and Japan "the two biggest threats" replacing the Soviet Union. Quoted in George Wilson, "U.S. Begins Revamping the Military," *Washington Post*, November 26, 1989, p. A12.

41. The ROK should not feel threatened by that strategy. As argued later, the shared interests that make international relationships strong are going to remain far more extensive between the United States and the South than between the United States and the North for years to come.

42. Russia has proposed a formal conference on the Koreas, and others have proposed a more structured framework. See, for example, Robert Manning, "Clinton and the Korea Question: A Strategy for the Endgame," Progressive Policy Institute Policy Briefing, July 7, 1994, p. 8.

43. See, for example, Randall Ashley, "South Korea Mulls Treaty with North," *Washington Times*, July 26, 1995, p. A3. Such proposals are relatively common. See, for example, Seong Ho Jhe, "How to Build a New Peace Structure on the Korean Peninsula," *Korean Journal of National Unification* 4 (1995): 20–22; and Kim Dae-Jung

[Kim Dae Jung], "The Impact of the US–North Korean Agreement on Korean Reunification," *Korean Journal of Defense Analysis* 6, no. 2 (Winter 1994): 93.

44. *Defense White Paper: 1994–1995*, pp. 43–44.

45. It was not just military occupation, of course. It was also "Japan's attempt in the last decade of its rule to eliminate Korean identity altogether—by enforced Shintoism and taking of Japanese names, plus a language ban." *South Korea, North Korea: 1994–1995* (London: The Economist Intelligence Unit, 1994), p. 4. The second-class treatment of ethnic Koreans in Japan also creates bitterness in the ROK.

46. Baldwin, pp. 19–20.

47. R. Mark Bean, *Cooperative Security in Northeast Asia* (Washington: National Defense University Press, 1990), p. 139.

48. Byung-joon Ahn [Ahn Byung-joon], "Regionalism and the US-Korea-Japan Partnership in the Asia-Pacific," in *US-Korean Relations at a Time of Change* (Seoul: Research Institute for National Unification, 1994), p. 130.

49. For a discussion of the tension in this relationship, see Clough, pp. 221–37.

50. Compare *Defense White Paper: 1994–1995*, pp. 48–49, and *Defense White Paper: 1992–1993*, pp. 47–48, with Ministry of National Defense, *Defense White Paper: 1991–1992* (Seoul: Republic of Korea, 1992), pp. 60–61, 63–64. Cited hereafter as *Defense White Paper: 1991–1992*. Indeed, the latter speaks of Japan's "carrying out a policy of equidistance toward South and North Korea and . . . promoting economic cooperation and the establishment of relations with North Korea as part of its policy of maintaining the status quo on the Korean peninsula" (p. 60).

51. Private meeting with the author during a visit to Seoul in July 1995. See Doug Bandow, "Time to End the Korean Protectorate," *Conservative Chronicle*, August 16, 1995, p. 27. Similar sentiments were voiced two decades ago as Korean officials argued against Richard Nixon's partial pullout. Buss, pp. 142–43.

52. A decade or two ago the idea of Japanese financial aid had a lot more appeal. See, for example, Weinstein and Kamiya, pp. 103–4.

53. Henry Kissinger, *Diplomacy* (New York: Simon and Schuster, 1994), p. 827.

54. *Defense White Paper: 1994–1995*, p. 21.

55. See, for example, Ahn, "Regionalism and the US-Korea-Japan Partnership," pp. 100–101. Henry Kissinger particularly doubts the viability of large-scale multilateral arrangements in this region. Kissinger, p. 828.

56. For a supporter of cooperative arrangements, see Ahn, "Regionalism and the US-Korea-Japan Partnership," p. 114.

57. Kissinger, p. 826.

58. Quoted in Ahn, "Regionalism and the US-Korea-Japan Partnership," p. 120.

59. U.S. Department of Defense, *United States Security Strategy for the East Asia–Pacific Region* (Washington: U.S. Department of Defense, February 1995), p. 1.

60. Ibid., p. 31.

61. *Defense White Paper: 1994–1995*, p. 127.

62. Quoted in Nigel Holloway, "Fast Friends," *Far Eastern Economic Review*, August 10, 1995, p. 22. So do some Americans. William Taylor, "US National Security and North Korea," in *US-Korean Relations at a Time of Change*, p. 29. More generally, see Ronald McLaurin, "Security Relations: Burden-Sharing in a Changing Strategic Environment," in *Alliance under Tension: The Evolution of South Korean–U.S. Relations*, ed. Manwoo Lee, Ronald McLaurin, and Chung-in Moon (Boulder, Colo.: Westview, 1988), pp. 166–67.

63. Seongwhun Cheon, "Some Problems of the US-DPRK Agreed Framework: A South Korean View," Presented at Research Institute for National Unification–Cato Institute Workshop on U.S.-ROK Relations, Washington, September 5, 1995, p. 7.

64. Quoted in "'We Are Truly Blood Allies,'" *Newsweek*, July 31, 1995, p. 27. Similarly, Seoul's Ministry of National Defense has called the two nations' relationship a "blood-forged alliance" arising out of the Korean War. Ministry of National Defense, *Defense White Paper: 1990* (Seoul: Republic of Korea, 1991), p. 131.

65. Some South Korean analysts acknowledge the likelihood of Seoul's continued diplomatic supremacy. See, for example, Chung Min Lee, "The North Korean Nuclear Issue and the Korean-American Alliance," *Korean Journal of National Unification* 4 (1995): 31.

66. An example of poll data is provided in Kim, pp. 180–81.

67. Selig Harrison, "Confederation or Absorption? Key Issues for South Korea and the United States," *Korean Journal of National Unification*, Special Edition (1993): 117–19; and Weinstein and Kamiya, pp. 163–70.

68. Selig Harrison, Speech to "Face-to-Face" meeting, Carnegie Endowment for International Peace, October 16, 1995, p. 3.

69. One estimate is that the North's economy has been contracting at almost 10 percent annually, a trend that is clearly unsustainable. Hakjoon Kim, "North Korea's Nuclear Development Program and the Future," in *US-Korean Relations at a Time of Change*, p. 68.

70. *Defense White Paper: 1992–1993*, p. 23.

71. See, for example, *Defense White Paper: 1994–1995*, p. 145. The accord and accompanying compliance protocols are reproduced in *Defense White Paper: 1992–1993*, pp. 219–40.

72. See, for example, *Defense White Paper: 1994–1995*, pp. 141–56; and *Defense White Paper: 1991–1992*, p. 133. For more general discussions of confidence-building and arms control issues, see James Macintosh, "A Confidence-Building Framework for the Korean Peninsula," *Korean Journal of Defense Analysis* 7, no. 1 (Summer 1995): 155–81; Young-koo Cha and Kang Choi, "Land-Based Confidence-Building Measures in Northeast Asia: A South Korean Perspective," *Korean Journal of Defense Analysis* 6, no. 2 (Winter 1994): 249–60; and Yong-Sup Han, "Breaking Off the Cold War Chains on the Korean Peninsula: The Relevance of Arms Control Measures," *Korean Journal of National Unification* 4 (1995): 51–85.

73. Past contacts are reviewed in Jinwook Choi, "Inter-Korean Economic Cooperation: A Vital Element of Seoul's Unification Policy," *Korean Journal of National Unification* 4 (1995): 133–50.

74. See, for example, Seong Ho Jhe, pp. 7–27. North Korea's attempt to replace the armistice is covered in Hideya Kurata, "The International Context of North Korea's Proposal for a 'New Peace Arrangement': Issues after the US-DPRK Nuclear Accord," *Korean Journal of Defense Analysis* 7, no. 1 (Summer 1995): 251–73. Obviously, there are many potential roadblocks to genuine arms reduction and peace. Han, pp. 58–68.

75. Obviously, there are many plans for reunification. See, for example, Li Cong, "Some Views on the Reunification of South Korea and North Korea on the Korean Peninsula," *Korean Journal of National Unification*, Special Edition (1993): 39–42; and Harrison, pp. 97–125. Enthusiasm for quick reunification is, however, low in both nations. The North's elite fears being "swallowed," as they expressed it during my visit to Pyongyang in August 1992. And ROK leaders worry about the expense of

economic investment and social welfare, as well as a massive population migration southward. One estimate is that Seoul would have to spend nearly $1 trillion after "acquiring" North Korea, roughly 2.5 times the South's current annual GDP. Harrison, p. 115. In fact, Germany's costly experience has caused some South Koreans to hope that they can prop up the DPRK for some time, allowing it to begin growing on its own. But, as Germany's experience also shows, once reunification becomes feasible, it may be impossible to slow down a highly emotional and popular process.

76. North Korea has long been willing to talk to little effect. Consider the prior experience with the South-North Military Committee. See, for example, *Defense White Paper: 1992–1993*, pp. 84–89. And no one knows for sure what to make of the DPRK's behavior, which seems to exemplify the phrase "mixed messages": requests for aid and then insulting and imperious treatment of those delivering the aid, for instance. Alleged kidnappings, armed infiltrations, refusal to let visiting Korean-Americans see family members, threats to rip up the armistice, and recalcitrance in the ongoing nuclear talks all suggest that Pyongyang is locked in a difficult policy struggle or that brinkmanship remains the North's negotiating modus operandi, or both.

77. *Defense White Paper: 1991–1992*, p. 31.

78. *Defense White Paper: 1994–1995*, p. 103.

79. Weinstein and Kamiya, p. 70.

80. *Defense White Paper: 1991–1992*, pp. 142–43.

81. U.S. Arms Control and Disarmament Agency, *World Military Expenditures and Arms Transfers: 1993–1994* (Washington: Government Printing Office, 1995), p. 68; U.S. Arms Control and Disarmament Agency, *World Military Expenditures and Arms Transfers: 1987* (Washington: Government Printing Office, 1988), p. 63; and U.S. Arms Control and Disarmament Agency, *World Military Expenditures and Arms Transfers: 1970–1979* (Washington: Government Printing Office, 1982), p. 63.

Chapter 6

1. Robert Manning, "The US, ROK and North Korea: Anatomy of a Muddle," Paper presented to Carnegie Council on Ethics and International Affairs conference, "Peace and Stability in Korea: Prospects and Pitfalls," Washington, October 31, 1995, p. 1.

2. On the beginning of the nuclear effort, see Ministry of National Defense, *Defense White Paper: 1994–1995* (Seoul: Republic of Korea, 1994), p. 67.

3. For a more detailed listing, see ibid., p. 6.

4. Quoted in John Fialka, "North Korean Nuclear Effort Tests U.S.," *Wall Street Journal*, November 14, 1991, p. A10.

5. Paul Shin, "Defector Says N. Korea Building Atom Bomb," *Washington Post*, September 14, 1991, p. A20.

6. Robert Hall and Ian Kemp, eds., "North Korea: The Final Act," *Jane's Intelligence Review*, Special Report no. 2, 1994, p. 6.

7. Among the summaries of the painful negotiations, promises, inspections, denunciations, and threats are Michael Mazarr, *North Korea and the Bomb: A Case Study in Nonproliferation* (New York: St. Martin's, 1995); William Berry, *North Korea's Nuclear Program: The Clinton Administration's Response* (Colorado Springs: Institute for National Security Studies, 1995), pp. 2–31; Hakjoon Kim, "North Korea's Nuclear Development Program and the Future," in *US-Korean Relations at a Time of Change* (Seoul: Research

Institute for National Unification, 1994), pp. 53–64; "Promises, Promises (While Building the Bomb)," *New York Times*, March 20, 1994, p. E4; and Byung Chul Koh, "Confrontation and Cooperation on the Korean Peninsula: The Politics of Nuclear Nonproliferation," *Korean Journal of Defense Analysis* 6, no. 2 (Winter 1994): 53–83.

8. The IAEA monitoring process is described in F. R. Cleminson, "Ongoing Monitoring and Verification: Learning from the IAEA/UNSCOM Experience in Iraq," *Korean Journal of Defense Analysis* 7, no. 1 (Summer 1995): 129–54.

9. Quoted in David Easter, "Korea Talks Gain amid Nuke Scare Campaign," *Guardian*, November 20, 1991, p. 17.

10. Quoted in Edward Neilan, "Talks Topped by North Korea Nuclear Agenda," *Washington Times*, November 19, 1991, p. A7.

11. Quoted in David Sanger, "U.S. Officials Step Up Warnings to North Korea on Nuclear Arms," *New York Times*, November 21, 1991, p. A6.

12. Stephen Chapman, "A Nuclear North Korea: The Danger We Can't Ignore," Creators Syndicate, November 14, 1991.

13. Compare Stephen Chapman, "What Could Be Worse Than a North Korean Bomb?" Creators Syndicate, March 25, 1993, and Stephen Chapman, "Let's Not Panic over North Korea," *Orange County Register*, June 14, 1994, p. Metro 7.

14. For years the United States refused to formally confirm the presence of such weapons, but it was generally believed that Washington maintained between 100 and 150 nuclear artillery shells and air-delivered bombs on South Korean soil.

15. Quoted in David Rosenbaum, "U.S. to Pull A-Bombs from South Korea," *New York Times*, October 20, 1991, p. 3.

16. Quoted in Don Oberdorfer, "North Korean A-Arms Danger Is Downgraded," *Washington Post*, November 1, 1992, p. A34.

17. Pyongyang went to great lengths to camouflage the two waste depositories in an unsuccessful attempt to fool the IAEA. See Nayan Chanda, "Bomb and Bombast," *Far Eastern Economic Review*, February 10, 1994, pp. 16–17.

18. Democratic People's Republic of Korea, "Statement of the Government of the Democratic People's Republic of Korea," no. 7, March 12, 1993, p. 1.

19. DPRK diplomats made similar representations to William Taylor of the Center for Strategic and International Studies. Taylor, "Cool Off Korean Tensions," *New York Times*, March 27, 1993, p. 21.

20. Quoted in Warren Strobel, "North Korea Risks Sanctions, Christopher Warns," *Washington Times*, March 26, 1993, p. A7.

21. Quoted in Nicholas Kristof, "China Opposes U.N. over North Korea," *New York Times*, March 24, 1993, p. A6.

22. Paul Greenberg, "Unhappy Precedent," *Washington Times*, March 19, 1993, p. F3. See also William Rusher, "Genuine Threat to Peace," *Washington Times*, March 19, 1993, p. F3. Ken Adelman simply said that the DPRK "must be punished—fast and hard." Adelman, "Bearding the Spoiler," *Washington Times*, March 17, 1993, p. G1.

23. [Frank Gaffney,] "What to Do about North Korea's Nuclear Threat: Execute the 'Osirak' Remedy," Center for Security Policy, Decision Brief 93-D 20, March 19, 1993, p. 3.

24. Quoted in ibid., p. 3.

25. See, for example, Jack Anderson and Michael Binstein, "McCain's Korea Warning," *Washington Post*, May 29, 1994, p. C7; Frank Gaffney, "What to Do about North Korea's Nuclear Threat: Hold the 'Carrots,' Apply the 'Stick,' " Speech to the American Enterprise Institute, November 2, 1993; Henry Kissinger, "No Compromise, But a

Rollback," *Washington Post,* July 6, 1994, p. A19; Charles Krauthammer, "North Korea's Coming Bomb," *Washington Post,* November 5, 1993, p. A27; William Safire, "Reactor Roulette," *New York Times,* June 2, 1994, p. A23; Brent Scowcroft, "Korea: Time for Action," *Washington Post,* June 15, 1994, p. A25; and Lally Weymouth, "North Korea and the Specter of War," *Washington Post,* April 6, 1994, p. A19.

26. Quoted in Robert D. Novak, "Aborted Ultimatum," *Washington Post,* December 16, 1993, p. A25.

27. For some of the president's remarks, such as threatening "the end of their country as they know it," see "Clinton's Warning Irks North Korea," *New York Times,* July 13, 1993, p. A6; and Berry, pp. 13–14.

28. Quoted in Bill Gertz, "Shalikashvili Tells Fears on Korea," *Washington Times,* March 16, 1994, p. A6.

29. Quoted in Bill Gertz, "U.S. and Allies Discuss Sanctions on North Korea," *Washington Times,* June 6, 1994, p. A4.

30. Quoted in Rowan Scarborough, "Air Strike Rejected in Taming N. Korea," *Washington Times,* April 4, 1994, p. A4.

31. Quoted in Gertz, "U.S. and Allies Discuss Sanctions on North Korea."

32. Quoted in David Usborne, "Pentagon Talks War to N Korea," *Independent,* April 1, 1994, p. 13.

33. Quoted in Steven Holmes, "Clinton Still Supports Yeltsin, Despite Shift on the Election," *New York Times,* November 8, 1993, p. A6.

34. Quoted in Art Pine, "U.S. Moving to Ready Public for Korea Tensions," *Los Angeles Times,* May 3, 1994, Washington edition, p. 1.

35. James Fallows, "The Panic Gap," *National Interest* (Winter 1994–95): 41.

36. Ibid. Those sentiments were frequently expressed when I visited Seoul in May 1993. Indeed, the calm in East Asia has been widely observed, except, apparently, by policymakers in Washington. See, for example, Pete Engardio et al., "North Korea: Why Asia Is So Calm As Sabers Rattle in Washington," *Business Week,* June 20, 1994, p. 58; Merrill Goezner, "North Korea Neighbors Hoping Crisis with U.S. Is Really Over," *Chicago Tribune,* June 20, 1994, p. 6; R. Jeffrey Smith, "S. Korea Takes Softer Stand Than U.S. on the North," *Washington Post,* April 24, 1994, p. A22; R. Jeffrey Smith, "U.S. Tough Talk Rattles Nerves in Asia," *Washington Post,* April 4, 1994, p. A14; Steven Greenhouse, "South Korean Cautious on Sanctions," *New York Times,* February 12, 1994, p. 3; David Sanger, "North Korea's Nuclear Program Provokes No Panic in the South," *New York Times,* December 21, 1993, p. A1; Thomas Friedman, "U.S. and Seoul Differ on Offer to North," *New York Times,* November 24, 1993, p. A16; Michael Breen, "Seoul Fears U.S. Impatience with North Korea," *Washington Times,* November 11, 1993, p. A13; David Sanger, "Seoul's Big Fear: Pushing North Koreans Too Far," *New York Times,* November 7, 1993, p. A16; and David Sanger, "Neighbors Differ on How to Chasten North Korea," *New York Times,* March 31, 1993, p. A9.

37. Selig Harrison describes his trip in "The North Korean Nuclear Crisis: From Stalemate to Breakthrough," *Arms Control Today,* November 1994, pp. 18–20. For a detailed discussion of the Carter mission, see Young Whan Kihl, "Confrontation or Compromise on the Korean Peninsula: The North Korean Nuclear Issue," *Korean Journal of Defense Analysis* 6, no. 2 (Winter 1994): 112–18.

38. "Agreed Framework between the United States of America and the Democratic People's Republic of Korea," October 21, 1994; "Agreement on the Establishment of the Korean Peninsula Energy Development Organization," October 21, 1994; and

"US-DPRK Framework Agreement Time Line for Implementation (Briefed to Foreign Embassies on 10/20/94)," October 20, 1994. All were provided by the U.S. Department of State.

39. William Perry, "Korea: The Deal Is Working," *Washington Times*, January 24, 1995, p. A17.

40. Frank Gaffney, "Whistling Past Galluci Gulch," *Washington Times*, October 24, 1994, p. A20.

41. Paul Greenberg, "Trusting a Tyrant," *Washington Times*, October 24, 1994, p. A20.

42. Office of Robert Dole, "North Korea," Press release, October 19, 1994.

43. U.S. Senate Committee on Foreign Relations, *North Korea Nuclear Agreement: Hearings before the Committee on Foreign Relations*, 104th Cong., 1st sess., January 24–25, 1995, p. 41.

44. Ibid., p. 46.

45. Quoted in "U.S. Resuming Work under N. Korea Pact," *Washington Post*, June 16, 1995, p. A17.

46. See, for example, Steven Greenhouse, "North Korea Issues Threat over Reactor," *New York Times*, October 1, 1995, p. 9.

47. Quoted in R. Jeffrey Smith, "Year after Deal, U.S. and N. Korea Debating Details of Reactor Project," *Washington Post*, October 21, 1995, p. A26.

48. Quoted in Douglas Jehl, "U.S. Outlines Concern over North Korean A-Arms," *New York Times*, February 25, 1993, p. A7. The *Washington Post* goes even further, declaring that "the only explanation that makes sense . . . is that the latest inspections demanded by the International Atomic Energy Agency would have uncovered evidence of the bomb the North Koreans deny they're working on." "Nuclear Cheat," editorial, March 25, 1993, p. A24. Similar is the *Wall Street Journal*'s opinion that "the only possible conclusion is the obvious one: North Korea wants to have nukes." "North Korea's Bomb Threat," editorial, March 17, 1993, p. A14.

49. Paul Quinn-Judge, "Doubts Voiced over Threat of North Korea," *Boston Globe*, April 5, 1994, p. 8; "The North Korean Threat," advertisement, *New York Times*, February 28, 1994, p. A12; "Hide and Seek," *Far Eastern Economic Review*, February 10, 1994, pp. 18–19; Bruce Nelan, "A Game of Nuclear Roulette," *Time*, January 10, 1994, p. 4; David Sanger, "Despite Atom Accord, U.S. Asks: Does North Korea Have a Bomb?" *New York Times*, January 9, 1994, p. 1.; Stephen Engelberg and Michael Gordon, "Intelligence Study Says North Korea Has Nuclear Bomb," *New York Times*, December 26, 1993, pp. 1, 8; and William Claiborne, "N. Korea Is Not Trying to Build More Nuclear Bombs, Aspin Says," *Washington Post*, December 13, 1993, p. A13.

50. "This Week with David Brinkley," January 9, 1994, Reuter Transcript Report, p. 1.

51. "Seoul: North Has No Bomb," *Washington Post*, December 29, 1993, p. A16.

52. Steve Pagani, "Korean Defector's Tale Dismissed by Probers," *Washington Times*, July 30, 1995, p. A9; James Sterngold, "Defector Says North Korea Has Five A-Bombs and May Make More," *New York Times*, July 28, 1994, p. A7; and Steve Glain, "Defector Claims North Korea Has Five Bombs," *Wall Street Journal*, July 28, 1995, p. A8.

53. Jim Lea, "ROK Says N. Korea Expanding Its Military," *Pacific Stars & Stripes*, October 4, 1995, p. 7.

54. "North Korea's Nuclear Program: Challenge and Opportunity for American Policy," United States Institute of Peace, undated, p. 11. See also David Albright,

"How Much Plutonium Does North Korea Have?" *Bulletin of the Atomic Scientists,* September–October 1994, pp. 46–53; and "North Korea Suspected of Hiding Plutonium," *Chemical & Engineering News,* April 11, 1994, p. 5.

55. Robert Manning, "Clinton and the Korea Question: A Strategy for the Endgame," Progressive Policy Institute Policy Briefing Paper, July 7, 1994, p. 4.

56. Manning, "The US, ROK and North Korea," p. 5. Manning believes that "Kim Il Sung made a strategic decision to pursue an opening to the United States sometime in 1990 or 1991" (p. 4).

57. Selig Harrison, "Breaking the Nuclear Impasse: How North Korea Views the Nuclear Problem," Paper presented to Carnegie Endowment for International Peace symposium, "The United States and North Korea: What Next?" November 16, 1993, pp. 4–8.

58. William Taylor, "Prospects for the Agreed Framework: What Do We Do Now?" *Korean Journal of Defense Analysis* 7, no. 1 (Summer 1995): 76.

59. David Sanger, "North Korea's Motives Baffle U.S. and the South," *New York Times,* June 6, 1994, p. A8.

60. Charles Krauthammer, "Get Ready for War," *Washington Post,* June 3, 1994, p. A23.

61. Robert Manning, "Clinton and Korea: From Cross-Recognition to Trilateral Package," *Korean Journal of National Unification* 3 (August 1994): 66.

62. Richard Fisher, "North Korea's Nuclear Threat Challenges the World and Tests America's Resolve," Heritage Foundation Asian Studies Center Backgrounder no. 129, February 23, 1994, pp. 8–9.

63. Chung Min Lee, "The North Korean Nuclear Issue and the Korean-American Alliance," *Korean Journal of National Unification* 4 (1995): 43.

64. Asia Society, *Preventing Nuclear Proliferation in South Asia* (New York: Asia Society, 1995), p. 2.

65. International Institute for Strategic Studies, *Military Balance: 1993–1994* (London: Brassey's, 1993), p. 232.

66. All numbers involving the North are guesstimates, and work by Nicholas Eberstadt of the American Enterprise Institute shows a smaller gap between the two. Eberstadt, *Korea Approaches Reunification* (Armonk, N.Y.: M. E. Sharpe, 1995), p. 12. However, other analyses consistently show a larger difference. Compare the International Institute for Strategic Studies, which figured the respective GDPs in 1994 to be $379.6 billion and $20.9 billion, with the National Unification Board and Bank of Korea, which estimated $328.7 billion and $20.5 billion for the respective GNPs in the same year. International Institute for Strategic Studies, *The Military Balance: 1995–1996* (Oxford: Oxford University Press, 1995), pp. 185, 183; and Young Namkoong, "Assessment of the North Korean Economy: Status and Prospects," in *US-Korean Relations at a Time of Change,* p. 26.

67. Harrison, p. 3.

68. Few people admit to such concerns publicly, just as few publicly admit to fearing Japanese rearmament. But in private conversations with the author, several scholars and government officials have cited the possibility of ROK aggression as yet another reason to maintain American forces on the peninsula.

69. Taewoo Kim, "The United States and North Korea: A South Korean Perspective," Paper presented to Carnegie Endowment for International Peace symposium, p. 4. See also Franklin Weinstein and Fuji Kamiya, eds., *The Security of Korea: U.S. and Japanese Perspectives on the 1980s* (Boulder, Colo.: Westview, 1980), pp. 113–49.

One member of South Korea's ruling party claims that his nation intended to make atomic weapons as late as 1991. Paul Shin, "U.S. Said to Stop South Korea's Nuke Bomb Plans," *Washington Times*, March 28, 1994, p. A11.

70. Sang Hun-choe, "S. Korea Was Close to Having A-Bomb," *Washington Times*, October 6, 1995, p. A17.

71. Peter Hayes, *Pacific Powderkeg: American Nuclear Dilemmas in Korea* (Lexington, Mass.: Lexington Books, 1990), p. 211.

72. "Japan's Moves to Become a Nuclear Power," Institute for International Affairs (Pyongyang) *Bulletin Information* 28, no. 7 (July 1993): 7. See also "N. Korea Hits Japan on Nuclear Remarks," *Washington Times*, June 29, 1994, p. A11.

73. Merrill Goozner, "Koreas Ask Why As Japan Pushes Nuclear Program," *Chicago Tribune*, June 29, 1994, pp. 1, 10; and Barbara Opall, "S. Korea Fears Japanese Nuclear Capability," *Defense News*, December 13–19, 1993, p. 6.

74. "Japan: Nuclear-Capable," *Far Eastern Economic Review*, June 30, 1994, p. 13. See also Charles Radin, "In Japan, Quiet Talk of Nuclear Arms," *Boston Globe*, September 19, 1993, pp. 1, 15; Clayton Jones, "Korea Prompts Japan to Review No-Nukes Policy," *Christian Science Monitor*, August 10, 1993, pp. 1, 14; and Sam Jameson, "Official Says Japan Will Need Nuclear Arms if N. Korea Threatens," *Los Angeles Times* July 29, 1993, p. A4.

75. *Jane's Intelligence Review*, Special Report no. 2, p. 3.

76. Quoted in Shin, "Defector Says N. Korea Building Atom Bomb," p. A20.

77. Quoted in Haynes Johnson, "Lessons from the Gulf War," *Washington Post*, January 17, 1992, p. A2.

78. Quoted in Edith Lederer, "Report: N. Korea Sees a Low-Cost Deterrent," *Philadelphia Inquirer*, March 22, 1994, p. 8. For one summary of reasons other than military aggression for which the DPRK may have pursued the nuclear option, see Hakjoon Kim, "North Korea's Nuclear Development Program and Future," in *US-Korean Relations at a Time of Change*, pp. 64–75.

79. Lee Chung Min, "Seoul's Uncertain Trumpet," *Far Eastern Economic Review*, December 2, 1993, p. 23.

80. Arnold Kanter, "Carrot and Stick: The Nuclear Problem and the Normalization of Relations," Paper presented to Carnegie Endowment for International Peace symposium, p. 3.

81. Denny Roy, "North Korea and the 'Madman' Theory," *Security Dialogue* 25, no. 3 (September 1994): 309.

82. As Scott Snyder of the U.S. Institute of Peace puts it, the North's recent decisions "are all indications of a coherent policy and political order in Pyongyang." Snyder, "A Framework for Achieving Reconciliation on the Korean Peninsula," *Asian Survey* 35, no. 8 (August 1995): 701.

83. Barbara Starr, "N Korea Casts a Longer Shadow with TD-2," *Jane's Defense Weekly*, March 12, 1994; Clark Sorensen, "The Folly of Isolating a Nuclear North Korea," *New York Newsday*, December 5, 1993, p. 37; and David Wright and Timur Kadyshev, "The North Korean Missile Program: How Advanced Is It?" *Arms Control Today*, April 1994, pp. 9–12.

84. Martin Sieff, "Domino Effect Triggers Seoul, Tokyo Nuke Plans," *Washington Times*, March 23, 1994, pp. A1, A17.

85. "President Roh Unveils Bold New Nuclear Policy Initiative," Statement no. 91–58, issued by South Korean embassy, Washington, November 7, 1991.

86. Quoted in Easter.

87. See what purports to be a worst-case scenario that offers no concrete harm worse than that. "Caught Red-Handed," *Far Eastern Economic Review*, March 31, 1994, p. 5.

88. The United States and its allies do need a strategy. Robert Manning complains that the Clinton administration has operated largely without one, having instead "lurched from crisis to crisis." Manning, "The US, ROK and North Korea," p. 3.

89. "South Korea's Nuclear Program," p. 14.

90. Quoted in Jim Hoagland, "The Trojan Horse at North Korea's Gate," *Washington Post*, August 2, 1995, p. A25.

91. Indeed, as Secretary of State Warren Christopher observed in early 1995, if the North "had intended to do that, they probably would have had four or five years prior to now to do it, so I don't think the present agreement makes that situation any worse than it is." U.S. Senate Committee on Foreign Relations, p. 56.

92. South Koreans are frustrated by the lack of progress. Dong-bok Lee, "An Overview of ROK-DPRK Relations," Paper presented at Center for Strategic and International Studies and Research Institute for National Unification conference, Washington, September 20, 1995.

93. See, for example, Seongwhun Cheon, "Some Problems of the US-DPRK Agreed Framework: A South Korean View," Paper presented at Research Institute for National Unification–Cato Institute workshop on U.S.-ROK relations, Washington, September 5, 1995.

94. In fact, the accord appeared close to collapse in April 1995. Rowan Scarborough, "N. Korean Nuclear Deal Unravels," *Washington Times*, April 24, 1995, pp. A1, A20. Then negotiations started again. Willis Witter, "Nuclear Pact Leaves N. Koreans Gleeful," *Washington Times*, June 16, 1995, p. A15. There were also hints that the North wants to switch to nonnuclear energy plants. Steve Glain, "North Korea May Seek Overhaul of Nuclear Pact in Talks with U.S.," *Wall Street Journal*, May 18, 1995, p. A12. That will probably prove to be a recurring pattern, especially as the time for the IAEA to conduct its special inspections approaches.

95. For some assessments of the benefits and costs, see Byung Chul Koh, "Confrontation and Cooperation on the Korean Peninsula: The Politics of Nuclear Nonproliferation," *Korean Journal of Defense Analysis* 6, no. 2 (Winter 1994): 75–83; Jung Yong-suk, "Problems Left Behind by U.S.–N. Korean Nuclear Accord," *Korea Focus* 2, no. 5 (September–October 1994): 5–7; Ronald Lehman, "Some Considerations on Resolving the North Korean Nuclear Question," *Korean Journal of Defense Analysis* 6, no. 2 (Winter 1994): 11–33; Larry Niksch, "Opportunities and Challenges in Clinton's Confidence-Building Strategy towards North Korea," *Korean Journal of Defense Analysis* 6, no. 2 (Winter 1994): 145–56; Kim Dae-jung [Kim Dae Jung], "The Impact of the US–North Korean Agreement on Korean Reunification," *Korean Journal of Defense Analysis* 6, no. 2 (Winter 1994): 85–89; Walter Slocombe, "The Agreed Framework with the Democratic People's Republic of Korea," Institute for National Strategic Studies, Strategic Forum no. 23, March 1995; Jessica Mathews, "A Sound Beginning with North Korea," *Washington Post*, October 21, 1994, p. A25; Taylor, "Prospects for the Agreed Framework," pp. 69–94; and William Taylor, "US National Security Strategy and North Korea," in *US-Korean Relations at a Time of Change*, pp. 39–52.

96. Quoted in Ben Barber, "Hands Off Korea Pact, GOP Told," *Washington Times*, December 10, 1994, p. A14.

97. Georgie Anne Geyer, "Nuclear Deal Revisited," *Washington Times*, July 30, 1995, p. B4.

98. See, for example, Steve Glain, "North Korea's Position Is Hardening in Talks on Reactors, Liaison Offices," *Wall Street Journal*, October 17, 1995, p. A17.

99. Robert Manning, "Economic Sanctions or Economic Incentives?" Paper presented at Carnegie Endowment for International Peace symposium, pp. 8–14.

100. See, for example, Steve Glain, "Evolving North Korea Attracts Foreigners Seeking Business Deals," *Wall Street Journal*, September 20, 1995, pp. A1, A8.

101. Li Cong, "Some Views on the Reunification of South Korea and North Korea on the Korean Peninsula," *Korean Journal of National Unification*, Special Edition (1993): 34–36.

102. Manning, "Clinton and the Korea Question," p. 6.

103. Manning, "The US, ROK and North Korea," p. 9.

104. An increasingly promising economic dialogue was essentially halted as the nuclear crisis burgeoned in 1993. Shim Jae Hoon, "Dangerous Deadlock," *Far Eastern Economic Review*, June 22, 1995, p. 50; Jinwook Choi, "Inter-Korean Economic Cooperation: A Vital Element of Seoul's Unification Policy," *Korean Journal of National Unification* 4 (1995): 133–50; and *South Korea, North Korea: 1994–95* (London: The Economist Intelligence Unit, 1994), pp. 5–7.

105. Various inspection options are covered by Seong Cheon, "North Korea's Nuclear Problem: Current State and Future Prospects," *Korean Journal of National Unification* 2 (1993): 100–101.

106. The framework includes a provision that appears to offer a pledge of no first use, but the provision's meaning is disputed by some. See, for example, Cheon, pp. 1–7.

107. See, for example, "North Korea's Nuclear Program," pp. 20–21.

108. Kim Kyung-won, "Need for a Realistic Approach to North Korea," *Korea Focus* 2, no. 5 (September–October 1994): 10.

109. Kim, "The United States and North Korea," p. 7.

110. There are others as well. See Taylor, "Prospects for the Agreed Framework," p. 72.

111. Ibid., pp. 73–74.

112. Bill Gertz, "Warning Sounded on North Korea," *Washington Times*, April 25, 1995, p. A1.

113. "Buckley's View on Bombing China," *New York Times*, October 26, 1968, p. 16.

114. "Should We Bomb Red China's Bomb?" editorial, *National Review*, January 12, 1965, p. 9.

115. William F. Buckley Jr., "Meanwhile, Over in the East," *Washington Times*, June 11, 1993, p. F3.

116. Clark Sorensen, "The Folly of Isolating a Nuclear North Korea," *New York Newsday*, December 5, 1993, p. 37.

117. Taylor, "Prospects for the Agreed Framework," p. 80.

118. See, for example, Patrick Tyler, "Japanese Hears China Oppose Korea Sanctions," *New York Times*, June 13, 1994, p. A5; John Burton et al., "Seoul Sanctions Plea Is Snubbed," *Financial Times*, June 9, 1994, p. A6; and Peter Grier, "At UN, China Stalls US Drive for Action against North Korea," *Christian Science Monitor*, April 1, 1994, p. 4.

119. Much of this money comes from Pachinko gambling shops and export-import firms, which dominate foreign investment in the North. See, for example, Manning, "Economic Sanctions or Economic Incentives?" pp. 7–8. A far lower estimate comes from Marcus Noland, "Prospects for the North Korean Economy," Paper presented

to Workshop on North Korea, Claremont McKenna College, Claremont, California, February 2–3, 1996, pp. 12–16.

120. See, for example, David Sanger, "Tokyo Reluctant to Levy Sanctions on North Koreans," *New York Times,* June 9, 1994, pp. A1, A7; T. R. Reid, "Japan Weighs Own Embargo of North Korea," *Washington Post,* June 7, 1994, p. A13; David Sanger, "Japan Split over Role in a North Korea Showdown," *New York Times,* April 24, 1994, p. A3; and Willis Witter, "Japan Can Ease Effect of N. Korea Sanction," *Washington Times,* February 11, 1994, p. A18.

121. Quoted in Lee Michael Katz, "Tricky Path Ahead on N. Korea," *USA Today,* June 3, 1994, p. 4A. See also Alessandra Stanley, "Moscow Is Miffed by U.S. Draft on Korea," *New York Times,* June 17, 1994, p. A10.

122. For a detailed look at the German experience and possible parallels with Korea, see *Economic Problems of National Unification* (Seoul: Research Institute for National Unification, 1993).

123. John Keegan, *The Second World War* (New York: Viking, 1989), p. 249.

124. See, for example, Robert Dallek, *Franklin D. Roosevelt and American Foreign Policy, 1932–1945* (New York: Oxford University Press, 1979), p. 302.

125. Quoted in William Henry Chamberlin, *America's Second Crusade* (Chicago: Regnery, 1950), p. 154. See also George Friedman and Meredith Lebard, *The Coming War with Japan* (New York: St. Martin's, 1991), p. 394.

126. Hisahiko Okazaki, "Thoughts on the North Korean Nuclear Issue," *Korean Journal of National Unification,* Special Edition (1993): 26. Obviously, there are a number of forms of economic pressure, which entail varying risks of pushing the peninsula to war. Taylor, "US National Security Strategy and North Korea," p. 51.

127. Manning, "Clinton and Korea," p. 69.

128. David Hamilton, "North Korea Threatens War against Japan," *Wall Street Journal,* June 10, 1994, p. A6; Paul Shin, "N. Korea Repeats Threat of War over Sanctions by U.N.," *Washington Post,* June 7, 1994, p. A18; and Teruaki Ueno, "N. Korea Lashes Out at Sanctions," *Washington Post,* February 13, 1994, p. A18.

129. R. Jeffrey Smith, "North Korea Bolsters Border Force," *Washington Post,* November 6, 1993, p. A19; and "N. Korea Brings Out Big Guns to Guard Nuke Facility," *Washington Times,* January 11, 1994, p. A11.

130. "Word for Word," *Defense News,* May 23–29, 1994, p. 30. See also Richard Allen, "Ten Steps to Address North Korea's Nuclear Threat," Heritage Foundation Executive Memorandum no. 378, March 31, 1994, p. 1.

131. Taylor, "US National Security Strategy and North Korea," p. 52. Richard Haass of the Carnegie Endowment for International Peace applied the same argument to proposals for military strikes: "Retaliation would be made less threatening and less likely if the U.S. and South Korea accelerated military preparations." Haass, "Keep the Heat on North Korea," *New York Times,* June 17, 1994, p. A31.

132. Anthony Lewis, "On Korea, Resolve," *New York Times,* June 13, 1994, p. A15.

133. Quoted in David Sanger, "Clinton, in Seoul, Tells North Korea to Drop Arms Plan," *New York Times,* July 11, 1993, p. 8. See also Joachim Scholz, "Military Options on the Korean Peninsula," in *US-Korean Relations at a Time of Change,* p. 140.

134. Mark Helprin, "My Brilliant Korea," *Wall Street Journal,* July 25, 1994, p. A14.

135. Quoted in Don Phillips, "Sanctions a First Step, U.S. Warns North Korea," *Washington Post,* April 4, 1994, p. A15.

136. John McCain, "Statement on United States Policy and the Crisis in Korea," May 24, 1993, pp. 12–13.

137. Okazaki, p. 25.

138. Richard McCormack, "Charting a Nuclear Course," *Washington Times*, July 15, 1995, p. A21.

139. A dissonant note comes from Robert Gaskin, who formerly served in the U.S. Department of Defense Office of Net Assessment. Gaskin, "Faulty Assessment of the Dangers," *Washington Times*, November 30, 1993, p. A15. He is, however, in a decided minority. See, for example, *Jane's Intelligence Review*, pp. 21–24; Bruce Bennett, "The Prospects for Conventional Conflict on the Korean Peninsula," *Korean Journal of Defense Analysis* 7, no. 1 (Summer 1995): 95–127; "Seoul Is Confident: North Couldn't Win," *International Herald Tribune*, March 29, 1994, p. 4; William Taylor, "Heading Off a Korea Showdown," *Washington Post*, November 21, 1993, p. A29; and Eugene Carroll, "Overstating the Danger of North Korea," *Washington Post*, April 22, 1994, p. A25.

140. Chongwook Chung, "The Korean War and Inter-Korean Relations," in *The Korean War: 40-Year Perspectives*, ed. Chae-Jin Lee (Claremont, Calif.: Claremont McKenna College, 1991), p. 73.

141. The 1961 Mutual Aid, Cooperation and Friendship Treaty, which commits China to support the DPRK in the event the latter is attacked, theoretically remains in force, but it envisions a defensive war. Whether Beijing would live up to its obligation in this limited case is by no means certain, though the possibility may offer a useful restraint on the temptation for the ROK to unify the peninsula by force at some future date. In any case, columnist William Safire's fear about Chinese "volunteers" streaming forth to aid DPRK invasion forces is really a paranoid fantasy. Safire, "Reactor Roulette," *New York Times*, June 2, 1994, p. A23. More measured is American Enterprise Institute scholar Nicholas Eberstadt, who worries that proximity might force China, Japan, and Russia all to intervene. Eberstadt, p. 142. However, nonnuclear warfare would pose no obvious threat to neighboring nations, and the lethality of the combat—in contrast to the typical UN peacekeeping mission—would make them hesitant to enter. If they did, it is by no means certain that even China would favor the North.

On Russian intervention, see Vladimir Miasnikov, "Russian–South Korean Security Cooperation," *Korean Journal of Defense Analysis* 6, no. 2 (Winter 1994): 313–41.

On the probable duration of a war, see Taylor, "Prospects for the Agreed Framework," p. 83.

142. Quoted in David Ignatius, "The Secret Korea Debate," *Washington Post*, June 12, 1994, p. C2.

143. Bennett, p. 121. See also Taylor, "US Security Strategy and North Korea," pp. 49–50.

144. Richard Fisher, "North Korea's Nuclear Threat: A Test for Bill Clinton," Heritage Foundation Backgrounder Update no. 190, March 23, 1993, p. 3.

145. Chapman, "A Nuclear North Korea."

146. Iraq's later Scud assaults on Israel were really directed at the multilateral coalition against Saddam Hussein. Moreover, he attacked with the knowledge that the United States would try to restrain Tel Aviv's response.

147. Quoted in Steven Weisman, "North Korea Adds Barriers to A-Plant Inspections," *New York Times*, October 24, 1991, p. A11.

148. "N Korea's 'Sea of Fire' Threat Shakes Seoul," *Financial Times*, March 22, 1994, p. 6.

149. Taylor, "Prospects for the Agreed Framework," p. 79.

150. Kevin Sullivan, "All Eyes—and Ears—On N. Korea," *Washington Post*, October 27, 1995, pp. A27, A30.

151. Shim Jae Hoon, "Empty Driver's Seat," *Far Eastern Economic Review*, October 26, 1995. There has long been much speculation about splits in Pyongyang between moderates and hard-liners. See, for example, Hyun In-taek and Masao Okonogi, "Security Cooperation in East Asia," *Korea Focus* 2, no. 5 (September–October 1994): 53–54; and Yinhay Ahn, "Elite Politics and Policy Making in North Korea: A Policy Tendency Analysis," *Korean Journal of National Unification* 2 (1993): 63–84. While such a division likely exists, most North Korean "moderates" would probably look rather hard-line to anyone living in the democratic, capitalist West. The progeny of older, long-ago-suppressed factions might also play a role in any political infighting. See, for example, Alexander Zhebin, "North Korea after Kim Il Sung: Hard Choices," *Korean Journal of Defense Analysis* 7, no. 1 (Summer 1995): 211–32. Indeed, Kim Jong Il faces a host of problems caused by supposed loyalists, let alone possible opponents, if he attempts to navigate the path to genuine reform in North Korea. For one look at the people and factions surrounding him, see Adrian Buzo, "The DPRK and Late De-Stalinization," *Korean Journal of National Unification* 4 (1995): 151–71.

152. Richard Macke, Testimony before U.S. Senate Armed Services Committee, February 16, 1995 (photocopy), p. 4.

153. Quoted in Fallows, p. 44.

154. Conversations during the author's trip to Seoul in July 1995.

155. George Melloan, "America the Feeble?—You Ain't Seen Nothing Yet," *Wall Street Journal*, March 28, 1994, p. A13.

156. Quoted in Thomas Friedman, "China Stalls Anti-Atom Effort on Korea," *New York Times*, November 15, 1991, p. A12.

157. See, for example, Jim Mann, "China Helped Bring About N. Korea's Change of Heart," *Los Angeles Times*, June 29, 1994, p. 1; and Steven Strasser, "Cooperate on Nukes, China Urges N. Korea," *Washington Times*, January 7, 1994, p. A15.

158. Jeffrey Parker, "Japan Nudges N. Korea on Ties," *Washington Times*, October 1, 1995, p. A7.

159. Officials freely acknowledged their economic problems during the author's trip to Pyongyang in August 1992.

160. Quoted in Sullivan, p. A30.

161. Quoted in Damon Darlin, "Roh's Nuclear-Free Pledge May Advance Effort to Inspect North Korean Facilities," *Wall Street Journal*, November 11, 1991, p. A10.

162. That sentiment was expressed by a number of officials during the author's trip to Seoul and Tokyo in July 1995.

163. Georgie Anne Geyer, ". . . Cautious Listeners," *Washington Times*, June 8, 1994, p. A14.

164. The U.S. Department of Defense is set to spend about $12 billion on theater missile defense between 1995 and 1999. South Korea first discussed participation in the Reagan administration's Strategic Defense Initiative a decade ago; concerns raised about the impact on relations with the Soviet Union obviously no longer apply. See, for example, Kang Suk Rhee, "South Korea's Participation in the SDI," *Armed Forces and Society* 14, no. 3 (Spring 1988): 391–406.

165. Stefan Halper, "The Imperatives and Alternatives," *Washington Times*, June 11, 1994, p. D3.

166. "What to Do about North Korea's Nuclear Threat," p. 2.

167. U.S. Senate Committee on Foreign Relations, p. 16.

168. "What Does North Korea Want?" editorial, *Washington Times*, March 28, 1994, p. A22.

169. See, for example, David Kay, "Don't Wait for a Change of Heart in North Korea," *Wall Street Journal*, March 18, 1993, p. A12; Frank Gaffney, "Patriots to Korea: Is That All There Is?" *Washington Times*, January 28, 1994, p. A21; James George, "U.S. Should Deploy SSGN to Deter North Korean Threat," *Defense News*, December 20–26, 1993, p. 14; Seth Cropsey, "Clinton's Retreat on North Korea Invites Aggression," Heritage Foundation Backgrounder Update no. 210, January 14, 1994, p. 2; Kanter, p. 12; and Richard Fisher, "North Korea's Nuclear Threat Challenges the World and Tests America's Resolve," Heritage Foundation Asian Studies Center Backgrounder no. 129, February 23, 1994, p. 12.

170. Fisher, "North Korea's Nuclear Threat: A Test for Bill Clinton," p. 3.

171. Quoted in "Woolsey's Visit, Patriots Prompt N. Korean Threat," *Washington Times*, January 31, 1994, p. A13.

172. Ignatius, p. C2.

173. Michael Breen, "U.S. Officials Reassure S. Korea," *Washington Times*, October 20, 1994, p. A13.

174. Naturally, one South Korean analyst insists that the United States "must not weaken its remaining nuclear umbrella over South Korea." Kim, "The United States and North Korea," p. 10.

175. For a detailed analysis of the risks of America's alliance with Pakistan, see Ted Galen Carpenter, *A Search for Enemies: America's Alliances after the Cold War* (Washington: Cato Institute, 1992), pp. 113–25.

176. See, for example, Seymour Hersh, "On the Nuclear Edge," *New Yorker*, March 29, 1993, pp. 56–73; "Report: Kashmir Nuke War Was Near," *Washington Times*, March 22, 1993, p. A5; and Douglas Jehl, "Assertion India and Pakistan Faced Nuclear War Is Doubted," *New York Times*, March 23, 1993, p. A3.

177. See, for example, R. Jeffrey Smith, "U.S., Ukraine, Russia Near Deal on Arms," *Washington Post*, January 9, 1994, pp. A1, A33; Bill Gertz, "Shaky Security Guarantees Could Undermine Nuke Pact," *Washington Times*, January 13, 1994, p. A14; and Ted Galen Carpenter, "Staying Out of Potential Nuclear Crossfires," Cato Institute Policy Analysis no. 199, November 24, 1993, pp. 13–14.

178. Quoted in Doug Bandow, "Let 'Em Have Nukes," *New York Times Magazine*, November 13, 1994, p. 56.

179. "About That Ukraine Agreement," editorial, *Washington Post*, January 14, 1994, p. A22.

180. Hall and Kemp, pp. 11–15.

181. "Nukes within Reach of Taiwan, Lee Says," *Washington Times*, August 1, 1995, p. A17.

182. See the concerns cited in Michael Mandelbaum, "Lessons of the Next Nuclear War," *Foreign Affairs* 74, no. 2 (March–April 1995): 27–28. The contrary argument, made by some, is that the spread of nuclear weapons would be stabilizing. See, for example, Richard Rhodes, "Echoes of the Big Bang," *New York Times*, July 15, 1995, p. 21; and Kenneth Waltz, "The Spread of Nuclear Weapons: More May Be Better," International Institute for Strategic Studies, Adelphi Paper no. 171, 1981. The latter argument has some force but underestimates the potential of an expensive breakdown of a multipolar nuclear regime.

183. Richard Fisher, "Price of Failure in North Korea," *Washington Times*, January 18, 1994, p. A17.

184. The nuclear capabilities of China and Russia are discussed in Gerald Segal, "What Can We Do about Nuclear Forces in Northeast Asia?" *Korean Journal of Defense Analysis* 6, no. 2 (Winter 1994): 36–39. See also Gerald Segal, "China's Nuclear Posture for the 1980s," in *Security in East Asia,* ed. Robert O'Neill (New York: St. Martin's, 1984), pp. 70–77; and Dunbar Lockwood, "The Status of the U.S., Russian and Chinese Nuclear Forces in Northeast Asia," *Arms Control Today,* November 1994, pp. 21–24.

185. "Japan Freezes Grant Aid to China," *Washington Post,* August 30, 1995, p. A17.

186. See, for example, Greenpeace International, *The Unlawful Plutonium Alliance: Japan's Supergrade Plutonium and the Role of the United States* (Amsterdam: Greenpeace International, 1994), pp. 27–31; Robert Manning, "Rethinking Japan's Plutonium Policy: Key to Global Non-Proliferation and Northeast Asian Security," *Journal of East Asian Affairs* 9, no. 1 (Winter–Spring 1995): 121–23; Charles Smith, "Touchy Subject," *Far Eastern Economic Review,* September 29, 1994, pp. 16, 18; and Michael Williams, "Japan Was Urged to Keep Potential for Nuclear Weapons," *Wall Street Journal,* August 2, 1994, p. A10.

187. Kim, "The United States and North Korea," p. 13.

188. Fallows, p. 42.

189. Kanter, p. 3.

190. Quoted in Jack Anderson and Michael Binstein, "McCain's Korea Warning," *Washington Post,* May 29, 1994, p. C7.

191. Stefan Halper, "Picking a Path through the Nuke Field," *Washington Times,* April 7, 1994, p. A17.

192. Ted Galen Carpenter, "A New Proliferation Policy," *National Interest* (Summer 1992): 67–68.

193. Anti-missile technologies are a matter of some interest throughout East Asia. Jae Kyu Park and Byung-joon Ahn [Ahn Byung-joon], eds., *The Strategic Defense Initiative: Its Implications for Asia and the Pacific* (Boulder, Colo.: Westview, 1987); and Richard Fisher, "Building a More Secure Asia through Missile Defense," Heritage Foundation, Asia Studies Center Backgrounder no. 138, October 24, 1995. For an expression of Japanese interest, see Okazaki, p. 29.

194. Carpenter, "A New Proliferation Policy," pp. 70–71.

Chapter 7

1. Ministry of National Defense, *Defense White Paper: 1994–1995* (Seoul: Republic of Korea, 1995), p. 127.

2. Ibid., p. 44. For slightly lower estimates, see Defense Agency, *Defense of Japan: 1994* (Tokyo: Defense Agency, 1994), p. 35. Cited hereafter as *Defense of Japan.*

3. Quoted in Jim Lea, "N. Korea Threat Alive, Official Says," *Pacific Stars & Stripes,* September 9, 1995, p. 1.

4. Selig Harrison, *The Widening Gulf: Asian Nationalism and American Policy* (New York: Free Press, 1978), pp. 376–78.

5. Ronald McLaurin, "Security Relations: Burden-Sharing in a Changing Strategic Environment," in *Alliance under Tension: The Evolution of South Korean–U.S. Relations,* ed. Manwoo Lee, Ronald McLaurin, and Chung-in Moon (Boulder, Colo.: Westview, 1988), p. 162.

6. James Kelly, "U.S. Security Policy in East Asia: Fighting Erosion and Finding a New Balance," *Washington Quarterly* 18, no. 3 (Summer 1995): 23.

7. U.S. Department of Defense, *United States Security Strategy for the East Asia–Pacific Region* (Washington: U.S. Department of Defense, February 1995), p. 1. Cited hereafter as *United States Security Strategy*.

8. See, for example, ibid. p. iv; and International Institute for Strategic Studies, *The Military Balance: 1995–1996* (Oxford: Oxford University Press, 1995), pp. 30–31. Cited hereafter as *The Military Balance: 1995–1996*.

9. *United States Security Strategy*, p. 30.

10. During a visit by the author to Tokyo in July 1995, Japanese officials in both the Defense and Foreign Ministries were quite explicit about their expectation of American involvement in those sorts of potential conflicts. Oddly enough, China is another nation with which the United States has forged a modest military relationship.

11. *United States Security Strategy*, p. 6.

12. Chang-Il Ohn, "South Korea's New Defense Policy and Military Strategy," *Korean Journal of Defense Analysis* 6, no. 1 (Summer 1994): 231.

13. Michael Baier, "From Forward Defense to Forward Presence: Military Factors Influencing the ROK and US Combined Forces in the Approaching Era," *Korean Journal of Defense Analysis* 6, no. 2 (Winter 1994): 261–84.

14. Quoted in Richard Fisher, "The Clinton Administration's Early Defense Policy toward Asia," *Korean Journal of Defense Analysis* 6, no. 1 (Summer 1994): 107. Perhaps the only surprise is that Washington would be influenced by the welcome accorded U.S. soldiers.

15. For a general discussion of this issue, see Ted Galen Carpenter, *A Search for Enemies: America's Alliances after the Cold War* (Washington: Cato Institute, 1992), pp. 161–65; and Doug Bandow and Ted Galen Carpenter, "Preserving an Obsolete NATO," *Cato Policy Report* 12, no. 5 (September–October 1990): 1, 10–12.

16. *United States Security Strategy*, p. 2.

17. George Will, "History Revs Its Engine," *Newsweek*, September 18, 1995, p. 90.

18. Robert Scalapino, "A Framework for Regional Security Cooperation in Asia," *Korean Journal of Defense Analysis* 5, no. 2 (Winter 1993): 12.

19. *United States Security Strategy*, p. 3.

20. See Mike Mochizuki and Michael O'Hanlon, "We Don't Need Okinawa," *Washington Times*, December 27, 1995, p. A15.

21. McLaurin, p. 163.

22. See, for example, the lament of A. James Gregor of the University of California at Berkeley, "The People's Republic of China and U.S. Security Policy in East Asia," in *Collective Defense or Strategic Independence? Alternative Strategies for the Future*, ed. Ted Galen Carpenter (Lexington, Mass.: Lexington Books, 1989), pp. 109–15.

23. *The Military Balance: 1995–1996*, p. 113; International Institute for Strategic Studies, *The Military Balance 1989–1990* (London: Brassey's, 1989), p. 32; and International Institute for Strategic Studies, *The Military Balance: 1986–1987* (London: International Institute for Strategic Studies, 1986), p. 33. See also U.S. Arms Control and Disarmament Agency, *World Military Expenditures and Arms Transfers: 1993–1994* (Washington: Government Printing Office, 1995), pp. 79, 81.

24. The latter remains a potent force but has shrunk markedly in just six years. Compare *The Military Balance: 1995–1996*, p. 118, with International Institute for Strategic Studies, *The Military Balance: 1989–1990*, p. 42. In fact, Japan is not overly worried about Moscow's modernizing its forces while reducing force levels. *Defense of Japan*, p. 43.

25. Hyon-Sik Yon, "The Russian Security Interests in Northeast Asia," *Korean Journal of Defense Analysis* 6, no. 1 (Summer 1994): 157.

26. Ministry of National Defense, *Defense White Paper: 1993–1994* (Seoul: Republic of Korea, 1994), p. 45.

27. One observer points to the precedents of the Japanese-Russian treaty of 1905 and the Camp David accord for the Mideast. Thomas Robinson, "Post–Cold War Security in the Asia-Pacific Region," in *The Chinese and Their Future: Beijing, Taipei, and Hong Kong*, ed. Zhiling Lin and Thomas Robinson (Washington: American Enterprise Institute, 1994), pp. 401–2. For Russia's view of the issue, see Yon, pp. 166–69.

28. Writes Thomas McNaugher of the Brookings Institution: "U.S. forces will play a major role in balancing China in the worst case that China indeed emerges as a threat to its neighbors." He also writes of applying "international discipline" to the Chinese military build-up. McNaugher, "U.S. Military Forces in East Asia: The Case for Long-Term Engagement," in *The United States, Japan, and Asia: Challenges for U.S. Policy*, ed. Gerald Curtis (New York: Norton, 1994), p. 212.

29. See, for example, Susan Lawrence and Tim Zimmermann, "A Political Test of When Guns Matter," *U.S. News & World Report*, October 30, 1995, p. 48; Keith Richburg, "China Bitterly Attacks Critics in U.S.," *Washington Post*, August 24, 1995, p. A29; "Asia-Pacific Region Uneasy over U.S.-China Tensions," *Washington Times*, August 21, 1995, p. A9; and Seth Faison, "Beijing Sees U.S. Moves as Plot to Thwart China," *New York Times*, August 1, 1995, p. A2.

30. A. James Gregor, "East Asian Security in the Gorbachev Era," in *The U.S.–South Korean Alliance: Time for a Change*, ed. Doug Bandow and Ted Galen Carpenter (New Brunswick, N.J.: Transaction Publishers, 1992), p. 166. For his critical review of America's relationship with Beijing, see A. James Gregor, *Arming the Dragon: U.S. Security Ties with the People's Republic of China* (Washington: Ethics and Public Policy Center, 1987).

31. Will. Columnist Arnold Beichman says that the PRC "is driven by an appetite for hegemony." Beichman, "Echoes of Past China Policies that Failed," *Washington Times*, October 11, 1995, p. A17. Al Santoli of Freedom House calls Beijing "a ruthless giant." Santoli, "China's Rapid Military Rise Threatens U.S.," *Insight*, April 24, 1995, p. 35. Somewhat more restrained, but still worried, is Nicholas Kristof, "The Real Chinese Threat," *New York Times Magazine*, August 27, 1995, pp. 50–51.

32. Jeffrey Hart, "Is War with China in America's Future?" *Conservative Chronicle*, August 2, 1995, p. 26. Sino-American conflict is also the stuff of novels. Steve Pieczenik, *Pax Pacifica* (New York: Warner Books, 1995).

33. Those arms sales, of course, have occasioned some controversy. See, for example, Martin Lasater, "Chinese Military Modernization," in *Security in Northeast Asia: Approaching the Pacific Century*, ed. Stephen Gibert (Boulder, Colo.: Westview, 1988), pp. 172–77. For a look at recent U.S.-PRC relations, see Harry Harding, *A Fragile Relationship: The United States and China since 1972* (Washington: Brookings Institution, 1992).

34. "Should We Bomb Red China's Bomb?" editorial, *National Review*, January 12, 1965, p. 9.

35. Robert Sutter, "Implications of China's Modernization for East and Southeast Asian Security: The Year 2000," in *China's Global Presence: Economics, Politics, and Security*, ed. David Lampton and Catherine Keyser (Washington: American Enterprise Institute, 1988), pp. 204–9.

36. For example, trade between China and South Korea ran $15 billion in 1995, an almost 50 percent increase over the year before. "Visit from China Leader Strengthening Seoul Ties," *New York Times*, November 14, 1995, p. A7.

37. William Clark, "Bilateral Security Arrangements in a Regional Perspective: Time for New Thinking May Be Short," in *US-Korean Relations at a Time of Change* (Seoul: Research Institute for National Unification, 1994), pp. 91–92.

38. Hammond Rolph, "China's Changing World View," in *Chinese Defence Policy*, ed. Gerald Segal and William Tow (London: Macmillan, 1984), p. 167. For other discussions of Beijing's weaknesses and fears, see, for example, Ralph Cossa, "China's Changing Security Environment: Implications for Northeast Asia Security," *Korean Journal of Defense Analysis* 6, no. 1 (Summer 1994): 149; Matt Forney, "Under Fire," *Far Eastern Economic Review*, August 31, 1995, p. 38; and Carpenter, *A Search for Enemies*, pp. 49–50.

39. Larry Niksch, "Southeast Asia," in *Chinese Defense Policy*, p. 239.

40. June Teufel Dreyer, "China's Military Power in the 1980s," in *The Challenge of China and Japan: Politics and Development in East Asia*, ed. Susan Shirk and Kevin Kennedy (New York: Praeger, 1985), pp. 429–37.

41. *The Military Balance: 1995–1996*, pp. 176, 181, 185. The International Institute for Strategic Studies' estimates fall in the middle of a wide range of estimates. Under Secretary of Defense, "China in the Near Term," August 1–10, 1994 (photocopy), p. 21. See also *United States Security Strategy*, p. 15.

42. U.S. Arms Control and Disarmament Agency, p. 58.

43. Paul Humes Folta, *From Swords to Plowshares? Defense Industry Reform in the PRC* (Boulder, Colo.: Westview, 1992), pp. 18–20.

44. Shunji Taoka, "A Shrinking Tiger," *Newsweek*, November 15, 1993, p. 19, Asian edition. But compare Stefan Halper, "Failing to Scale Summits of Possibility," *Washington Times*, November 5, 1995, p. B3. See also Arthur Waldron, "Deterring China," *Commentary*, October 1995, p. 19.

45. See, for example, Chong Yoon, "Problems of Modernizing the PLA: Domestic Constraints," in *China's Military Modernization: International Implications*, ed. Larry Wortzel (Westport, Conn.: Greenwood, 1988), pp. 2–25; and Carpenter, *A Search for Enemies*, pp. 49–50.

46. *Defense of Japan*, p. 51. See also Steven Mufson, "China's New Muscle: Military or Monetary?" *Washington Post*, July 24, 1995, pp. A1, A16.

47. Taoka.

48. For a discussion of political-military relations in the PRC, see Ellis Joffe, "Civil-Military Relations," in *Chinese Defense Policy*, pp. 18–35; and Feng Shengbao, "Party and Army in Chinese Politics—Neither Alliance nor Opposition," in *The Chinese and Their Future*, pp. 58–81.

49. Robinson, p. 392.

50. See, for example, Kelly, p. 27.

51. Which is not to say that Moscow is indifferent to events in China. See, for example, Alexei Voskressenski, "Russia's China Challenge," *Far Eastern Economic Review*, June 22, 1995, p. 34. However, even the most enthusiastic interventionist has not yet suggested making Russia an American defense dependent.

52. For a discussion of the latter, more recent, conflict, see Takashi Tajima, "China and South-East Asia: Strategic Interests and Policy Prospects," in *Security in East Asia*, ed. Robert O'Neill (New York: St. Martin's, 1984), pp. 101–2.

53. This seems to be the preponderant, though not unanimous, view in Tokyo. See, for example, *Japanese-American Security Cooperation in the Post–Cold War Era*, Policy Studies Report 2, no. 1 (Washington: George Washington University, 1994), pp. 9–10.

Among the volumes covering Sino-Japanese relations are Chae-Jin Lee, *China and Japan: New Economic Diplomacy* (Stanford, Calif.: Hoover Institution, 1984); R. K. Jain, *China and Japan: 1949–1980*, 2d ed. (Atlantic Highlands, N.J.: Humanities Press, 1981); and Peter Mueller and Douglas Ross, *China and Japan—Emerging Global Powers* (New York: Praeger, 1975), pp. 116–25.

54. A. Doak Barnett, *China and the Major Powers in East Asia* (Washington: Brookings Institution, 1977), p. 147.

55. *Defense of Japan*, pp. 50–53. Obviously, not all Japanese analysts are so sanguine.

56. See, for example, Chae-Jin Lee, "Japan and China: From Hostility to Accommodation," in *Northeast Asian Security after Vietnam*, ed. Martin Weinstein (Urbana: University of Illinois Press, 1982), pp. 95–127.

57. See, for example, William Tow, "China's Modernization and the Big Powers: Strategic Implications," in *China's Global Presence*, pp. 184–86. However, judging from private conversations, that sentiment seems to have waned some.

58. Quoted in Kathy Wilhem, "China's Li Thumps Nationalist Drum," *Washington Times*, October 1, 1995, p. A9.

59. Toshiyuki Shikata, "Japan's Security Strategy in a New Era," Paper presented to the Trilateral (Germany-USA-Japan) Conference, "Challenges of the 21st Century," Berlin, June 12, 1995, p. 12.

60. Thomas Robinson contends that "no Asian state—even a heavily rearmed Japan—could cope with the new Chinese power by itself." Robinson, p. 393. However, why that would be the case is not clear. It will undoubtedly be decades before the PRC surpasses Japan's GDP; it will be more years before China can aspire to match Tokyo's technological edge. And even with an inferior army, Japan could construct sufficient air and naval forces to protect sea lanes and its own territory.

61. For that reason some analysts believe that Beijing would impose a blockade rather than invade the island nation. See, for example, Paul Godwin, "The Use of Military Force against Taiwan: Potential PRC Scenarios," in *If China Crosses the Taiwan Strait: The International Response*, ed. Parris Chang and Martin Lasater (Lanham, Md.: University Press of America, 1993), pp. 15–33.

62. See Scalapino, pp. 18–20. And Beijing certainly expressed its concern after the visit of Taiwan's Lee Teng-hui to the United States. See, for example, Patrick Tyler, "China Warns U.S. Again on Taiwan," *New York Times*, November 11, 1995, p. 6; Lorien Holland, "China Threatens to Take Taiwan by Force if Pushed," *Washington Times*, October 20, 1995, p. A15; and Kathy Chen, "Taiwan Looms over U.S.-China Summit," *Wall Street Journal*, October 11, 1995, p. A10.

63. Compare Frank Ching, "China Impact on Taiwan Election," *Far Eastern Economic Review*, November 9, 1995, p. 59; Keith Richburg, "Taiwan Candidates Muffle Freedom Call to Calm Voters Fearful of China Backlash," *Washington Post*, November 7, 1995, p. A19; Patrick Tyler, "Tough Stance toward China Pays Off for Taiwan Leader," *New York Times*, August 29, 1995, pp. A1, A8; and Julian Baum, "A Case of Nerves," *Far Eastern Economic Review*, July 20, 1995, p. 26; with Guocang Huan, "Changing China-Taiwan Relations," in *The Chinese and Their Future*, pp. 418–41; and Douglas Habecker, "Cool Feet," *Far Eastern Economic Review*, October 12, 1995, pp. 148, 150. Perhaps the best evidence of change is the fact that the Taiwanese

islands of Quemoy and Matsu, once under daily artillery attack, are now largely demilitarized. Patrick Tyler, "For Taiwan's Frontier Islands, the War Is Over," *New York Times*, October 4, 1995, p. A3.

64. " 'The Problem Is Political Will,' " *U.S. News & World Report*, October 23, 1995, p. 72.

65. Robinson, p. 403.

66. On Lee's threat, see "Nukes within Reach of Taiwan, Lee Says," *Washington Times*, August 1, 1995, p. A17. Beijing has reportedly told the Clinton administration that it is prepared to use military force against Taiwan unless that island nation lowers its international profile. "China Threatens Taiwan," *New York Times*, January 25, 1996, p. A20. But whether the threat is more than an attempt to intimidate is unknowable. Still, China has to realize that it would pay a very high price for any military strike.

67. Beichman.

68. For a critique of U.S. relations with the Republic of China, see William Bader and Jeffrey Bergner, eds., *The Taiwan Relations Act: A Decade of Implementation* (Indianapolis: Hudson Institute, 1989). Not surprisingly, Taipei is lobbying hard to weaken the State Department's traditional commitment to the mainland's "one-China" policy. Leon T. Hadar, "The Sweet-and-Sour Sino-American Relationship," Cato Institute Policy Analysis no. 248, January 23, 1996, p. 10; Don Oberdorfer, "Juggling the Two Chinas," *Washington Post*, October 22, 1995, p. C4; and Robert Greenberger, "Taiwan, Trying to Win Status in Washington, Targets Grass Roots," *Wall Street Journal*, May 16, 1995, pp. A1, A12.

69. Somewhat similar is the case of the Paracel Islands, which are occupied by China but claimed by Vietnam.

70. Robinson, p. 391. See also Philip Shenon, "China Signals Willingness to Settle Islands Dispute," *New York Times*, July 31, 1995, p. A3; and Murray Hiebert, "Comforting Noises," *Far Eastern Economic Review*, August 10, 1995, p. 16.

71. See, for example, Abby Tan, "Manila's Plan to Build Lighthouses in Spratlys May Make China See Red," *Christian Science Monitor*, July 5, 1995, p. 8; Rigoberto Tiglao, "Remote Control," *Far Eastern Economic Review*, June 1, 1995, pp. 20–21; and Reginald Chua, "Chinese, Filipinos Stage a Stare-Down at Sea in Disputed Pacific Reef Area," *Wall Street Journal*, May 17, 1995, p. A14.

72. *United States Security Strategy*, p. 20.

73. Ibid., p. 23.

74. On that perception, see Hadar, pp. 13–17.

75. Ibid., p. 19. For a discussion of just one of those obscure disputes, over Sipidan Island, see Michael Vatikiotis, "Isle of Contention," *Far Eastern Economic Review*, March 17, 1994, p. 32.

76. Lloyd Vasey, "Collision in the China Sea," *Christian Science Monitor*, June 22, 1995, p. 19.

77. Michael Lind, "Asia First: A Foreign Policy," *New York Times*, April 18, 1995, p. A25. A somewhat more benign view of China's potential as a superpower comes from William Overholt, *The Rise of China: How Economic Reform Is Creating a New Superpower* (New York: W. W. Norton, 1993).

78. *United States Security Strategy*, p. 15.

79. Under Secretary of Defense, p. 29. Other analysts have made similar arguments in the past. Victor Louis, *The Coming Decline of the Chinese Empire* (New York: Times

Books, 1979). That potentially messy transition bothers some analysts the most. Waldron, pp. 17–21.

80. One military analyst warns that a U.S. withdrawal might end movement toward economic and political liberalization in China (as well as prevent the unification of Korea), though he doesn't explain how American troops in South Korea and Japan are able to influence the factional struggle within Zhongnanhai's red walls. Gary Anderson, "Why Okinawa Still Needs American Troops," *Washington Times*, November 2, 1995, p. A17.

81. Edward Olsen, "The U.S.-Japan Alliance in Disrepair? A Revisionist Critique," in *The United States, Japan, and East Asia*, ed. Kyongsoo Lho (Seoul: Korean Institute of International Studies, 1995), p. 73.

82. One analyst has gone so far as to argue that the presence of American forces in a united Korea "would increase the potential for conflict between China and the U.S.," citing Beijing's entry into the Korean War. Jim Mann, "The Struggle for Korea Begins," *Japan Times*, July 13, 1995, p. 18. However, the PRC is likely to view Washington's intentions and capabilities very differently today than it did in 1950.

83. J. N. Mak and B. A. Hamzah, "Navy Blues," *Far Eastern Economic Review*, March 17, 1994, p. 30.

84. Steven Strasser et al., "A New 'Anti-China Club'?" *Newsweek*, July 17, 1995, pp. 30–31. Even the hawkish editors of the *Far Eastern Economic Review* call this an "encouraging" sign. "The Sun Also Sets," *Far Eastern Economic Review*, August 24, 1995, p. 7.

85. Sheila Tefft, "China's Shot across Bow of Taiwan Riles Asians," *Christian Science Monitor*, July 24, 1995, p. 6; and Patrick Tyler, "Sound and Fury in East Asia," *New York Times*, August 23, 1995, p. A12.

86. On Chinese nationalism, see, for example, Nayan Chanda and Kari Huus, "The New Nationalism," *Far Eastern Economic Review*, November 9, 1995, pp. 20–26; and Marcus Brauchli and Kathy Chen, "Bolstered by Economy, Chinese Are Resisting Policies of the West," *Wall Street Journal*, June 23, 1995, pp. A1, A6.

87. Quoted in George Wilson, "U.S. Begins Revamping the Military," *Washington Post*, November 26, 1989, p. A12. Similar were the comments of Marine Corps Gen. Henry Stackpole, who opined that "no one wants a rearmed, resurgent Japan" and termed America's Cold War role in Japan "the cap in the bottle." Quoted in Fred Hiatt, "Marine General: U.S. Troops Must Stay in Japan," *Washington Post*, March 27, 1990, pp. A14, A20. Similar sentiments have emerged from the Department of Defense and the Central Intelligence Agency. "Excerpts from Pentagon's Plan: Prevent the Emergence of a New Rival," *New York Times*, March 8, 1992, p. A14; and Andrew Dougherty, Rochester Institute of Technology, "Japan 2000," Preliminary draft, February 11, 1991, p. 145.

88. Carpenter, *A Search for Enemies*, p. 47.

89. *United States Security Strategy*, pp. 25, 26.

90. Ibid., p. 9.

91. Resentment of Chinese immigrants was probably the worst. See, for example, Philip Choy et al., *The Coming Man: 19th Century American Perceptions of the Chinese* (Seattle: University of Washington Press, 1995).

92. Arthur Waldron, ed., *How the Peace Was Lost* (Stanford, Calif.: Hoover Institution, 1992), p. 128.

93. John Dower, *War without Mercy: Race and Power in the Pacific War* (New York: Pantheon, 1986), p. 10. Of course, the Japanese used equally debasing images of allied soldiers.

94. For a discussion of that ugly episode in American history, see Peter Irons, *Justice at War: The Story of the Japanese American Internment Cases* (New York: Oxford University Press, 1983).

95. John Maki, *Japanese Militarism* (New York: Alfred A. Knopf, 1945), p. 4. Some of the same themes are evident in Hillis Lory, *Japan's Military Masters: The Army in Japanese Life* (New York: Viking, 1943).

96. For a detailed discussion of American policy and its implementation, see Meirion Harries and Susie Harries, *Sheathing the Sword: The Demilitarization of Postwar Japan* (New York: Macmillan, 1987). See also Carpenter, *A Search for Enemies*, pp. 50–52.

97. The pressure on a then very reluctant Japan started even before ratification of the peace treaty between the two nations. See, for example, Michael Yoshitsu, *Japan and the San Francisco Peace Settlement* (New York: Columbia University Press, 1983), pp. 39–66; and Harries and Harries, pp. 228–42.

98. Haruhiro Fukui, "Beyond Korea: The Future of the US-Japan Partnership," in *US-Japan Partnership in Conflict Management: The Case of Korea*, ed. Chae-jin Lee and Hideo Sato (Claremont, Calif.: Keck Center for International and Strategic Studies, 1993), p. 152.

99. A strict reading of article 9 suggests that the Japan Socialist Party was right. Even some nationalists admit as much, scorning the subterfuge of "opportunistic legal interpretation." Harries and Harries, p. 289. However, Japan's government, with American support, has always accepted an elastic reading of the constitution. Carpenter, *A Search for Enemies*, pp. 54–55. That allows Tokyo to build the force that it wants, while deflecting American pressure for additional spending. For the current interpretation, see *Defense of Japan*, pp. 62–63.

100. Detailed discussions of Japanese defense policy are provided by Joseph Keddell, *The Politics of Defense in Japan: Managing Internal and External Pressures* (Armonk, N.Y.: M. E. Sharpe, 1993); James Buck, ed., *The Modern Japanese Military System* (Beverly Hills: Sage Publications, 1975); John Emmerson and Leonard Humphreys, *Will Japan Rearm? A Study in Attitudes* (Washington: American Enterprise Institute, 1973); and Yukio Satoh, "The Evolution of Japanese Security Policy," in *Security in East Asia*, pp. 19–61. Japan's growing involvement in UN operations is covered in *Defense of Japan*, pp. 117–37.

101. Tetsuya Kataoka, *Waiting for a "Pearl Harbor": Japan Debates Defense* (Stanford, Calif.: Hoover Institution, 1980), p. 1.

102. Shinichi Okawa, "Significance of the Post–Cold War US-Japan Alliance and Prospects for Security Cooperation," *Korean Journal of Defense Analysis* 6, no. 1 (Summer 1994): 71–72.

103. Quoted in Emmerson and Humphreys, p. 45. Oddly, this hasn't stopped Beijing from promoting a very modest level of military cooperation. See, for example, Joachim Claubitz, "Japan," in *Chinese Defense Policy*, pp. 228–31.

104. Yon, pp. 164–65.

105. Ministry of National Defense, *Defense White Paper: 1990* (Seoul: Republic of Korea, 1991), pp. 53, 54. See also Ministry of National Defense, *Defense White Paper: 1992–1993* (Seoul: Republic of Korea, 1993), p. 38.

106. Quotation from Ministry of National Defense, *Defense White Paper: 1991–1992* (Seoul: Republic of Korea, 1992), p. 61.

107. Quoted in Damon Darlin, "South Korea, Fearing Japan's Military, Wants U.S. to Remain as Peace Keeper," *Wall Street Journal*, November 20, 1991, p. A12. Opposition leader Kim Dae Jung equates the potential threats from China and Japan. Kim Dae

Jung, "The Once and Future Korea," *Foreign Policy*, no. 86 (Spring 1992): 53. For detailed discussions of the painful relationship between the two countries, see Chong-Sik Lee, *Japan and Korea: The Political Dimension* (Stanford, Calif.: Hoover Institution, 1985), pp. 1–42; Soong-Hoom Kil, "Japan in American-Korean Relations," in *Korea and the United States: A Century of Cooperation,* ed. Youngnok Koo and Dae-Sook Suh (Honolulu: University of Hawaii Press, 1984), pp. 152–71; and Ralph Clough, *Embattled Korea: The Rivalry for International Support* (Boulder, Colo.: Westview, 1987), pp. 221–37. Japan tends to trail only the DPRK as the nation most disliked by South Koreans. Pyong-Choon Hahm, "The Korean Perception of the United States," in *Korea and the United States,* p. 45.

108. Quoted in Karen Elliott House, "Asia's Stability Depends on Relationship of Japan and U.S., Singapore's Lee Says," *Wall Street Journal,* May 18, 1989, p. A13. See also Lee's comments quoted in Edward Olsen and David Winterford, "Asian Multilateralism: Implications for US Policy," *Korean Journal of Defense Analysis* 6, no. 1 (Summer 1994): 31.

109. Quoted in Emmerson and Humphreys, p. 54.

110. William Price, *The Japanese Miracle and Peril* (New York: John Day, 1971), p. 332.

111. See, for example, Edwin Hoyt, *The Militarists: The Rise of Japanese Militarism since WWII* (New York: Donald I. Fine, 1985); and Harold Hakwon Sunoo, *Japanese Militarism: Past and Present* (Chicago: Nelson Hall, 1975). A more cautious view is found in Harries and Harries, pp. 245–304.

112. George Friedman and Meredith Lebard, *The Coming War with Japan* (New York: St. Martin's, 1991), p. 395.

113. *The Military Balance: 1995–1996,* pp. 181–83.

114. *Defense of Japan,* p. 98.

115. *The Military Balance: 1995–1996,* p. 181.

116. *Defense of Japan,* p. 99.

117. Ibid.

118. Stockholm International Peace Research Institute, *SIPRI Yearbook 1995: Armaments, Disarmament and International Security* (New York: Oxford University Press, 1995), pp. 417–19; Ted Galen Carpenter, "Paternalism and Dependence: The U.S.-Japanese Security Relationship," Cato Institute Policy Analysis no. 244, November 1, 1995, p. 11; William Dawkins, "Japan Agrees First Defence Review since 1976," *Financial Times,* November 29, 1995, p. 8; and *Japanese-American Security Cooperation in the Post–Cold War Era,* p. 16.

119. Edward Olsen, "U.S.-Japan Security Relations after Nakasone: The Case for a Strategic Fairness Doctrine," in *Collective Defense or Strategic Independence?* p. 75.

120. Ibid., pp. 75, 73.

121. *United States Security Strategy,* p. 25.

122. In 1993, $1.7 billion of $4 billion in Japanese support, or 43 percent, was forgone land rental costs and similar expenses. Japan Defense Agency, *Do You Know . . .* (Tokyo: Japan Defense Agency, March 1993), p. 15.

123. Yet one prominent Japanese parliamentarian, Junichiro Koizumi, has sarcastically suggested that if Americans can't afford the "stationing costs" of U.S. forces, then Tokyo, rather than paying more in host-nation support, should "ask them to reduce military personnel and bases to a size [the United States] can afford to maintain." "Hashimoto, Koizumi Debate Japan-U.S. Ties," FNN Television Network, September 16, 1995, *Foreign Broadcast Information Service Daily Report—East Asia,* September 19, 1995, p. 2.

124. Carpenter, "Paternalism and Dependence," p. 9.

125. Quoted in Doug Bandow, "Reordering Defense for East Asia," *Washington Times*, August 9, 1995, p. A15. This and similar quotes are from private meetings in July 1995.

126. Carpenter, "Paternalism and Dependence," p. 2.

127. *United States Security Strategy*, p. 7.

128. Curiously, Japanese defense analyst Shinichi Ogawa argues that the U.S.-Japanese alliance "provides the US with grounds for asking Japan to do more in defending the sea lines of communication." Ogawa, p. 59. But Tokyo would have to do more if Washington was not generously performing Japan's job. Moreover, much of Japan's heavy reliance on Mideastern oil has stemmed from Washington's perverse ban on the export of Alaskan crude oil—a policy implemented to enrich American maritime unions. Congress has finally lifted that prohibition, allowing Tokyo to purchase Alaskan oil, which will be transported across the Pacific Ocean, a de facto American lake.

129. Olsen, "U.S.-Japan Security Relations after Nakasone," p. 77. Or as Thomas Robinson observes, "Relying so completely on the United States has paid off handsomely for the Japanese Foreign Ministry for many years, and it cannot be blamed for being reluctant to change." Robinson, p. 395.

130. Ralph Cossa et al., *The Japan-U.S. Alliance and Security Regimes in East Asia: A Workshop Report* (Washington: Institute for International Policy Studies, 1995), p. 9.

131. Nicholas Kristof, "Japan to Cut Own Military, Keeping G.I.'s," *New York Times*, November 29, 1995, p. A9.

132. *Japanese-American Security Cooperation in the Post–Cold War Era*, p. 5.

133. Ogawa, pp. 58–59.

134. Ibid., p. 59. In the same article he goes on to argue that the Mutual Security Treaty also benefits America by helping to improve Tokyo's military (p. 62).

135. Bandow, "Reordering Defense for East Asia." Ted Galen Carpenter calls this the "stop us before we conquer again" argument. Carpenter, "Paternalism and Dependence," p. 14.

136. Quoted in Kenneth Pyle, "The Japanese Question," in *Japan and the World: Considerations for U.S. Policymakers* (Seattle: National Bureau of Asian and Soviet Research, 1990), p. 7.

137. See, for example, Carpenter, "Paternalism and Dependence," pp. 20–23; and Frank Ching, "A Partnership under Strain," *Far Eastern Economic Review*, March 17, 1994, p. 33. The media in both nations play a role. Stanley Budner and Ellis Krauss, "Newspaper Coverage of U.S.-Japan Frictions," *Asian Survey* 35, no. 4 (April 1995): 336–56.

138. David Sanger, "U.S. Won't Admit or Explain Its Trade Espionage to Japan," *New York Times*, October 28, 1995, p. 4; and Paul Blustein and Mary Jordan, "U.S. Eavesdropped on Talks, Sources Say," *Washington Post*, October 17, 1995, pp. B1, B7.

139. See, for example, Chalmers Johnson and E. B. Keehn, "The Pentagon's Ossified Strategy," *Foreign Affairs* 74 (July–August 1995): 103–14.

140. See, for example, Andrew Pollack, "One Guilty Plea in Okinawa Rape; 2 Others Admit Role," *New York Times*, November 8, 1995, p. A3; Nicholas Kristof, "Tokyo Fails to Resolve Bases Impasse," *New York Times*, November 5, 1995, p. 13; Sheryl WuDunn, "More Okinawans Dislike U.S. Military Presence," *New York Times*, November 4, 1995, p. 3; Nicholas Kristof, "U.S. Apologizes to Japan for Rape of 12-Year-Old in Okinawa," *New York Times*, November 2, 1995, p. A7; Mary Jordan,

"Perry Rules Out Reducing Troops in Japan Despite Groundswell of Opposition," *Washington Post*, November 2, 1995, p. A25; Robert Burns, "U.S., Japan Agree to Panel in Wake of Rape," *Washington Times*, November 1, 1995, p. A11; "U.S. May Move Some Troops from Okinawa," *Washington Post*, October 28, 1995, p. A18; Nicholas Kristof, "U.S. to Turn Over Troops Accused of Murder or Rape to Japan," *New York Times*, October 26, 1995, p. A14; Paul Eckert, "85,000 Protest Military Bases on Okinawa," *Washington Times*, October 22, 1995, pp. A1, A10; Andrew Pollack, "Okinawa Governor Takes on Both Japan and U.S.," *New York Times*, October 5, 1995, p. A3; Willis Witter, "Japan Requests Fewer GIs in Okinawa," *Washington Times*, October 4, 1995, p. A19; Steven Butler, "An Alliance under Fire," *U.S. News & World Report*, October 2, 1995, pp. 54–56; Edward Desmond, "Rape of an Innocent, Dishonor in the Ranks," *Time*, October 2, 1995, pp. 51–52; and Andrew Pollack, "Rape Case in Japan Turns Harsh Light on U.S. Military," *New York Times*, September 20, 1995, p. A3.

141. *Japanese-American Security Cooperation in the Post–Cold War Era*, p. 3.

142. Ibid., pp. 18, 19.

143. When are old relationships ever said not to be "more important now than ever"? Henry Kissinger says much the same thing about U.S. cooperation with China, despite the collapse of the Soviet Union and the Cold War, which made rapprochement with Beijing seem so important. Henry Kissinger, "Heading for a Collision in Asia," *Washington Post*, July 26, 1995, p. A23.

144. Cossa, p. 22.

145. *A National Security Strategy of Engagement and Enlargement* (Washington: The White House, February 1995), p. 28.

146. Hisayoshi Ina, "Role of Security Treaty with U.S. Discussed," *Foreign Broadcast Information Service Daily Report—East Asia*, September 27, 1995, p. 7.

147. Caspar Weinberger, "The Pentagon Gets It Right," *Forbes*, September 11, 1995, p. 33.

148. Quoted in Lea.

149. Olsen, "The U.S.-Japan Alliance in Disrepair?" p. 73.

150. For instance, see Olsen, "U.S.-Japan Security Relations after Nakasone," pp. 80–82.

151. Quoted in Bandow, "Reordering Defense for East Asia."

152. See Carpenter, *A Search for Enemies*, pp. 62–63.

153. Quoted in Bandow, "Reordering Defense for East Asia."

154. One disengagement strategy is suggested in Carpenter, "Paternalism and Dependence," pp. 23–27.

155. Carpenter, *A Search for Enemies*, p. 57.

156. Quoted in Bandow, "Reordering Defense for East Asia."

157. Quoted in ibid.

158. Ibid.

159. Ibid. See also Shikata, p. 26.

160. On Japanese participation in peacekeeping missions, see Carpenter, "Paternalism and Dependence," pp. 19–20. Given Japan's economic influence, it should be given a seat on the UN Security Council, which it has requested. Eugene Lee, "Japan's Quest for Global Leadership," *Korean Journal of National Unification* 2 (1993): 219–33. Sending medics to, say, Bosnia, is no substitute for the purchase of additional frigates and AWACS aircraft to help patrol sea lanes in the South China Sea.

On diversion of U.S. resources, see Jason Glashow and Naoaki Usui, "Host Japan Intends to Strengthen Support of U.S. Troops," *Defense News*, September 25–October 1, 1995, p. 18.

161. For a brief description of Tokyo's depredations, see Harries and Harries, pp. 97–99. The saga of the "comfort women" seeking compensation has become a particularly emotional issue today. For a discussion of that aspect of Japanese imperialism, see George Hicks, *The Comfort Women: Japan's Brutal Regime of Enforced Prostitution in the Second World War* (New York: Norton, 1995).

162. On defenders of Japan's conduct, see Frank Ching, "Hiroshima: 50 Years Later," *Far Eastern Economic Review*, August 24, 1995, p. 31. Michio Watanabe, a one-time foreign minister and influential member of the Liberal Democratic Party, said in June 1995 that the Koreans had consented to annexation by Japan. Andrew Pollack, "Michio Watanabe, 72, of Japan; Powerful Minister Despite Gaffes," *New York Times*, September 16, 1995, p. 11. Four months later Prime Minister Tomiichi Murayama, followed by Management and Coordination Agency Minister Takami Eto, who quickly resigned, made similar statements. See, for example, Nicholas Kristof, "Japanese Aide Quits after Citing 'Good' of Korean Occupation," *New York Times*, November 14, 1995, p. A14; Kevin Sullivan, "Remark Costs Tokyo Aide His Job," *Washington Post*, November 14, 1995, p. A14; "Japan Jilted," *Far Eastern Economic Review*, November 2, 1995, p. 13; and Brian Williams, "Tokyo Gropes to End Tiff with Seoul," *Washington Times*, November 12, 1995, p. A9. Tokyo obviously would have a lot less to apologize for if its current officials learned to keep their mouths shut.

On Japan's apology, see, for example, Morton Keller, "Amnesia Day," *New Republic*, September 18 and 25, 1995, p. 14; Emily Thorton, "Final Mea Culpa?" *Far Eastern Economic Review*, August 24, 1995, p. 18; "Japan's Many Memories of War," *The Economist*, August 19, 1995, pp. 29–30; Willis Witter, "Japan Apology Welcomed," *Washington Times*, August 16, 1995, p. A10; Sheryl WuDunn, "Japanese Apology for War Is Welcomed and Criticized," *New York Times*, August 16, 1995, p. A3; T. R. Reid, "Asia Underwhelmed by Japan's Apology," *Washington Post*, August 16, 1995, pp. A21, A22; Willis Witter, "War Criminals among Japan's Gods," *Washington Times*, August 15, 1995, p. A9; "Japan Denies Making World War II Apology," *Washington Times*, August 13, 1995, p. A6; "The Japan That Cannot Say Sorry," *The Economist*, August 12, 1995, pp. 31–33; Eldon Griffiths, "Will Japan Ever Face Up to Its WWII Shame?" *Orange County Register*, July 28, 1995, p. Metro 6; T. R. Reid, "Japan to Apologize to 'Comfort Women,'" *Washington Post*, July 13, 1995, p. A18; Steven Mufson, "All the Yen for China Can't Heal War Wounds," *Washington Post*, July 10, 1995, p. A12; and Nicholas Kristof, "Why Japan Hasn't Said That Word," *New York Times*, May 7, 1995, p. E3.

Properly dismissive of the entire notion are Kenneth Auchincloss, "No Apologies," *Newsweek*, July 24, 1995, p. 41; and "Remorseful Japan," editorial, *Wall Street Journal*, June 19, 1995, p. A10.

163. Historian Mark Peattie calls that the lesson "seared most deeply into the Japanese consciousness by the devastation in the Pacific war." Peattie, *A Historian Looks at the Pacific War* (Stanford, Calif.: Hoover Institution, 1995), p. 7. See also Richard Halloran, "Is Japan a Military Threat to Asia?" *Arms Control Today*, November 1994, pp. 15–17.

164. For a discussion of how attitudes toward Japan vary by nation, see Simon Elegant et al., "Memory and Apathy," *Far Eastern Economic Review*, August 24, 1995,

pp. 36–38; and Marcus Eliason, "Generations Split on Views of Japan," *Washington Times*, August 11, 1995, p. A13.

165. "Memory and Apathy" and "Indicators," *Far Eastern Economic Review*, November 9, 1995, p. 15. Emblematic of the troubles is Seoul's plan to demolish the building that once housed the Japanese governor-general. Shim Jae Hoon, "Brother Enemy," *Far Eastern Economic Review*, August 24, 1995, p. 39. And, it must be said, the South Koreans have much to be angry about. See *South Korea, North Korea: 1994–95* (London: The Economist Intelligence Unit, 1994), p. 4.

166. Author's conversations with a number of South Korean analysts and officials over the years.

167. Ivan Hall, "Japan's Asia Card," *National Interest*, no. 38 (Winter 1994–95): 23. See also Elegant et al.; and Eliason.

168. Carpenter, *A Search for Enemies*, p. 68.

169. Conversation with the author in July 1995.

170. Kataoka, p. 64.

171. Michael Nacht, "Multinational Naval Cooperation in Northeast Asia: Some Plausible Considerations for 2010 Based on What We Know in 1994," *Korean Journal of Defense Analysis* 7, no. 1 (Summer 1995): 39. Nacht thinks such a step will be more feasible in 15 years than it is today.

172. Quoted in Doug Bandow, "Time to End the Korean Protectorate," *Conservative Chronicle*, August 16, 1995, p. 27. From a private meeting in July 1995. Such sentiments, though widespread, are not unanimous. President Park Chung Hee, who actually served with Japanese forces in Manchuria, was widely viewed as having a less hostile attitude toward Japan. See, for example, Harrison, pp. 215–16.

173. The paucity of past contacts is evident from the description of them. See, for example, *Defense of Japan*, pp. 138–39.

174. Very different are proposals for multilateral exercises tied to the existing bilateral treaties. See, for example, Nacht, p. 41. The ultimate goal would be to reduce Washington's role. Compare Sung Hwan Wie et al., *Prospects for U.S.-Korean Naval Relations in the 21st Century* (Alexandria, Va.: Center for Naval Analysis, 1995).

175. See, for example, Edward Olsen, "Security in Northeast Asia," *Naval War College Review*, January–February 1985, p. 21.

176. See Chong-Sik Lee, pp. 105–39.

177. For a discussion of the role of the DPRK and the Korean minority in Japan, see Ralph Clough, *Embattled Korea: The Rivalry for International Support* (Boulder, Colo.: Westview, 1987), pp. 233–37.

178. ASEAN has a more venerable history. M. Rajeendran, *ASEAN's Foreign Relations: The Shift to Collective Action* (Kuala Lumpur: Arenaburku, 1985). In contrast, the name APEC suggests a desire to eschew formal organization, but one seems to be arising anyway. Andrew Pollack, "A Pacific Vision in Search of Reality," *New York Times*, November 14, 1995, p. D5.

179. Quoted in Olsen and Winterford, p. 31. The term "vacuum" has been used by many people to oppose almost any reconfiguration of U.S. commitments and forces. See William Taylor, "The Military Balance on the Korean Peninsula: Trends, Linkages, and the Dangers of Premature Judgments," in *The U.S.–South Korean Alliance*, p. 33; Defense Secretary Richard Cheney, quoted in Marcus Corbin et al., "Mission Accomplished in Korea: Bringing U.S. Troops Home," *Defense Monitor* 19, no. 2 (1990): 5; and former national security adviser Richard V. Allen, "Fifty Years after

Pearl Harbor: The Future of U.S.-Japan Relations," Heritage Foundation Lecture no. 356, December 3, 1991, p. 3.

180. Scalapino, p. 7. On the problems of this approach, see also Young Sun Song, "Prospects for a New Asia-Pacific Multilateral Security Arrangement," *Korean Journal of Defense Analysis* 5, no. 1 (Summer 1993): 188–90; Byung-joon Ahn [Ahn Byung-joon], "Regionalism and the US-Korea-Japan Partnership in the Asia-Pacific," in *US-Korean Relations at a Time of Change*, pp. 100–101; and Olsen and Winterford, pp. 36–37. Those problems are not new. Sheldon Simon, *Asian Neutralism and U.S. Policy* (Washington: American Enterprise Institute, 1975), pp. 31–48.

181. See, for example, Kyu-Roon Kim, "Economic Cooperation in Northeast Asia: The Role of Asia," *Korean Journal of National Unification*, Special Edition (1993): 167–77.

182. See Scalapino, pp. 23–26.

183. How far ASEAN is willing to go in confronting China remains to be seen. Compare Steven Strasser, "The Neighbors Are Restless," *Newsweek*, July 17, 1995, pp. 8–14, with Adam Schwarz, "Joining the Fold," *Far Eastern Economic Review*, March 16, 1995, pp. 20–21, and Robert Manning and James Przystup, "The China Challenge," *Far Eastern Economic Review*, July 6, 1995, p. 30. For a useful, albeit dated, look at ASEAN's military policy, see Donald Weatherbee, "ASEAN Defense Programs: Military Patterns of National and Regional Resilience," in *Security, Strategy, and Policy Responses in the Pacific Rim*, ed. Young Whan Kihl and Lawrence Grinter (Boulder, Colo.: Lynne Rienner, 1989), pp. 182–220.

184. For a discussion of ASEAN's increasing activities, see Olsen and Winterford, pp. 24–28.

185. Ralph Clough, *East Asia and U.S. Security* (Washington: Brookings Institution, 1975), p. 232.

186. Hyun In-tack and Masao Okonogi, "Security Cooperation in East Asia," *Korea Focus* 2, no. 5 (September–October 1994): 60. See also Robert Manning, "Clinton and the Korea Question: A Strategy for the Endgame," Progressive Policy Institute Policy Briefing, July 7, 1994, p. 8.

187. See, for example, Song, pp. 195–98.

188. For the position of the Bush administration, see Carpenter, *A Search for Enemies*, p. 60.

189. *Japanese-American Security Cooperation in the Post–Cold War Era*, p. 12.

190. James Lasswell, "Presence—Do We Stay or Do We Go?" *Joint Force Quarterly* (Summer 1995): 85.

191. See, for example, Mueller and Ross, pp. 108–15.

192. Henry Kissinger, *Diplomacy* (New York: Simon and Schuster, 1994), p. 827.

193. Franklin Weinstein and Fuji Kamiya, eds., *The Security of Korea: U.S. and Japanese Perspectives in the 1980s* (Boulder, Colo.: Westview, 1980), p. 133.

194. Richard Holbrooke, "Japan and the United States: The Unequal Partnership," *Foreign Affairs* 70 (Winter 1991–92): 53.

195. Harries and Harries, p. 308.

196. Friedman and Lebard, pp. 378–403.

197. Persistent trade disputes are probably the most poisonous part of the current relationship. See, for example, Carpenter, *A Search for Enemies*, pp. 64–65.

198. Young-Koo Cha and Kang Choi, "Land-Based Confidence-Building Measures in Northeast Asia: A South Korean Perspective," *Korean Journal of Defense Analysis* 6, no. 2 (Winter 1994): 248.

199. Robinson, pp. 400–401.

200. *Defense of Japan,* p. 34.

201. *United States Security Strategy,* p. 12.

202. Ibid., p. 11.

203. See, for example, Doug Bandow, "ANZUS: A Case of Strategic Obsolescence," in *Collective Defense or Strategic Independence?* pp. 121–32; and Carpenter, *A Search for Enemies,* pp. 95–103.

204. *United States Security Strategy,* p. 32.

205. Ibid., p. 5.

206. Ibid., p. 23.

207. Kelly, p. 31.

208. Meeting with the author in July 1995.

209. *United States Security Strategy,* pp. 23–24.

210. Ibid., p. 24.

211. Cossa et al., p. 12.

212. Baier, p. 282.

213. Edward Olsen, "Are Allies Necessary?" *Chronicles,* October 1995, p. 43.

214. Ministry of National Defense, *Defense White Paper: 1991–1992,* p. 323.

215. James Kelly worries about the "tyranny of distance" and therefore advocates forward military deployments. Kelly, p. 31. However, terminating security guarantees that implicitly rely on ground forces, especially the one with Korea, lessens the problem. Air power could arrive quickly and American fleets could remain on patrol. And, as noted earlier, even Army units could be deployed relatively quickly in an emergency. Harrison, *The Widening Gulf,* pp. 376–78.

216. The threat to the sea lanes has receded with the collapse of the USSR. See, for example, Michael Leifer, "The Security of Sea-Lanes in South-East Asia," in *Security in East Asia,* pp. 166–74.

217. Clark, p. 85.

218. The bases long ago outlived their usefulness. Ted Galen Carpenter, "The U.S. Military Presence in the Philippines: Expensive and Unnecessary," Cato Institute Foreign Policy Briefing no. 12, July 28, 1991. Nevertheless, Gary Anderson argues that "our withdrawal from the Philippines was a profoundly disturbing event for regional leaders, even though the issue was a dispute over the cost of the bases rather than a manifestation of the lack of U.S. interest. Those leaders knew that another major U.S. withdrawal from the western Pacific would be potentially disastrous to regional stability." Anderson. However, the very fact that there was no disastrous impact on regional stability despite such fears has demonstrated that there is a lot more to East Asian stability than American bases and soldiers.

219. Weinstein and Kamiya, pp. 86–88.

220. Olsen, "The U.S.-Japan Alliance in Disrepair?" p. 59.

221. Carpenter, *A Search for Enemies,* p. 172.

222. Kelly, p. 21.

Chapter 8

1. U.S. Department of Defense, *United States Security Strategy for the East Asia–Pacific Region* (Washington: U.S. Department of Defense, February 1995), p. 6.

2. U.S. Department of Defense, *United States Security Strategy for Europe and NATO* (Washington: U.S. Department of Defense, June 1995), p. 1.

3. U.S. Department of Defense, *United States Security Strategy for Sub-Saharan Africa* (Washington: U.S. Department of Defense, August 1995), p. 24.

4. Ted Galen Carpenter, *A Search for Enemies: America's Alliances after the Cold War* (Washington: Cato Institute, 1992).

5. Anthony Lewis, letter to the author, September 18, 1995.

6. Hong-Choo Hyun, "Korea's Heroes Come Home," *Wall Street Journal*, July 28, 1995, p. A14.

7. Quoted in "S. Korean President Voices War Fears," *Washington Times*, October 1, 1995, p. A9.

8. See M. Frederick Nelson, *Korea and the Old Orders in Eastern Asia* (Baton Rouge: Louisiana State University Press, 1946).

9. Ibid., p. 269.

10. Quoted in ibid., p. 264.

11. Ministry of National Defense, *Defense White Paper: 1989* (Seoul: Republic of Korea, 1990), p. 28.

12. Ministry of National Defense, *Defense White Paper: 1994–1995* (Seoul: Republic of Korea, 1995), p. 127.

13. Quoted in "Kim Endorses U.S. Troop Presence," *Washington Post*, July 27, 1995, p. A23.

14. Nicholas Eberstadt, *Korea Approaches Reunification* (Armonk, N.Y.: M. E. Sharpe, 1995), p. 153. For similar sentiments, see Robert Dujarric, "Taiwan and East Asian Security," Hudson Institute Briefing Paper no. 186, February 1996, p. 9.

15. Carpenter, p. 204.

16. That distinction is not as harsh as it might at first sound. According to one Council of Foreign Relations poll, more than twice as many "leaders" as members of the public are willing to send troops to defend the South from a North Korean invasion. *American Public Opinion and U.S. Foreign Policy 1995* (Chicago: Chicago Council on Foreign Relations, 1995), p. 35.

17. Seth Cropsey, "Clinton's Retreat on North Korea Invites Aggression," Heritage Foundation Backgrounder Update no. 210, January 14, 1994, p. 3.

18. Edward Olsen, "Are Allies Necessary?" *Chronicles*, October 1995, p. 43.

19. *A National Security Strategy of Engagement and Enlargement* (Washington: The White House, February 1995), p. 28.

20. William Taylor, "The Military Balance on the Korean Peninsula: Trends, Linkages, and the Dangers of Premature Judgements," in *The U.S.–South Korean Alliance: Time for a Change*, ed. Doug Bandow and Ted Galen Carpenter (New Brunswick, N.J.: Transaction, 1992), p. 27.

21. Earl Ravenal, "The Way Out of Korea: A Genuine Alternative to the Nixon-Carter Doctrine in Asia," *Inquiry*, December 5, 1977, p. 16.

22. Kim Dae-jung [Kim Dae Jung], "The Impact of the US–North Korean Agreement on Korean Reunification," *Korean Journal of Defense Analysis* 6, no. 2 (Winter 1994): 94.

23. For one look at this issue, see Thomas Henriksen and Kyongsoo Lho, eds., *One Korea? Challenges and Prospects for Reunification* (Stanford, Calif.: Hoover Institution, 1994).

24. Scott Snyder, "A Framework for Achieving Reconciliation on the Korean Peninsula," *Asian Survey* 35, no. 8 (August 1995): 703.

25. Chongwook Chung, "The Korean War and Inter-Korean Relations," in *The Korean War: 40-Year Perspectives*, ed. Chae-Jin Lee (Claremont, Calif.: Keck Center for International and Strategic Studies, 1991), p. 74.

26. William Stueck, *The Korean War: An International History* (Princeton, N.J.: Princeton University Press, 1995), p. 353.

27. Quoted in Kevin Sullivan and Mary Jordan, "S. Korea Wants to Be Grown-Up Ally," *Washington Post*, October 19, 1995, p. A31.

28. Rowan Scarborough, "Perry Questions Plan to Defend Gulf Area," *Washington Times,* January 5, 1996, pp. A1, A20.

29. Ted Galen Carpenter, "Ending South Korea's Unhealthy Security Dependence," *Korean Journal of Defense Analysis* 6, no. 1 (Summer 1994): 194.

30. Ministry of National Defense, *Defense White Paper: 1994–1995,* p. 21.

31. Quoted in Frank Baldwin, "Japan: Roadblock on the Way Out of Korea," *Inquiry,* April 3, 1978, p. 21.

Index

Acheson, Dean, 2, 19, 66, 84
Agreement on Reconciliation, Nonaggression and Exchanges and Cooperation
  proposed implementation of, 99–100, 126
Ahn Byung-joon, 93
ANZUS, 175, 178
Armistice, ROK-DPRK, 22, 37
Asian Development Bank, 27
Asia-Pacific Economic Cooperation (APEC), 95, 171
Aspin, Les, 110, 115
Association of Southeast Asian Nations (ASEAN), 95, 150–51, 160
  political and security actions, 171
  recommended discussions under auspices of, 171
Australia
  isolation of, 6, 151
  U.S. alliance with, 2, 147, 175
  See also ANZUS

Bahnsen, John, 36
Baldwin, Frank, 93
Barnett, A. Doak, 156
Bean, R. Mark, 93
Beichman, Arnold, 158
Bennett, Bruce, 70
Bermudez, Joseph, 104, 120
Blair, Clay, 21, 22
Bohlen, Charles, 3
Bosnia, 45
Brown, Hank, 113
Brown, Harold, 87
Buckley, James, 71, 128
Buckley, William F. Jr., 128
Burke, J. Herbert, 162–63
Burma, 174
Burns, Arthur, 45, 52
Burstein, Daniel, 54
Bush, George
  assurances to South Korea, 5
  on U.S. military presence in ROK, 29

Bush administration
  planned reduction in troop strength in ROK, 88, 100
  position on DPRK nuclear program, 106
Buss, Claude, 74, 83

Cambodia, 174
Carpenter, Ted Galen, 10, 40, 63, 65, 66, 144, 164, 167, 170, 179, 182, 185, 189
Carter, Jimmy
  proposal to withdraw U.S forces from Korea, 90
  visit to Pyongyang, 112
Carter administration
  commitment to ROK, 90
  policy of troop withdrawal from South Korea, 26, 39, 41, 97, 179, 187
  policy toward DPRK, 26, 28
Central Treaty Organization, 4
Chang Myon (John), 24
Chapman, Stephen, 106, 134
Cheney, Richard, 63
China
  assistance to DPRK uranium mining, 104
  containment of, 153–54
  current economic policy, 155–56
  current military strength, 66
  economic relations with ROK, 137
  foreign policy of, 154–55
  military spending, 163
  nuclear program of, 142
  policy toward DPRK, 34, 136–37
  post-Mao, 151
  potential threat of, 59
  as regional power, 136–37
  response to UN invasion of DPRK, 21–22
  ROK military relations with, 69–70
  role in proposed agreement related to Korea, 92–94
  Spratly Islands dispute, 158–60

247

North Korea as member of, 103–4
planned special inspections in DPRK,
124
refused access to DPRK nuclear
waste sites, 107–8
Intervention policy, U.S.
cost of, 47–48, 140
lack of benefits to America, 46,
185–86
motivation for, 11, 75
response to North Korean invasion
of South Korea, 1

Japan
argument for U.S. military presence,
175
defense burden sharing, 163–68
impact of hypothetical sanctions
against DPRK, 129–30
potential security role in East Asia,
93–96
potential to acquire nuclear weapons,
119, 141–42, 172–73
recommendations for regional
cooperation, 170–72
as regional power, 137
relations with China, 156–57
relations with DPRK, 137
role in proposed agreement related
to Korea, 92–94
as threat to peace, 160
U.S. defense subsidy for, 52, 164–65
U.S. security commitment to and
forces in, 2, 35, 147, 164–65
See also Military forces, Japan
Johnson, Louis, 3
Johnson administration, 24, 128
Jordan, Amos, 72

Kangwha Treaty (1876), 16
Kanter, Arnold, 120–21, 143
Kashmir, 141
Kataoka Tetsuya, 162, 170
Kazakhstan, 124
Kelly, James, 148, 176, 179
Kennan, George, 3
Kennedy, Paul, 47, 48
Kennedy administration, 24
Kim, Sung-Hoon, 58
Kim Dae Jung, 77, 150, 188
conditions for support of troop
withdrawal, 98
as exile from ROK, 27
kidnapping of, 25

political actions of, 27
Kim Eulkwon, 72
Kim Il Sung
death of, 112
initiates war with South Korea, 20
offer to freeze nuclear program, 112
Kim Jae Kyu, 27
Kim Jong Il
on economic problems of DPRK, 137
as leader of DPRK, 37, 114
on opening to the West, 135
Kim Jong Nam, 106
Kim Jong Pil, 27, 29, 83
Kim Kook Chin, 137
Kim Kyung-won, 126
Kim Taewoo, 142
Kim Young Sam, 27
on DPRK nuclear program, 115, 122
on effect of DPRK's economic
decline, 70
on necessity of U.S. military
presence, 184
as president of ROK, 29, 42, 77, 81
visit to Washington, 5
warning of renewed military action,
183
Kirkpatrick, Jeane, 5
Kissinger, Henry, 94, 96, 110
Koo Cha Young, 162
Koo Young Nok, 23
Korea
as colony of Japan, 17
concentration of military power in,
37
conditions for reunification, 99–100
consequences of new war in, 133–36
current status of Demilitarized Zone,
4
early U.S. contacts and relations
with, 15–17
as post–World War II trusteeship,
17–19
See also Democratic People's Republic
of Korea (DPRK); Republic of
Korea (ROK)
Korea Peninsula Energy Development
Organization, 112–13
Korean people
costs of Korean War, 23
in Japan, 129
ties with and in United States, 30–31
Korean War
costs to United States and United
Nations of, 22–23, 37

About the Author

A senior fellow at the Cato Institute, Doug Bandow is a nationally syndicated columnist with Copley News Service. He formerly served as a visiting fellow at the Heritage Foundation, editor of *Inquiry* magazine, and special assistant to President Reagan. Bandow has written and edited several books including *The U.S.–South Korean Alliance: Time for a Change* (Transaction), *Human Resources and Defense Manpower* (National Defense University), *Perpetuating Poverty: The World Bank, the IMF, and the Developing World* (Cato Institute), and *The Politics of Plunder: Misgovernment in Washington* (Transaction). He has also been widely published in such periodicals as *Foreign Policy*, *Harper's*, *National Interest*, *National Review*, *New Republic*, and *Orbis* as well as leading newspapers, including the *New York Times*, the *Wall Street Journal*, and the *Washington Post*, and has appeared on numerous television and radio programs. Bandow received his B.S. in economics from Florida State University in 1976 and his J.D. from Stanford University in 1979.

Cato Institute

Founded in 1977, the Cato Institute is a public policy research foundation dedicated to broadening the parameters of policy debate to allow consideration of more options that are consistent with the traditional American principles of limited government, individual liberty, and peace. To that end, the Institute strives to achieve greater involvement of the intelligent, concerned lay public in questions of policy and the proper role of government.

The Institute is named for *Cato's Letters*, libertarian pamphlets that were widely read in the American Colonies in the early 18th century and played a major role in laying the philosophical foundation for the American Revolution.

Despite the achievement of the nation's Founders, today virtually no aspect of life is free from government encroachment. A pervasive intolerance for individual rights is shown by government's arbitrary intrusions into private economic transactions and its disregard for civil liberties.

To counter that trend, the Cato Institute undertakes an extensive publications program that addresses the complete spectrum of policy issues. Books, monographs, and shorter studies are commissioned to examine the federal budget, Social Security, regulation, military spending, international trade, and myriad other issues. Major policy conferences are held throughout the year, from which papers are published thrice yearly in the *Cato Journal*. The Institute also publishes the quarterly magazine *Regulation*.

In order to maintain its independence, the Cato Institute accepts no government funding. Contributions are received from foundations, corporations, and individuals, and other revenue is generated from the sale of publications. The Institute is a nonprofit, tax-exempt, educational foundation under Section 501(c)3 of the Internal Revenue Code.

CATO INSTITUTE
1000 Massachusetts Ave., N.W.
Washington, D.C. 20001